SHAPE IT! 3 COMBO

STUDENT'S BOOK
WITH DIGITAL PACK

Samantha Lewis and Daniel Vincent
with Andrew Reid

CAMBRIDGE
UNIVERSITY PRESS

CONTENTS

STARTER

WELCOME!

VOCABULARY

Technology

1 Match the words with the photos (1–6). Then listen, check, and repeat. S.01

app	1	emoji		social media	
device		screen		video chat	

Use It!

2 Circle the correct words to complete the questions. Then ask and answer with a partner.

1 What's your favorite *screen* / *app* on your phone?
2 Which *emoji* / *screen* do you use the most in messages to your friends?
3 Which *device* / *social media* sites do you use?
4 How often do you use *video chat* / *device*?

Explore It!

Guess the correct answer.

What was the most popular emoji in 2017?

a b c

Find another interesting fact about emojis. Then write a question for your partner to answer.

Feelings

3 Write the words in the box next to the emojis in the sentences. Then listen, check, and repeat. S.02

angry	~~bored~~	embarrassed
excited	nervous	upset

1 Help! He's talking about his favorite computer game again! I'm so bored.

2 Oops! Clothing disaster this morning. One red sock, one pink sock. I feel ________.

3 Andi's ________ with me. I forgot to reply to his text.

4 Feeling ________ before my presentation. Wish me luck!

5 Video chat isn't working – again! Feeling ________.

6 This birthday boy is feeling ________. Party at my house tonight!

LEARN TO LEARN

Recording Vocabulary

Writing new words in example sentences can help you remember them.

4 Write the words from Exercise 3 in example sentences. Then read your sentences to your partner.

I always feel excited when the weekend starts.

____

____

____

____

READING

A Message on an App

1 Look at the photos and answer the questions.

1 What can you see?
2 How do the people feel?
3 Which is more difficult? Skateboarding or making a robot?

S.03 **2 Read the messages. What do Dylan and Izzy do at their summer camps every day?**

Izzy: Hey, Dylan! How's tech camp? Are you having fun?

Dylan: It's awesome. I'm never bored here.

Izzy: What do you do every day?

Dylan: In the morning we usually study computer languages, and in the afternoon we learn how to write apps. But we don't always do the same thing. Today we're building robots!

Izzy: That sounds cool!

Dylan: It is, but it isn't as easy as it looks!

Izzy: **I bet**.

Dylan: There's a competition tomorrow. I'm excited but also **kind of** worried. My robot isn't working very well. Anyway, how's skateboarding camp?

Izzy: I'm **having the time of my life**. I'm learning a lot of new **tricks**. I always feel nervous before I do one, and I sometimes feel embarrassed when I fall down. 😳

Dylan: I feel nervous when my robot falls down! 😬

Izzy: Oh, don't be nervous!

Dylan: Listen, do you have any photos of you on your skateboard? I'm making an app for social media. I need some cool photos to put on it.

Izzy: No. I hardly ever take photos.

Dylan: OK, don't worry. Anyway, gotta go. The next class is starting and everyone's waiting for me.

Izzy: You're never **on time**! Listen, we always use this messaging app to talk. Next time, let's do a video chat.

Dylan: Good idea! Bye!

Izzy: Bye! Good luck with your robot!

3 Read the conversation again. Write *D* (Dylan) or *I* (Izzy).

Who …

1 thinks their camp is always interesting? D
2 has an important event soon? __
3 sometimes falls down? __
4 needs help with a project? __
5 talks about a different way to communicate? __

4 Write the words and phrases in bold in the conversation that mean …

1 clever, fun acts. tricks
2 I believe that's true. ____________
3 a little. ____________
4 enjoying myself a lot. ____________
5 not late. ____________

Voice It!

5 Discuss the questions.

1 Which summer camp do you think is more interesting?
2 Are summer camps popular in your country?

GRAMMAR IN ACTION

Simple Present and Present Continuous with Adverbs of Frequency

Watch video S.1
Where is he? What does he usually do during the day?

	Simple Present	Present Continuous
+	I **need** some cool photos.	The next class [3] ___is___ **starting**.
–	We [1] ______ **always do** the same thing.	My robot **isn't working** very well.
?	What [2] ______ you **do** every day?	[4] ______ you **having** fun?

⊖ ---------- **Frequency** ---------- ⊕

never – hardly ever – sometimes – often – usually – always

1 **Complete the examples in the chart above. Use the messages on page 5 to help you.**

Get It Right!

Adverbs of frequency go before the main verb, but after *to be*.

We usually study computer languages. *I am never late.*

S.04 2 **Complete the phone message with the correct form of the verbs in the box. Then listen and check.**

call ~~have~~ have learn make not believe play sing

Hi Anna! How's it going? [1] ___Are you having___ a good vacation? Guess where I [2] __________ from! Summer camp! I [3] __________ an amazing time here. During the day, we [4] __________ sports and in the evening, we [5] __________ songs by the fire. Oh, and guess what! We [6] __________ our own food every day, so I [7] __________ how to cook! I'm sure you [8] __________ me, but it's true! Talk to you soon! Bye!

3 **Write the adverbs of frequency in the correct places.**

1 I clean my computer screen. (hardly ever)
   I hardly ever clean my computer screen.
2 Do you feel nervous when you speak English? (sometimes)
   ____
3 A video chat is as good as a face-to-face chat. (never)
   ____
4 New skateboard tricks aren't easy to do. (always)
   ____

Use It!

4 **In your notebook, write sentences about your partner with the time expressions.**

at the moment in the evening on the weekend when it's sunny

You often go to the park on the weekend.

Simple Present and Present Continuous for Future

5 **Write *SP* (Simple Present) or *PC* (Present Continuous).**

1 The movie starts at 9 p.m. ___SP___
2 The train is leaving soon. ______
3 We're going on vacation next week. ______
4 The store opens at 11 a.m. ______

6 **Which sentences in Exercise 5 describe scheduled routines?**

Use It!

7 **Ask and answer the questions.**

1 What time does this class end?
2 Are you going on vacation soon?

1

2

3

4

5

6

7

8

9

10

VOCABULARY AND LISTENING

Music

S.05 **1 Match the words with the photos (1–10). Then listen, check, and repeat.**

bass guitar	☐	fans	☐	rap	☐
country	☐	heavy metal	☐	reggae	☐
DJ	☐	jazz	☐		
drums	☐	keyboard	1		

S.06 **2 Listen and write the words from Exercise 1.**

1 bass guitar 5 ______ 9 ______
2 ______ 6 ______ 10 ______
3 ______ 7 ______
4 ______ 8 ______

3 Complete the chart with the words from Exercise 1.

Types of Music	country,
Instruments	
People	

Use It!

4 Read the questions and take notes.

1 How often do you listen to music?
2 What are your favorite types of music?
3 Is the music you listen to different from the music that your parents like? Why?

5 Ask and answer the questions in Exercise 4.

How often do you listen to music?

I listen to music every day when I get home from school. What about you?

A Conversation

LEARN TO LEARN

Contextualizing Vocabulary

Listening to words in context helps you understand and remember them.

S.07 **6 Listen to the conversation. Which words from Exercise 1 do you hear?**

S.07 **7 Listen again and circle the correct answers.**

1 Most of the children like *pop* / *rap* music.
2 A lot of the children feel *excited* / *nervous* about hearing themselves on the radio.
3 On the radio, the children talk about their *hobbies* / *families*.
4 Sometimes *doctors* / *bands* give concerts in the hospital.

Voice It!

8 Would you like to be a DJ in a children's hospital? Why / Why not?

GRAMMAR IN ACTION
Simple Past

Watch video S.2
What did she listen to on her way to school? What's her favorite music?

	Regular Verbs	Irregular Verbs
+	I **played** a lot of music.	They **gave** a concert.
–	They **didn't want** to be in the hospital.	They [1] ________ **speak** to me.
?	Where **did** you **work** last summer?	What [2] ________ you **do**?

1 **Complete the examples in the chart above.**

2 **Complete the sentences about your summer. Use the correct form of the verbs in the box.**

get up	~~go~~	have	learn	listen	play	see	work

1 I _didn't go_ to the beach.
2 I ____________ soccer in the park.
3 I ____________ how to play the drums.
4 I ____________ at a swimming pool.
5 I ____________ to music every day.
6 I ____________ late every day.
7 I ____________ a party at my house.
8 I ____________ my friends every day.

3 **Write questions about the activities in Exercise 2. Then ask and answer them with a partner.**

Did you go to the beach last summer?
____
____
____
____
____
____
____

4 **Rewrite the paragraph in the simple past. Then read your paragraph to a partner.**

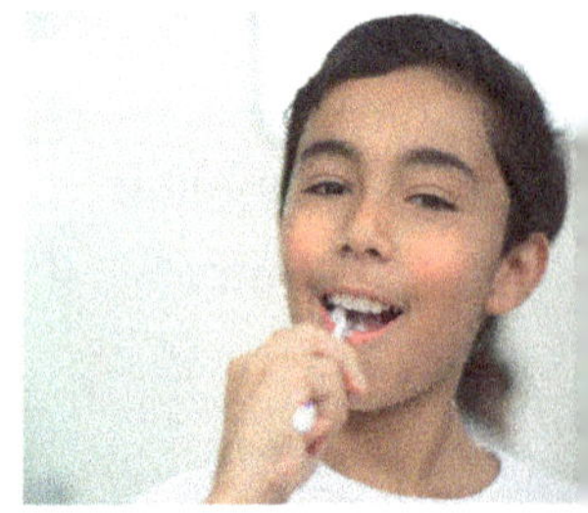

Matias gets up at seven o'clock to go to school. First, he gets dressed and then he has breakfast. He has cereal and toast. He doesn't have juice. Then he brushes his teeth and puts on his coat. He doesn't walk to school. He takes the bus. He meets his friends outside school, and they listen to music before school starts.

Matias got up at seven o'clock to go to school.
____
____
____
____
____
____
____

Use It!

5 **Write questions in the simple past with *you*.**

1 Where / go / on your last vacation?
Where did you go on your last vacation?
2 What / do / last weekend?
____
3 Who / see / yesterday?
____
4 Have / breakfast / yesterday morning?
____

6 **Ask and answer the questions in Exercise 5.**

Where did you go on your last vacation?

I went to Florida.

WRITING
A Review of an App

1 Which apps do you use every day? Discuss with a partner.

2 Read Sophia's review. Does she recommend this app?

1 ☐ PhotoFun is a photo-editing app. All my friends have it and they use it every day. Last week, I downloaded it on my phone.

2 ☐ It's great because it's free and very easy to use. I can change my photos and make them look better. I'm interested in photography, so it's a great way to make beautiful pictures and share them with my friends on the Internet. I upload new photos every week and my friends really like them.

3 ☐ In my opinion, there are a couple of problems with it. My phone is kind of old and the app is sometimes slow. Also, people sometimes post negative comments about my photos. That's not cool, and it makes me angry.

4 ☐ Overall, I think it's a great app and I really recommend it.

3 Match topics a–d with paragraphs 1–4.

a good things
b general opinion
c introduce the app
d bad things

4 Complete the phrases in the *Useful Language* box. Then check the review.

Useful Language

[1] ________ is a [2] ________ app.
It's great because [3] ________.
In my [4] ________, there are [5] ________ with it.
Overall, I think it's [6] ________.
I really [7] ________.

PLAN

5 Write your own review of an app. Take notes about an app you use.

What is it? ________

What's good about it? ________

What isn't good about it? ________

What's your general opinion? ________

6 Decide what information to include in each paragraph. Use the information in Exercise 3 to help you.

WRITE

7 Write your review. Remember to include four paragraphs, the simple present and the present continuous, and adverbs of frequency.

CHECK

8 Do you ...
- introduce the app in the first paragraph?
- write about good and bad things?
- give your general opinion?

1 What inspires you?

LEARNING OUTCOMES

I can ...

- understand texts about inspiring people
- interview someone
- write a letter to a magazine
- understand how to use different past tense forms
- describe people and use phrasal verbs
- identify opposites, take notes, and identify cause and effect
- set and achieve learning goals

Start It!

1 What can you see in the photo?
2 Before you watch, what do you think an entrepreneur is?
3 Which businesses are mentioned? Watch and check.
4 Can you invent a new business? What is it?

Watch video 1.1

p13 Grammar in Action 1.2

p15 Grammar in Action 1.3

p16 Everyday English 1.4

p18 Globetrotters 1.5

VOCABULARY

Describing People

a

b

c

d

e

f

1.01 **1 Read the definitions (1–6) and match them with the photos (a–f). Then listen and check.**

1. A **calm** person is relaxed and doesn't worry. [e]
2. An **active** person has a lot of energy. [ ]
3. A **cheerful** person is happy. [ ]
4. A **confident** person feels they can do something well. [ ]
5. A **sensitive** person understands how others feel. [ ]
6. A **helpful** person helps others. [ ]

1.02 **2 Listen and complete the definitions. Which adjectives are similar in your language? Which are different? How can you remember them?**

angry	~~decisions~~	feel	good at	people	successful

1. A **sensible** person makes good *decisions* .
2. An **ambitious** person wants to be ________ .
3. A **talented** person is naturally ________ something.
4. A **sociable** person likes being with other ________ .
5. A **patient** person doesn't get ________ when things take a long time.
6. An **inspiring** person makes you ________ motivated.

3 What kind of people do you like to be around? Why?

LEARN TO LEARN

Opposites

When you learn a new adjective, write the opposite.

4 Match the words from Exercises 1 and 2 with their opposites.

1	grumpy	*cheerful*	7	silly	________
2	anxious	________	8	unambitious	________
3	impatient	________	9	unhelpful	________
4	insensitive	________	10	uninspiring	________
5	lazy	________	11	unsociable	________
6	shy	________	12	untalented	________

5 Test a partner. Say a word. What's the opposite?

Use It!

6 In your notebook, write three adjectives to describe you and say why.

sociable: I'm sociable because I love making friends and being with people.

7 Tell your partner your answers from Exercise 6. Do they agree? Did you both choose the same adjectives?

Explore It!

Guess the correct answer.

Some people in Japan believe your … influences your personality.

a blood type b height c shoe size

Find another interesting idea about what can influence your personality. Then write a question for your partner to answer.

READING

An Article

The Man Who Taught Himself to See

We sometimes say that a person who cannot see is "as blind as a bat," but bats actually have an amazing ability to "see" the world. The inspiring Daniel Kish lost his sight when he was a baby, but he learned to use sound to become more independent.

When he was growing up, his friends all rode bikes to school. Daniel wanted to be active like his friends, so he decided to teach himself to ride a bike by riding next to a wall. Soon he was biking to school.

One day, while Daniel was riding his bike, one of his friends realized something incredible. Daniel was making clicking sounds with his tongue and using his ears to "see" objects around him. Bats make similar sounds, and the sound waves travel through the air until they hit something. The bats then listen to the sound waves as they bounce off the object and return to them with information. Using this technique, called echolocation, Daniel knows the size, position, and shape of an object so he can "see" it in his head.

Daniel believes anyone can train their brain to learn echolocation. While he was studying in college, he planned an echolocation training program. Now, he travels around the world giving talks and teaching the technique to other blind people. He inspires them to use echolocation so they can enjoy activities such as mountain biking, climbing, camping, and cooking, just like he does.

1.03 1 Mark (✓) the things in the box you think Daniel uses to "see." Read and check.

brain ☐	hands ☐	sticks ☐
dogs ☐	nose ☐	tongue ☐
ears ☐	sounds ☐	

2 Answer the questions.

1 Why is the phrase "as blind as a bat" strange?

____

2 What can Daniel do with sounds?

____

3 What does Daniel do now?

____

4 What does Daniel do in his free time?

____

3 Complete the chart with words from the article.

Verb	Noun	Adjective
1 believes	belief	believable
2 ______	inspiration	inspiring
	3 ______	active
see	4 ______	sighted
	independence	5 ______
amaze	amazement	6 ______

4 In your notebook, write sentences about Daniel with words from Exercise 3. Work in pairs. Compare your sentences.

Voice It!

5 Discuss the questions.

1 Do you think Daniel Kish is inspiring? Why / Why not?

2 Do you know any inspiring people? Why are they inspiring?

Finished? p118 Ex. 1

Watch video 1.2
Why did he start vlogging?
How does he describe himself?

GRAMMAR IN ACTION

Simple Past and Past Continuous with *When* and *While*

Past Continuous	Simple Past
Daniel **was riding** his bike	[1] ___when___ one of his friends realized something.
[2] ________ Daniel **was riding** his bike,	one of his friends **realized** something incredible.
[3] ________ he was **growing up**,	his friends all **rode** bikes to school.

Pronunciation p141

1 **Complete the examples in the chart above. Use the article on page 12 to help you.**

2 **Circle the correct words.**

1 What *did you do* / *were you doing* when I *called* / *was calling* you?

2 They *were leaving* / *left* when the phone *was ringing* / *rang*.

3 I *didn't see* / *wasn't seeing* Tom while I *played* / *was playing* soccer.

Get It Right!

We usually use **while** with the past continuous to emphasize an ongoing action in the past. We usually use **when** with the simple past to talk about an interrupting action.

I was walking my dog when it started to rain.

NOT ~~I walked my dog when it was starting to rain.~~

3 1.07 **Complete the text with the correct form of the verbs in parentheses. Then listen and check.**

Elvis Ingersoll, a 14-year-old from California, [1] ___was working___ (work) in his family's restaurant one day when suddenly, it [2] ________ (start) to rain. Elvis [3] ________ (look) out the window when he [4] ________ (see) an old man walking across the street without an umbrella. Immediately, Elvis [5] ________ (run) outside with an umbrella and [6] ________ (help) the man cross the street. Elvis and the old man [7] ________ (not know) that people in the restaurant [8] ________ (take) videos of them while they [9] ________ (cross) the street. Later, thousands of people [10] ________ (share) videos of the helpful teen and the old man online.

Use It!

4 **Complete the questions with the correct form of the verbs in parentheses.**

1 What ___did___ you ___see___ (see) when you ___were going___ (go) to school this morning?

2 ________ it ________ (snow) when you ________ (wake up)?

3 What ________ you ________ (talk) about when you ________ (see) your friends last week?

4 What ________ you ________ (do) when you ________ (get) home from school yesterday?

5 What ________ you ________ (think) about while you ________ (eat) breakfast this morning?

5 **Ask and answer the questions in Exercise 4.**

Finished? p118 Ex. 2

VOCABULARY AND LISTENING

Phrasal Verbs

1.08 **1** **Match the underlined phrasal verbs 1–8 with the definitions a–h. Then listen, check, and repeat.**

A

During summer break, most teenagers [1]hang out [h] with their friends, but Ben volunteers at a children's summer camp. He [2]takes care of [ ] the children. "I [3]get along with [ ] the other volunteers," he says. "It's great!"

B

"I really [4]look up to [ ] my best friend, Emma. Her mom is in a wheelchair, so she [5]depends on Emma [ ] for many things, like taking a shower. Emma is also busy with schoolwork. I don't know how she [6]deals with [ ] everything, but she never [7]gives up [ ]. She's really positive. When I'm feeling sad, she always [8]cheers me up [ ]."

a supervises or cares for
b makes me feel happier
c manages to do
d admire
e stops trying
f have a good relationship with
g needs Emma's help
~~h spend time relaxing~~

Use It!

2 **Write true and false sentences about your friends and family with the phrasal verbs from Exercise 1. Can your partner guess which sentences are false?**

A Radio Show

3 **Look at the photo. What do you think the man's special talent is?**

LEARN TO LEARN

Taking Notes

Writing key words can help you remember what the listening was about.

1.09 **4** **Listen to the radio show about Henry Fraser and take notes. Then compare with a partner. Whose notes are clearer? Why?**

His life before the accident:

The accident:

His life after the accident:

1.09 **5** **Listen again and circle the correct answers.**

1 Henry hit his head because …
  a the water wasn't deep.
  b he was running.
2 After the accident, Henry …
  a needed help with some things.
  b needed help with everything.
3 Henry paints pictures of …
  a animals and people.
  b animals, people, and things.
4 Jeremy looks up to Henry because he …
  a is positive about a difficult situation.
  b paints with his mouth.

Voice It!

6 **Discuss the questions.**

1 How do you think Henry felt after the accident?
2 Why do you think he didn't give up?
3 Do you think Henry is inspiring? Why / Why not?

GRAMMAR IN ACTION

Used To

Watch video 1.3
What did James use to be afraid of?
Is James still afraid?

+	Henry Fraser **used** [1] ________ be a rugby player.
–	He **didn't use to** be an artist.
?	What **did** he **use** [2] ________ be?

1 **Complete the examples in the chart above.**

2 **Complete the sentences with the correct form of *used to* and the phrases in the box.**

> be very active build things
> hate vegetables like coffee
> ~~live in the country~~ play with

1 Now my grandparents live in the city, but they *used to live in the country.*

2 I ________________________________,
but now I drink it every day.

3 These days, Caroline doesn't do much exercise, but she ________________________________.

4 I ________________________________,
but now I have a salad for lunch every day.

5 A ________________________________
blocks when you were little?
B Yes, I loved it. I ________________________________
all the time.

Get It Right!

To make negative sentences and questions, we use **did (not)** + **use to** + the base verb form.

He didn't use to live in the city. **NOT** ~~*He didn't used to live in the city.*~~

Did you use to walk to school? **NOT** ~~*Did you used to walk to school?*~~

1.10 **3** **Complete the conversation with the correct form of *used to* or the simple past and the verbs in parentheses. Then listen and check.**

ALEX What do you want to be when you're older, Mia?
MIA I [1] *used to want* (want) to be a tennis player, but now I want to be a scientist.
ALEX Why [2] ________ (change) your mind?
MIA I [3] ________ (see) a really interesting show about science on TV.
I [4] ________ (not pay) attention in science, but now I love it. What about you?
ALEX I want to be an English teacher, but when I was younger, I had a different idea.
MIA Really? What was that?
ALEX I [5] ________ (change) my mind all the time. For a while, I [6] ________ (want) to be a photographer. Then I thought about being a singer … or a painter.
MIA Well, we have a lot of time to decide!

Use It!

4 **In your notebook, write sentences about what you used to do when you were younger. Think about the things in the box.**

> elementary school food and drink
> games and toys vacations

When I was younger, I used to build things with blocks.

5 EXAM **Ask and answer the questions with a partner.**

Student A:
What toys did you use to play with when you were younger?
What fun activities do you do now that you didn't use to do?

Student B:
What fun activities did you use to do when you were younger?
What foods do you eat now that you didn't use to eat?

Finished? p118 Ex. 3

SPEAKING

Interviewing Someone

1.11 **1 What is a hero? Listen to the conversation. Do you agree with Sam?**

JARED Hey, Sam. [1] Can I ask you a few questions for the school magazine?

SAM Sure. Go ahead.

JARED [2] ______________, who's your hero and why?

SAM My friend Elena. Last month she saved a boy at the swimming pool.

JARED Really? [3] ______________ what happened?

SAM He was playing with a ball when he fell in the water. The thing is, Elena isn't a great swimmer, but she jumped in and pulled him out.

JARED Good for her! [4] ______________, in your opinion, what is a hero?

SAM I used to think all heroes were famous. Now I think when someone does something brave, they're a hero.

JARED I'm with you there. [5] ______________, Sam. Thanks!

1.11 **2 Complete the conversation with the phrases from the *Useful Language* box. Then listen and check.**

Useful Language

Can I ask you a few questions … ?
Can you tell us … ?
First of all …
One more thing …
That's all …

3 Match the uses (1–4) with the phrases in the *Everyday English* box.

We say this when we …

1 think someone did a good thing.
2 tell someone it's OK to start.
3 agree with someone.
4 introduce a problem.

Watch video 1.4
Everyday English

Go ahead. ☐
Good for (her)! ☐
I'm with you there. ☐
The thing is … ☐

PLAN

4 Read the interview again. Work in pairs. Think of a hero you both have. Discuss the questions and take notes.

1 Why is this person a hero?

____

____

2 What is this person like?

____

____

5 Plan an interview. One of you is the interviewer and the other answers questions about the hero. Think of questions and answers for your interview.

SPEAK

6 Practice an interview. Remember to use past tenses, *used to*, and phrases from the *Useful Language* and *Everyday English* boxes.

CHECK

7 Work with another pair. Listen to their interview and answer the questions from Exercise 4.

WRITING

A Letter to a Magazine

Dear Editor,

1 ☐ I am writing about your "Inspiring Person" competition. Personally, I think **Anoka Primrose Abeyrathne** should win the competition.

2 ☐ In 2004, **Anoka** was living in Sri Lanka when a tsunami destroyed a lot of the coast, so she decided to start a project to plant new trees. Now she works with other young people to take care of the environment and help people around the world. For me, her most exciting project is "Make It Green Again." For this project, **Anoka** made Sri Lanka's first environmental music video because she wanted people to think about the environment.

3 ☐ In my view, **Anoka** is an inspiring person because she's ambitious and helpful. I look up to her because she used to be a normal student and now she's changing the world. In my opinion, **Anoka** should win because she cares about the environment.

Thank you for reading this letter.

Yours truly,

Luke Black

1 Do you know any inspiring teens? What inspiring things do they do?

2 *Teen Magazine* is having a competition to find an inspiring person. Read Luke's letter. Who does he want to win?

3 Match questions a–c with paragraphs 1–3.

a Why should this person win the competition?

b Who should win the competition?

c What inspiring things does this person do?

4 Complete the phrases in the *Useful Language* box. Then check in the letter.

Useful Language

1 ________ me,

2 ________ ________ opinion,

3 ________ ________ view,

4 ________ , I think …

PLAN

5 Write your own letter to the editor about an inspiring person you know. Read the notes. Use them to write your own notes.

Who? my friend Gina

What does she do? runs a lot, raises money for sick children

Why should she win? never gives up, cheerful, talented

6 Decide what information to include in each paragraph. Use the questions in Exercise 3 to help.

WRITE

7 Write your letter. Remember to include three paragraphs, past tenses, *used to,* and phrases from the *Useful Language* box.

CHECK

8 Do you …

- introduce the person in the first paragraph?
- say why the person should win?
- use language for giving opinions?

Finished? p118 Ex. 4

AROUND THE WORLD

READING
An Article

1 Do you know where Freetown is? How do you think life in Freetown is different from where you live?

1.12 2 Read the article and check your answers from Exercise 1.

3 Put the events in order.

a ☐ He built a radio station.
b ☐ He made a battery.
c ☐ He played music on the radio.
d ☐ He found objects in the street.
e ☐ He went to a summer camp.
f 1 The lights in his community didn't always work.

Globetrotters
Watch video 1.5
Local Heroes

- Who is your hero? Why?
- Which heroes are mentioned? What did they do?
- What type of personality do heroes have?

Voice It!

4 Discuss the questions.

1 When you show initiative, you help in a big way when no one expects you to. How does Kelvin show initiative?
2 Is it easy to show initiative? Why / Why not?
3 Why is it important to show initiative?

The Boy Who Brought Light to Freetown

Can you imagine life with no TV? What about life without a computer, or music, or even lights?

Kelvin Doe is an inspiring young man from Freetown, Sierra Leone. When he was growing up, the electricity in his neighborhood didn't always work, so the lights only used to come on once a week.

As a boy, Kelvin was interested in how things worked and he used to get excited about making things. While he was hanging out with his friends, Kelvin used to find materials in the street and make useful things from them.

His mom used to get tired of finding pieces of garbage everywhere, but he made some amazing things. He used old electronic items to repair broken TVs and radios. At 13, he even made a battery so that his family and neighbors had lights at night.

When Kelvin was in high school, he participated in a summer innovation camp. Students had to think of a way to deal with a problem in their community. Radio is important in Sierra Leone, and Kelvin knew that his community would be proud of their own radio station. So, while he was there, Kelvin built a radio station. He played music on the radio and when he wasn't playing music, he interviewed people about life in Freetown. His radio show was very popular because Kelvin gets along well with everybody and was good at talking to people. People called him DJ Focus because he believes that when you focus on something, you can do anything.

LEARN TO LEARN

Cause and Effect

Identifying why something happened (the cause) and what happened (the effect) can improve your reading.

5 Use the correct form of the phrases in the box to complete the sentences about causes and their effects.

build a radio station	~~make a battery~~	not be happy	people like his radio show	repair broken things

1 The lights in Freetown worked only once a week, so Kelvin _made a battery_.
2 Kelvin's family didn't have much money, so he ________________.
3 Kelvin left garbage everywhere, so his mom ________________.
4 Kelvin knew radio was important, so he ________________.
5 Kelvin was good at talking to people, so ________________.

6 Complete the questions with the adjectives in the box. Then ask and answer them.

~~excited~~	good	interested	proud	tired

1 What are you _excited_ about doing next week?
2 What types of websites are you ________ in?
3 Which subjects are you ________ at?
4 What do you get ________ of doing?
5 What are you most ________ of?

Explore It!

Guess the correct answer.

The four main languages that people speak in Sierra Leone are: Mende, Temne, Krio, and …

a Spanish. b French. c English.

Find another interesting fact about Sierra Leone. Then write a question for your partner to answer.

SHAPE IT!

CULTURE PROJECT

A Presentation

Kelvin solves a problem in his community. Think of a problem in your community or country and research possible solutions. In groups, give a presentation about the problem.

Teacher's Resource Bank

1 REVIEW

VOCABULARY

1 Circle the correct words.

1 When I have problems with my homework, I ask my brother. He's very *helpful* / *ambitious*.
2 I've watched all her movies. I want to be just like her one day – she's so *calm* / *inspiring*.
3 Sophie is very *patient* / *confident*. She talks to everyone and is never shy.
4 When I have a lot of things to do, I feel *patient* / *stressed*. My mom says I need to relax more.
5 My best friend is very *sensible* / *sensitive*. He always plans things very carefully.
6 He has the most amazing voice. He's so *talented* / *sociable*.

2 Complete the sentences with the words in the box. Then match sentences 1–8 with sentences a–h.

cheer up	deal with	depend on	get along
give up	hang out	look up to	take care of

1 ☐ This is so difficult!
2 ☐ Your uncle's a firefighter? Wow!
3 ☐ Do you take your cat on vacation with you?
4 ☐ How do you ______ so much homework?
5 ☐ Hey, do you want to ______ after school?
6 ☐ ______! There's no school tomorrow!
7 ☐ Do you ______ with your sister?
8 ☐ Babies ______ adults for everything.

a Sure, let's watch a movie!
b Of course! She's like my best friend.
c No, silly! Our neighbors ______ it.
d They do. But they're really cute!
e Yes, but I have homework to do.
f Don't ______! You can do it.
g I make a list and do the most important things first.
h He's my hero. I really ______ him.

GRAMMAR IN ACTION

3 Complete the text with the simple past or past continuous form of the verbs in parentheses.

While I [1] ______ (play) tennis yesterday with Anna, a dog [2] ______ (run) onto the court. It chased the ball and [3] ______ (pick) it up in its mouth. While Anna [4] ______ (run) after it, the dog [5] ______ (wag) its tail. Then it [6] ______ (jump) on her. When I [7] ______ (go) to check if she was OK, I [8] ______ (see) that she was smiling. It was her cousin's dog!

4 In your notebook, write sentences about Leo's student life with *used to* or *didn't use to*. Use the phrases in the box.

get up late every day   not have a job
not have any money
share an apartment with friends
sometimes study in the afternoon

Self-Assessment

I can describe people in English.
I can use phrasal verbs to talk about people and what they do.
I can use the simple past and past continuous with *when* and *while*.
I can use *used to* to describe past habits.

LEARN TO ... SET AND ACHIEVE LEARNING GOALS

When you know what you want to achieve with English, you can take steps to get there.

1 Read what Tae Min says about his learning goal. What was it? Did he succeed?

Last year, five Australian students visited our school. Our teacher told us a month before their visit. I wanted to spend time with them, but my English wasn't very good. I was getting good grades in class, but conversations with real people were difficult. So my goal was to hang out with the Australian students and talk about things they were interested in. I spoke to my teacher and she helped me make an action plan. My plan was to learn some easy phrases and expressions to use in informal conversations and practice them every day with my sister – she speaks English really well. The plan worked! I spoke a lot of English with the Australians and we became good friends.

2 Look at the action plan below. Write Tae Min's answers to questions 1–3.

3 Read what Paola says about her learning goal. Write her answers to questions 1 and 2 in the action plan.

What's my learning goal? Well, in two months we have an important exam in English. It's on the vocabulary we're studying in class. I really want to do well on it. I'm very ambitious!

4 Circle the best answers to questions 3 and 4 for Paola and write them in the action plan.

Question 3

a Find the vocabulary I'm studying in a dictionary.

b Make vocabulary flash cards and use them every day.

c Study all the vocabulary the day before the exam.

Question 4

a I pass the exam.

b I fail the exam.

c I pass with a high score.

SHAPE IT!

5 Think of an English learning goal. Write your name and your answers to questions 1 to 4 in the action plan.

6 Tell your partner about your learning goal. Use the action plan to help you. Do they think it is realistic? Why / Why not?

Action Plan	NAME: *Tae Min*	NAME: *Paola*	NAME:
1 What do I want to do?			
2 How much time do I have?			
3 How do I achieve it?			
4 How do I know that I achieved my goal?	*I have some new Australian friends.*		

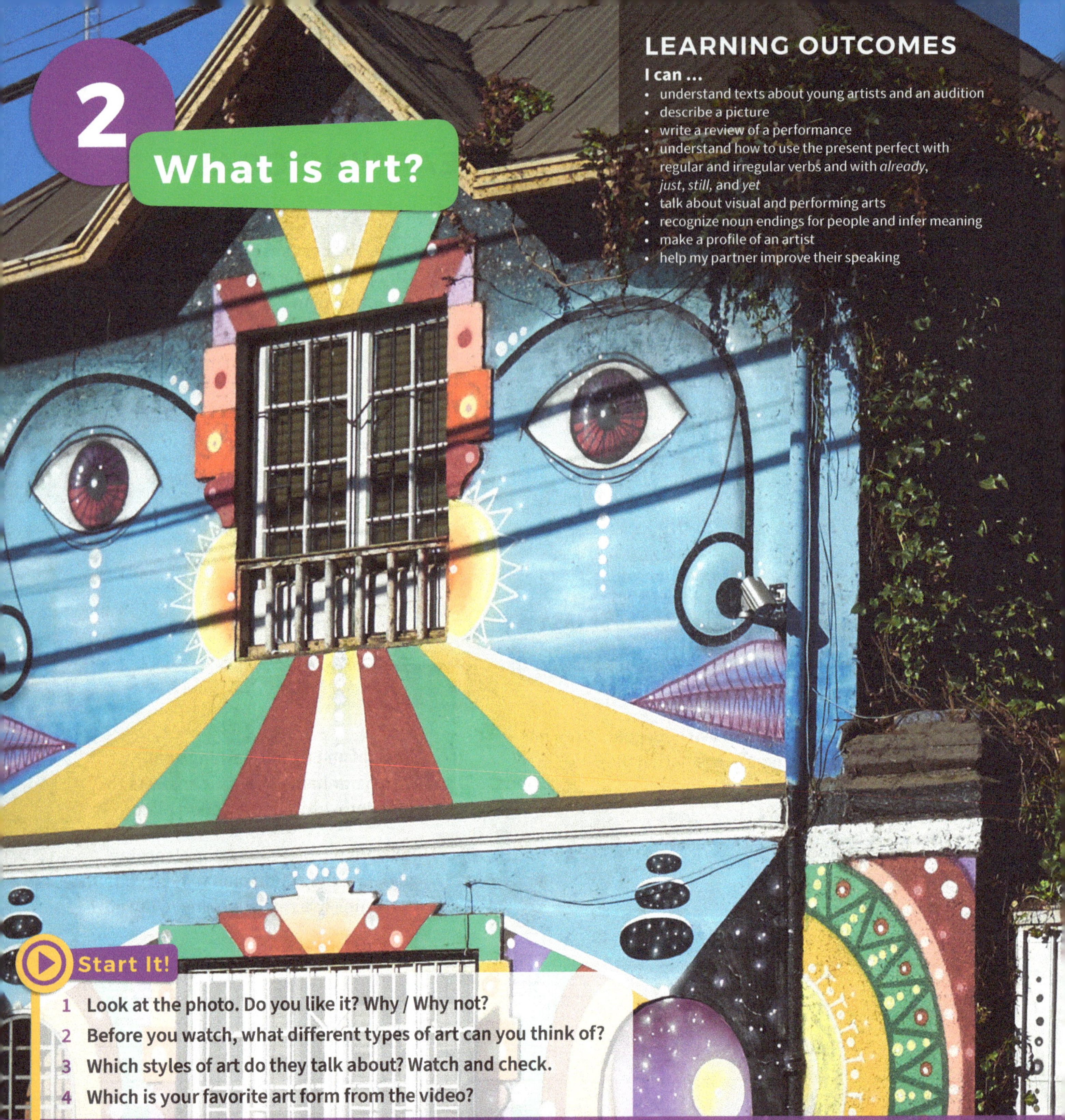

2 What is art?

LEARNING OUTCOMES

I can ...

- understand texts about young artists and an audition
- describe a picture
- write a review of a performance
- understand how to use the present perfect with regular and irregular verbs and with *already*, *just*, *still*, and *yet*
- talk about visual and performing arts
- recognize noun endings for people and infer meaning
- make a profile of an artist
- help my partner improve their speaking

Start It!

1 Look at the photo. Do you like it? Why / Why not?
2 Before you watch, what different types of art can you think of?
3 Which styles of art do they talk about? Watch and check.
4 Which is your favorite art form from the video?

Watch video 2.1

p25

Grammar in Action 2.2

p27

Grammar in Action 2.3

p28

Everyday English 2.4

VOCABULARY

Visual and Performing Arts

2.01 **1 Match the words with the photos (1–9) and definitions (10–12). Then listen, check, and repeat.**

architecture	☐	illustration	☐
contemporary dance	1	musical theater	☐
exhibition	☐	performance	☐
fashion design	☐	photography	☐
filmmaking	☐	sculpture	☐
gallery	☐	street art	☐

10 a room or building where you can see art
11 acting, singing, dancing, or playing music
12 an event where you can see paintings and other art forms

1

2

3

4

5

6

7

8

9

2 Complete the chart with the words from Exercise 1.

Visual Arts	Performing Arts
architecture	

LEARN TO LEARN

Making Nouns for People

We often use the endings *-ist*, *-er*, and *-or* for people.

3 Write the people who do these activities.

1 fashion design ___fashion designer___
2 filmmaking ________
3 illustration ________
4 performance ________
5 photography ________
6 sculpture ________
7 street art ________

Use It!

4 Put the words from Exercise 1 in order starting with your favorite. Then compare with your partner and say why.

My favorite art form is street art because it looks really cool. What's yours?

Explore It!

Guess the correct answer.

People won medals for architecture, painting, sculpture, and … at the Olympic Games between 1912 and 1948.

a music b filmmaking c fashion design

Find another interesting fact about an art form. Then write a question for your partner to answer.

WHAT DO YOU SEE?

TRASH, PASTA, OR ART?

Check out this talented street artist from Lisbon, Portugal!

Bordalo II, creator of "Big Trash Animals," has transformed the streets of Lisbon into an art gallery. When you first look, you see an enormous bear or a giant duck, but look again and you'll see a car wheel or an old toilet. [1]____ Bordalo II hasn't used normal paints, brushes, or rollers for a reason. [2]____

His animals are beautiful, but he has made them from ugly things. Fans have seen his creations at exhibitions and festivals in the U.S.A., Italy, and Sweden, but Lisbon is his favorite city.

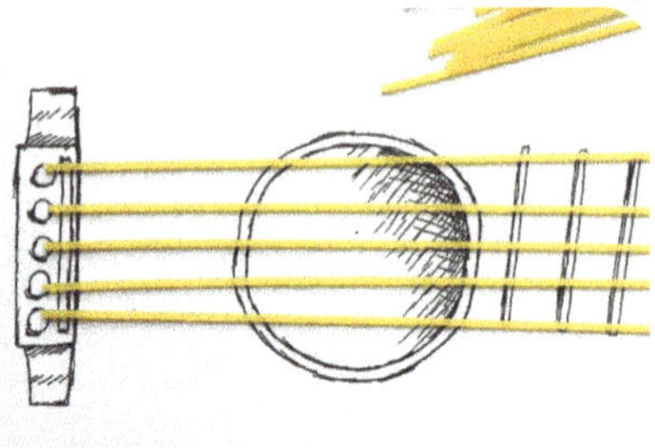

[3]____ Inspiring young illustrator Kristián Mensa, from Prague in the Czech Republic, takes ordinary objects and uses his imagination to change them into exciting visual art. For Kristián, an orange isn't just a fruit, it's a turtle's body, and spaghetti becomes guitar strings. His biggest gallery is social media, and followers have shared photos of his artwork thousands of times, but fans have also been to exhibitions of his illustrations in his home country and the U.S.A. Kristián loves dance, theater, and music. [4]____ So, next time you look at some pasta, imagine what else it could be!

We haven't finished talking about young, talented artists. Next week, you can read about Joshua Behrens and Shania McDonagh.

READING

A Magazine Article

1 **Look at the pictures. Which types of art can you see?**

2 **Read the magazine article and check your answers from Exercise 1.**

2.02 **3** EXAM **Four sentences have been removed from the article. For each gap (1–4), choose the correct answer. There is one extra sentence. Then listen and check.**

A He hasn't been to art school but would love to go.

B This is street art with a message.

C They are all objects from his house.

D Have you ever looked at a normal, everyday object and seen something else?

E He's used trash and spray paint because he wants us to think about all the things we throw away.

4 **Complete the chart with words from the article.**

People	artist, creator, ____, ____, ____
Art Materials	____, ____, ____, ____
Other Art Words	____, ____, ____, ____, ____, ____, ____, ____, ____, ____

Voice It!

5 **Discuss the questions.**

1 Do you prefer Bordalo II's art or Kristián's art? Why?

2 Which type of art do you like to create? Why?

Finished? p119 Ex. 1

Watch video 2.2
How does she describe São Paulo? What amazing things has she seen?

GRAMMAR IN ACTION

Present Perfect with Regular and Irregular Verbs

	I/You/We/They	He/She/It
+	Fans **have** [1] *seen* his creations at exhibitions.	He**'s** [4] ______ trash and spray paint.
–	We **haven't** [2] ______ talking about young, talented artists.	He **hasn't** [5] ______ to art school.
?	**Have** you **ever** [3] ______ at a normal, everyday object and seen something else? **Yes**, I **have**. / **No**, I **haven't**.	Where **has** he **been**?

1 **Complete the examples in the chart above. Use the article on page 24 to help you.**

Get It Right!

The verb **to go** has two past participles: **been** and **gone**.

She has been to a few exhibitions. (describes a completed experience) *She has gone to school.* (describes a physical action)

2 **Put the words in the correct order.**

1 had / has / exhibitions in the U.S.A. and Poland / Bordalo II
Bordalo II has had exhibitions in the U.S.A. and Poland.

2 Bordalo II / Has / had an exhibition in Italy / ever / ? ______

3 Bordalo II / sculptures of animals / made / hasn't ______

4 People / Kristián's work on social media / shared / have ______

5 Kristián / Has / been to art school / ? ______

3 **Correct the false sentences and answer the questions in Exercise 2.**

1 *False. Bordalo II hasn't had exhibitions in Poland.*
2 ______
3 ______
4 ______
5 ______

4 (2.03) **Complete the text with the correct form of the verbs in the box. Then listen and check.**

amaze appear create not finish ~~see~~ win

[1]*Have* you ever *seen* a photograph and then realized it was a drawing? Maybe you were looking at one of Shania McDonagh's illustrations. Shania is a young Irish artist who [2] ______ the world of art with her incredible pictures. She [3] ______ several drawings that look like photographs, with nothing more than a pencil. The talented student [4] ______ first prize in national art competitions, and her pictures [5] ______ in exhibitions in Ireland. Shania [6] ______ her education, but in the future, she wants to be an artist.

Use It!

5 **In your notebook, write questions with the present perfect and the phrases in the box or your own ideas.**

go to an exhibition ~~go to the theater~~ make a movie play a musical instrument win a competition

Have you ever been to the theater?

6 **Work in groups. Ask and answer your questions to complete the sentences about your group.**

All of us *have been to a concert* .
All of us ______ .
Some of us ______ .
None of us ______ .

Finished? p119 Ex. 2

VOCABULARY AND LISTENING

Music and Theater

2.04 **1 Read the sentences and put the words in bold in the correct category. Then listen and check.**

1. I'm playing the **part** of the sister, but I'm only in the opening **scene** of the play.
2. The **audience** stood up when the **orchestra** finished playing the last song.
3. I need to learn my **lines** for an **audition** I have next week.
4. I'm learning the **lyrics** to my favorite song.
5. We only had one **rehearsal** before the **show**.
6. She spent three months in the **studio** working on her latest album.

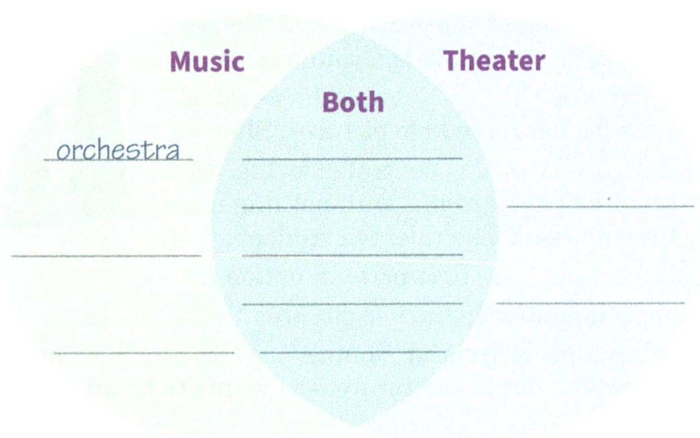

Use It!

2 In your notebook, write present perfect questions with words from Exercise 1. Then ask and answer the questions with a partner.

Have you ever seen a show?

A Conversation

3 Which emotions in the box can people feel before or after an audition? Why?

calm	cheerful	confident
sad	sensitive	stressed

LEARN TO LEARN

Inferring

Noticing the way people speak can help you to guess their feelings.

2.05 **4 Rosa and Pablo have had auditions. Listen and answer the questions.**

1. Did they get the parts they auditioned for?
   ____
2. How do Rosa and Pablo feel?
   ____
   ____

2.05 **5 Listen again. Mark (✓) the advice Pablo gives Rosa.**

1. ☐ practice every day
2. ☐ say your lines out loud
3. ☐ think about the meaning of the lines
4. ☐ say your lines in front of a mirror
5. ☐ record yourself with a camera
6. ☐ think about your audience
7. ☐ don't make any mistakes

Voice It!

6 Discuss the questions.

1. Which is the most important piece of advice?
2. What's difficult about performing?

GRAMMAR IN ACTION

Present Perfect with *Already*, *Just*, *Still*, and *Yet*

Watch video 2.3
When was the audition? Has he gotten the part?

+	I've [1] just **spoken** to my drama teacher. I've [2] ________ **had** my audition!
–	They [3] ________ **haven't decided** on the main parts. I **haven't heard** anything [4] ________ .
?	**Have** you **heard** anything [5] ________ ?

Pronunciation p141

1 Read the information below. Then complete the examples in the table above.

- We use *still* before *hasn't/haven't*.
- We use *just* and *already* between *has/have* and the past participle.
- We use *yet* at the end of the sentence.

Get It Right!

We use **just** to emphasize that an action has happened very recently.

I've just finished my project.

2 Choose a word and write it in the correct place in the sentences.

1. Have you heard the news? (still / yet)
   Have you heard the news yet?
2. I haven't finished my food. (already / still)
   ____
3. She's seen the new play at the theater. (already / yet)
   ____
4. They've gone to see a movie. (just / still)
   ____
5. They haven't learned their lines for the play. (already / yet)
   ____

3 Complete the conversation with the present perfect form of the verbs and *already*, *just*, *still*, or *yet*. Then listen and check.

2.08

PABLO Hey! Guess what? I [1] 've just seen (see) my drama teacher and …

ROSA You got the part?

PABLO Shh! Yes, but it's a secret. They [2] ________ (not tell) everyone ________ because they [3] ________ (not choose) all the parts.

ROSA So, why [4] ________ they ________ (tell) you?

PABLO Because they've decided they really want me for the part. I said at the audition that I [5] ________ (learn) all the lyrics to all the songs.

ROSA And [6] ________ you ________ (tell) your parents ________ ?

PABLO Not yet. I [7] ________ (send) my mom a message to call me, but she [8] ________ (not call).

Use It!

4 Write questions to help you find a person in your class who …

1. has already finished some homework.
   Have you finished your biology homework yet?
2. hasn't seen (movie name) yet.
   ____
3. has already tried (a sport you've never done).
   ____
4. has helped someone today.
   ____
5. still hasn't been to (a place in your town).
   ____

5 Ask your questions from Exercise 4.

Have you finished your biology homework yet?

No, not yet.

Finished? p119 Ex. 3

SPEAKING
Describing a Picture

1 **Look at the painting and answer the questions.**

1 What can you see?

2 Do you like it? Why / Why not?

2 (2.09) **Listen to Alex and Katya talking about the painting. Who do you agree with?**

ALEX Hey, Katya, have you done your art homework yet?

KATYA To write about the painting? No, I still haven't finished. There's tons to say!

ALEX Really? What?

KATYA I've seen *The Starry Night*. It's amazing! [1] It makes me feel calm and excited at the same time. What about you?

ALEX I dunno, [2] ______ a kid's painting. The clouds, stars, and moon are ginormous compared to the houses. [3] ______ strange.

KATYA Have you read about it yet? [4] ______ look real. The artist, Van Gogh, wanted to show how the sky made him feel.

ALEX Nope, sorry! I've just looked at it again and I don't understand why he used wavy lines and shapes.

KATYA He used them to show how light moves.

ALEX Oh, I see. And he combines a lot of bright and dark colors.

KATYA Right. [5] ______ his mixed emotions.

3 (2.09) **Complete the conversation with the phrases from the *Useful Language* box. Then listen and check.**

Useful Language

It isn't supposed to …
~~It makes me feel …~~
It seems a little …
It looks like …
It probably shows …

4 **Match the words and phrases (1–5) with the words in the *Everyday English* box.**

1 I don't know
2 no
3 child
4 a lot
5 enormous

Watch video 2.4
Everyday English

dunno ☐ ginormous ☐ kid ☐
nope ☐ tons ☐

PLAN

5 **Look at the painting of the artist's bedroom. Take notes.**

Object	Size	Color

Feelings: ______

6 **Work in pairs. Plan a conversation about the painting.**

SPEAK

7 **Practice a conversation. Remember to use the present perfect and phrases from the *Useful Language* and *Everyday English* boxes.**

CHECK

8 **Work with another pair. Listen to their conversation. Do they include the information from Exercise 5?**

WRITING

A Review

1 ☐ Have you seen **STOMP** yet?
You haven't? Then what are you waiting for? **STOMP** is perfect for adults and kids – it's the best show I've ever seen.

2 ☐ **STOMP** isn't a musical or a dance show. It's a unique performance. The performers create powerful rhythms with objects like brushes and newspapers. There are no lines, singing, or story, but the sounds and movements are amazing.

3 ☐ What I liked about it was that the performers were so talented. I've never seen anything like it before. It was a little loud sometimes but a lot of fun.

4 ☐ **STOMP** is playing at a theater near Broadway and tickets are a really good price. I recommend it because it's so creative and original.

1 Look at the photo and answer the questions with a partner.

1 What type of show is it?
2 Have you ever seen a similar performance?

2 Read Camila's review of the show. Did she enjoy it?

____

3 Match information a–d with paragraphs 1–4.

a a description of the event
b what she liked / didn't like about it
c where you can see it
d who it is for

4 Complete the phrases in the *Useful Language* box. Then check in the review.

Useful Language

I [1] ______________ it because …
It's the best show I'[2] ______________ seen.
I've never [3] ______________ anything like it before.
(STOMP) is [4] ______________ at …
[5] ______________ I liked / didn't like about it was …

PLAN

5 Write your own review of a performance. Look at the *School of Rock* poster or think of a performance you have been to. Take notes.

Where did you see it? ______________________________
____
Who was the performance for? ______________________________
____
What was it like? ______________________________
____
What did you like / not like about it? ______________________________
____

6 Decide what information to include in each paragraph. Use the information in Exercise 3 to help you.

WRITE

7 Write your review. Remember to include four paragraphs, the present perfect, and phrases from the *Useful Language* box.

CHECK

8 Do you …

- describe the event?
- say who it is for?
- say what you liked / didn't like about it?

Finished? p119 Ex. 4

ART PROJECT

A Profile of an Artist

1 Look at the photos and read the profile. Do you like Ben Heine's work? Why / Why not?

2 Read the profile again and complete the notes.

Nationality: ______________________

Education: ______________________

Interests: ______________________

Types of Art: ______________________

Exhibitions: ______________________

How to Do Online Research

3 Why is it important to think about these questions when you read information online?

a Who wrote the information?

____

b Who is the information for?

____

c How do I know it's true?

____

d Can you find the same information on a different website?

____

e When did they write it?

____

f Can I copy and paste this information into my own work?

____

2.10 4 Listen to the advice about doing online research and check your ideas from Exercise 3.

SHAPE IT!

Artist's Name: Ben Heine
Art Form: painting, illustration, and photography

1 He is Belgian and he lives and works in Brussels. He started drawing when he was 11. He's an artist and a music producer.

2 He studied at an art college in the UK and he taught himself photography. He has also taught himself how to play the drums and the piano, and he has learned how to speak French, English, Russian, and other languages.

3 In 2010, he invented a new art form that uses illustration and photography. He adds drawings to photos to make them come alive. This artwork has been so popular that art teachers around the world have used it to teach their students how to be creative.

4 He has created a range of paintings that use paintings and real-life models. Ben paints a model the same colors as the painting. Then the model stands in front of the painting so they look "invisible."

5 Ben's artwork has appeared in exhibitions and galleries in Africa, Asia, Europe, and the U.S.A. You can see his work all over the world.

PLAN

5 Work in pairs to make a profile of an artist. Choose an artist you like.

- Find information about the artist. Use the tips from Exercise 4.
- Take notes like the ones in Exercise 2.
- Find pictures of their artwork.
- Decide who will write the different parts of the profile.
- Write your part and then give it to your partner to check.
- Work with your partner to put together the information and pictures.
- Write two questions for your classmates to answer about your profile.

PRESENT

6 Present your profile to the class. Remember to include interesting facts and pictures and to use your own words.

CHECK

7 Look at your classmates' profiles. Do they include all the information from Exercise 2? Which artist is your favorite? Discuss with your partner.

2 REVIEW

VOCABULARY

1 Complete the words with vowels.

1 __rch__t__ct__r__
2 __xh__b__t__ __n
3 f__lmm__k__ng
4 sc__lpt__r__
5 __ll__str__t__ __n
6 m__s__c__l th__ __t__r
7 p__rf__rm__nc__
8 ph__t__gr__phy

2 Match the parts of the words.

1	aud	a	es
2	lin	b	ow
3	pa	c	rt
4	sh	d	sal
5	sce	e	ience
6	rehear	f	ne

3 Complete the text with the words from Exercise 2.

Yesterday I went to the final [1] __________ of my sister's school [2] __________. It was the last practice before the first performance tonight with a real [3] __________ watching. My sister plays the main [4] __________ and forgot some of her [5] __________ in the final [6] __________. I think she needs a lot more practice!

GRAMMAR IN ACTION

4 Circle the correct words.

1 Have you finished *still* / *yet*?
2 I've *already* / *still* been to that gallery twice.
3 Have you *just* / *still* learned some new lines?
4 She *already* / *still* hasn't heard how her audition went.
5 She's *just* / *still* sung the lyrics to the song.

5 Complete the text with the present perfect form of the verbs in parentheses.

Teenage artist Autumn de Forest sold her first painting when she was just six years old. People [1] __________ (compare) her to Pablo Picasso. She [2] __________ (teach) herself how to paint by studying famous artists. People from all over the world [3] __________ (buy) her paintings and she [4] __________ (sell) some of them for thousands of dollars. Autumn [5] __________ (give) interviews on TV and she [6] __________ (speak) to college students about the importance of art in school.

Self-Assessment

I can describe visual and performing arts in English.
I can talk about music and theater.
I can use the present perfect with regular and irregular verbs.
I can use the present perfect with *already*, *just*, *still*, and *yet*.

LEARN TO LEARN

LEARN TO ... HELP YOUR PARTNER IMPROVE THEIR SPEAKING

When you work in pairs, it's important to listen carefully so you can help each other improve.

1 **Do you agree with these ideas? Why / Why not?**

a Everyone in this class knows different things in English.

b Everyone in this class can help each other improve.

I agree with a. You already knew the word "filmmaking," but I didn't.

Yes, but you often know words I don't know!

2 **Read Lucy's notes for a presentation about the best show she's ever been to. Think about the best show, concert, or exhibition you've ever been to. Take notes and prepare a one-minute presentation.**

The Best Show I've Ever Been To

What: The Moon Circus
Where: Brisbane
When: January 27
Who With: Mom, Dad, older sister Maria
Other Information: amazing orchestra, funny clowns – audience loved them, not a traditional circus – no animals

The Best ______________ I've Ever Been To
What: ______________
Where: ______________
When: ______________
Who With: ______________
Other Information: ______________
____
____

3 **Take turns listening to each other's presentations. Student A, look at the checklist below. Then use your notes from Exercise 2 to give your presentation. Student B, listen carefully to Student A. Do they do the things on the checklist? Take notes. Then swap roles.**

- speak clearly ☐ ______________
- speak for one minute ☐ ______________
- use the present perfect to introduce the topic ☐ ______________
- use the simple past to talk about:
  - where it was ☐ ______________
  - when you went ☐ ______________
  - who you went with ☐ ______________
  - what it was like ☐ ______________
  - why you liked it ☐ ______________
- use adjectives to make your presentation interesting ☐ ______________

SHAPE IT!

4 **Use the checklist to talk to your partner about their presentation. Say what they did well and what they can do to improve next time.**

You spoke very clearly, but you didn't use the present perfect to introduce the topic.

5 **Use your partner's comments from Exercise 4 to help you improve. Then give your presentation again to a different student.**

6 **Next time you do a speaking activity, listen to your partner carefully and then tell them how they can improve.**

3 How do we communicate?

LEARNING OUTCOMES

I can ...

- understand texts about language and communication
- ask for something I need
- write a listicle
- understand how to use *can*, *could*, *will be able to*, the present perfect with *How long … ?* and *for/since*, and the simple past
- talk about ways of communicating and use expressions with *to say* and *to tell*
- use spidergrams and flash cards, skim texts, and record collocations in different ways

Start It!

1. What is the woman in the photo doing?
2. Before you watch, do you use emojis? Why / Why not?
3. Where did emojis come from originally? Watch and check.
4. Can you think of other ways people communicate?

Watch video 3.1

p37

Grammar in Action 3.2

p39

Grammar in Action 3.3

p40

Everyday English 3.4

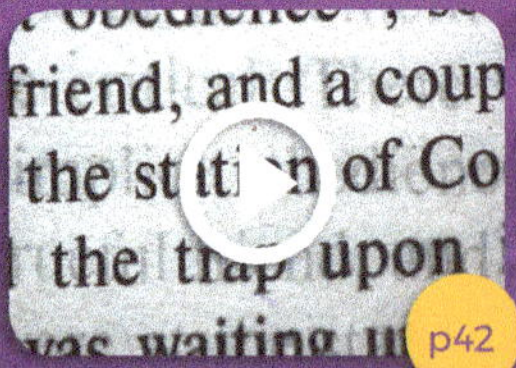

p42

Globetrotters 3.5

VOCABULARY
Communicating

3.01 **1 Match the words with the photos (1–8) and definitions (9–11). Then listen, check, and repeat.**

describe	☐	post	☐	translate	☐
gesture	☐	shake hands	☐	wave	☐
greet	1	shout	☐	whisper	☐
interpret	☐	smile	☐		

9 say what someone is saying in another language
10 put something on a blog or website
11 say what someone or something is like

LEARN TO LEARN
Using Spidergrams

When you learn new words, make spidergrams to help you remember the meaning.

2 Add other words from Exercise 1 to the spidergrams.

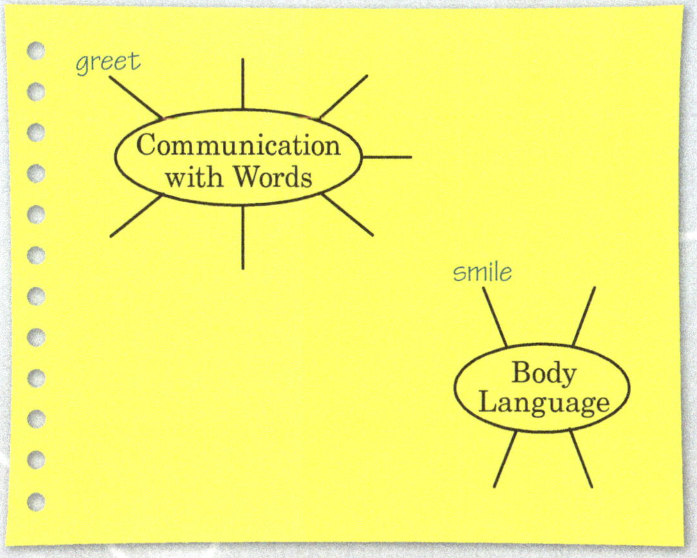

Use It!

3 When do people do the things in Exercise 1? Write four sentences.

whisper: People do this when they're in a movie theater.

4 Read your sentences from Exercise 3 to your partner. Can they guess the words?

Explore It!

Guess the correct answer.

How many messages do people around the world text every minute?

a 1.6 million b 16 million c 160 million

Find another interesting fact about how people communicate. Then write a question for your partner to answer.

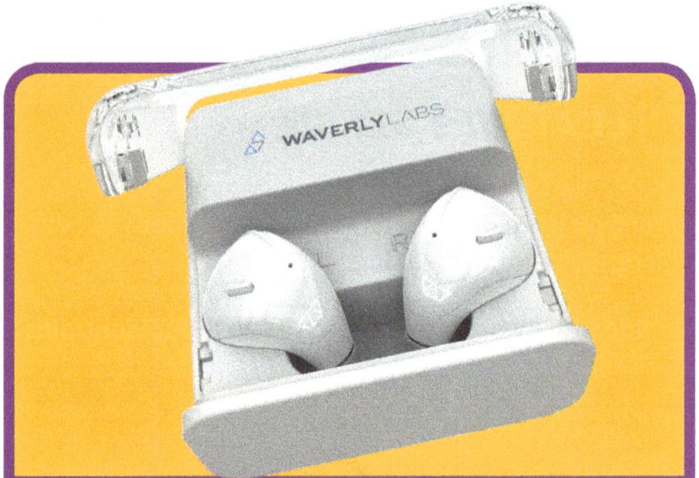

No More Language Lessons?

1 **Imagine you're traveling in a different country, but you can't speak the language. What can you do? Speak more slowly? Gesture with your hands? Well, you can try, but those things won't work for every situation. Luckily, now there's a solution: the Pilot, the world's first "smart earphones."**

2 It's really easy to use. You put the earphone in your ear and the other person puts one in theirs. When you speak, the earphone translates what you say, so the other person hears what you said but in their own language. As far back as the 1950s, machines could translate written texts, but they could not interpret spoken language. Things are very different today. The Pilot can already translate between English, French, Italian, Spanish, and Portuguese, and in the future, you'll be able to chat with speakers of many more languages.

3 Some scientists say that machine translation won't be able to replace human translation completely. Machines can understand people when they speak clearly, but they can't always understand people when they whisper or tell jokes. However, the technology uses artificial intelligence to learn and is improving rapidly, so maybe in a few more years, the Pilot will be able to do those things, too.

4 What does this mean for learning languages? Will tourists be able to travel without a dictionary or a guide? Will students be able to forget about grammar? Will we be able to understand every language perfectly? Not yet, but one thing is clear: devices like the Pilot will be able to help.

READING

An Article

1 How can we communicate with people who don't speak our language?

3.02 **2 Read the article. Does it mention any of your ideas?**

3 Circle the correct answers.

1 What is the writer trying to do in this text?
   a give advice about learning languages
   b describe a new invention
   c explain why they like machine translation
   d emphasize the importance of artificial intelligence

2 What does the writer say about machine-translation technology?
   a It works for all languages.
   b It is getting better all the time.
   c It is usually perfect.
   d It is helpful in all situations.

3 What does the writer say about learning languages?
   a We don't need dictionaries anymore.
   b In the future, only tour guides will speak different languages.
   c It is still necessary to study languages.
   d We will be able to learn a language very quickly.

4 Find the adverbs in the article for the adjectives.

1 lucky (paragraph 1) luckily
2 complete (paragraph 3) ______
3 clear (paragraph 3) ______
4 rapid (paragraph 3) ______
5 perfect (paragraph 4) ______

Voice It!

5 Discuss the questions.

1 Would you buy a set of these earphones? Why / Why not?
2 What are the advantages and disadvantages of these earphones?

Finished? p120 Ex. 1

GRAMMAR IN ACTION
Can, Could, Will Be Able To

Watch video 3.2
What tips does he give? Do you think they are good tips?

	Past
+	As far back as the 1950s, machines [1] could translate written texts.
	Present
–	They [2] ______ always understand people.
	Future
?	**Will** we **be** [3] ______ **to** understand every language perfectly?

Pronunciation p141

1 **Complete the examples in the chart above. Use the article on page 36 to help you.**

2 **Circle the correct options.**

1 Most people … Swahili, but they know the Swahili word *safari*. It means "journey."
   (a) can't speak b will be able to speak c could speak

2 Don't speak too quietly during the presentation tomorrow. People … hear you.
   a will be able to b won't be able to c won't be able

3 Many ancient Romans … speak both Latin and Greek.
   a could b can't c can

4 I … understand why he was shouting.
   a won't be able to b couldn't to c couldn't

5 … help me translate this report tomorrow?
   a Will you be able to b Will you can c Can you to

6 Carlos is bilingual. He … speak Spanish and English perfectly.
   a can't b can c could

3.05 **3** **Complete the text with the correct form of *can*, *could*, or *will be able to*. Then listen and check.**

For centuries, nobody [1] could read Egyptian hieroglyphics, but in 1799, archaeologists discovered a large black stone in the desert. They [2] ______ believe how lucky they were. On the stone there was a text written in hieroglyphics and two other languages. This meant they [3] ______ finally translate hieroglyphics. Today, you [4] ______ see the Rosetta Stone in the British Museum. Most visitors [5] ______ read the text (only the experts know how to do that!), but there are translations in different languages so you [6] ______ understand what it says. However, if you visit, go very early in the morning. It's so popular that you [7] ______ see it if you get there late.

Use It!

4 **In your notebook, write something you …**

1 could do in the past.
2 couldn't do in the past.
3 can sometimes do.
4 will be able to do in the future.
5 won't be able to do in the future.
   stand on my head

5 **Tell your partner your answers from Exercise 4. Can they guess what they are about?**

Stand on my head.

Is it something you won't be able to do in the future?

Finished? p120 Ex. 2

VOCABULARY AND LISTENING

A Radio Interview

3.06 **1** **Listen to a radio interview with James about conlangs (invented languages). Why do people invent languages like Elvish?**

3.06 **2** EXAM **Listen again and circle the correct answers.**

1 James says invented languages …
   A are similar to English.
   B can help people communicate.
   C are new.

2 James speaks Elvish with …
   A his family.
   B readers of *The Lord of the Rings*.
   C people at the conference.

3 Before he was 16, James spoke …
   A four languages.
   B five languages.
   C six languages.

4 Later, James is going to …
   A make a speech.
   B learn Turkish.
   C speak to the radio listeners.

Voice It!

3 **Discuss the questions.**

1 How many languages do you speak?
2 Is it important to learn other languages?
3 What's difficult about learning a language?

Collocations with *To Say* and *To Tell*

3.07 **4** **Complete the chart with the words and phrases in the box. Then listen, check, and repeat.**

~~hello~~ a joke a lie a story someone a secret something in Italian sorry the truth yes/no

To Tell	*To Say*
	hello

LEARN TO LEARN

Using Flash Cards

When you learn new collocations, make flash cards so you can test yourself on the words.

5 **Make flash cards for the collocations in Exercise 4. Write *to say* or *to tell* on one side and the rest of the collocation on the other. Then test your partner.**

Use It!

6 **In your notebook, write sentences about the last time you did the things in Exercise 4.**

The last time I said hello was when I came into class this morning.

7 **Compare your answers from Exercise 6 with your partner and ask for more information.**

When was the last time you said hello?

The last time I said hello was 15 minutes ago.

Really? Who did you say hello to?

GRAMMAR IN ACTION

Present Perfect with *How long ... ?* and *For/Since*

Watch video 3.3
Where has she gone?
Did she like the ice cream?

How long have you studied Elvish?
I've studied it [1] ________ about five years.
I've loved languages [2] ________ I was little.

1 Read the information below. Then complete the examples in the chart above.

Get It Right!

We use **for** with periods of time and **since** when we talk about a specific time.

I've been here for hours. **NOT** ~~*I've been here since hours.*~~

I've been here since 1 p.m. **NOT** ~~*I've been here for 1 p.m.*~~

2 Complete the sentences with *for* or *since*.

1 I've lived here __for__ about six months.
2 Billy has had the same phone ________ a long time.
3 Mr. Wilson has worked here ________ 2015.
4 I haven't eaten ________ hours.

3 Write questions and answers with *How long*, *for*, *since*, and the present perfect.

1 Elena / study French — ten years
How long has Elena studied French?
Elena has studied French for ten years.
2 Igor / live in Moscow — five months
____
____
3 Bill and Lucy / be married — 2010
____
____

Present Perfect and Simple Past

4 Look at the sentences. Which tense do we use for actions that started and finished in the past?

____

1 I**'ve studied** it for about five years.
2 This morning someone **told** a joke.

3.08 **5 Circle the correct answers. Then listen and check.**

BEN: How are you? I [1] *didn't hear* / *haven't heard* (circled) from you for nearly a week.
MARIANA: Sorry! I [2] *was* / *'ve been* so busy since I [3] *got* / *have gotten* here.
BEN: How's the conference?
MARIANA: It's great. There are so many cool people here.
BEN: [4] *Did you see* / *Have you seen* much of New York?
MARIANA: On my first day, I [5] *saw* / *'ve seen* the Empire State Building. Tomorrow I'm going to the Museum of Modern Art. I'm really excited.
BEN: Wow! How long [6] *did you want* / *have you wanted* to go there? Years?
MARIANA: I know! Anyway, I'm going to get a burger and fries with some friends I [7] *made* / *'ve made* last night. I haven't eaten anything [8] *since* / *for* this morning. Catch you later!

Use It!

6 In your notebook, write questions for your partner with *How long* and the ideas in the box.

go to this school	have your phone
know your best friend	study English

How long have you gone to this school?

7 Ask and answer the questions in Exercise 6. Use the prompts to ask simple past questions to find out more.

enjoy / first day?	where / buy?
where / meet?	who / first teacher?

Finished? p120 Ex. 3

SPEAKING

Asking for Something You Need

3.09 **1 Listen to the conversation. What does Cristina want to buy?**

SALESPERSON	Hello, can I help you?
CRISTINA	Um, oh, no! I'm sorry, I can't speak English very well, but I'm looking for … oh, what's it called? Sorry, I can't remember the word! [1] It's a kind of liquid. You put it on your face at the beach. [2] ________ protect your skin from the sun.
SALESPERSON	Do you mean sunscreen?
CRISTINA	Yep, that's it! Sunscreen. Thank you!
SALESPERSON	Sure thing. Here you go. Anything else?
CRISTINA	Yes. Do you have … oh, what's the word? [3] ________ earphones. You put them in your ears. You use them when it's noisy. [4] ________ be able to sleep!
SALESPERSON	You mean earplugs?
CRISTINA	Yes, thank you! Phew! Now I'll be able to sleep!

3.09 **2 Complete the conversation with the phrases from the *Useful Language* box. Then listen and check.**

Useful Language

I need them to …	~~It's a kind of …~~
They're similar to …	You use it to …

3 Match the sentences (1–4) with the correct responses in the *Everyday English* box.

1. Thanks for helping me with my homework.
2. Can you come to the party?
3. Don't worry. The spider's gone.
4. I broke my phone!

Watch video 3.4
Everyday English

Oh, no! ☐	Phew! ☐
Sure thing. ☐	Yep. ☐

PLAN

4 Look at the objects. Work in pairs. What do you use these things for?

5 Plan a conversation. One of you is a customer and the other is a salesperson.

1. Decide which object you want to ask for.
2. Think about how you can ask for the object when you don't know what it's called.

SPEAK

6 Practice a conversation. Remember to use *can*, *could*, *will be able to,* and phrases from the *Useful Language* and *Everyday English* boxes.

CHECK

7 Work with another pair. Listen to their conversation and decide which object they're talking about.

WRITING

A Listicle

1 **Look at the picture. How many languages can you name? Can you speak any of them?**

2 **Read the listicle. Which languages can Alex speak?**

____

____

____

Meet Alex, the Amazing Language Learner

Most of us can say "hello" and "thank you" in another language, but Alex Rawlings can speak many languages. Here are seven reasons why Alex is amazing.

- He has loved languages [1] ________________ and can speak 14 in total.
- He grew up speaking Greek and English.
- As a teenager, he learned languages for fun. [2] ________________ he was 18, he could speak French, German, Spanish, Catalan, Hebrew, Dutch, Afrikaans, and Italian.
- [3] ________________ he studied Russian and German in college. [4] ________________ then, he has learned Serbian, Hungarian, and Yiddish.
- In 2012, he became the UK's most multilingual student.
- [5] ________________, he has organized many conferences.
- [6] ________________, Alex is too busy working to study more languages, but he hopes to learn more [7] ________________.

Next time you're studying a language, don't think, "I won't be able to do this," but say "Yes, I can!"

3 **Put a–d in the order they appear in the listicle.**

a ☐ interesting facts about his life
b ☐ a short ending to make the reader think
c ☐ a title that makes you want to find out more
d ☐ a general introduction to the topic

4 **Complete the listicle with the words and phrases in the *Useful Language* box.**

Useful Language

all (his) life before later on
over the last few years since soon these days

PLAN

5 **Write your own listicle. Read the notes. Then write your own notes about a person who has an amazing talent.**

Title: David and His Amazing Memory

Introduction: My friend David. I've known him for five years.

Interesting Facts: He can remember every book he has ever read. He could remember phone numbers when he was a young child.

Short Ending: I hope David will be able to help me remember English vocabulary!

6 **Decide what information to include. Use the information in Exercise 3 to help you.**

WRITE

7 **Write your listicle. Remember to include an introduction, interesting facts and a short ending, *can*, *could*, *will be able to*, the correct past tenses, and words and phrases from the *Useful Language* box.**

CHECK

8 **Do you …**

- have an introduction to the topic?
- give interesting facts about the person's life?

Finished? p120 Ex. 4

AROUND THE WORLD

READING

A Magazine Article

1 Look at the photo and discuss the questions.

1. Where do you think the person is from?
2. What languages do people speak there?

Globetrotters
Watch video 3.5
Other Worlds, Other Words

- How many ways are there of saying that the weather is bad in your language?
- Can you explain what *tsundoku*, *sobremesa*, and *sturmfrei* mean?
- Invent a new word. What is it and what does it mean?

LEARN TO LEARN

Skimming

Practice reading texts quickly to understand the main points within a time limit. This will help you increase your reading speed.

3.10 **2 Skim the article and match the paragraphs (1–5) with the headings (a–e). Then listen and check.**

a ☐ Living in the Moment
b [1] Disappearing Languages
c ☐ Losing Language – Losing Culture
d ☐ A Language Like No Other
e ☐ There's an App for That!

Languages in DANGER

1 Do you know how many languages there are in the world? According to experts, the answer is about 7,000, but sadly, they predict that nearly half are likely to **die out** by the end of the century. This is often because speakers are elderly or because the main language of a country **has taken over**.

2 Luckily for us, some people are working to preserve a record of these languages for history. One of them is Steven Bird. He developed a phone app to translate Tembé, the language of a small tribe in Brazil's Amazon region. Tembé speakers recorded their voices on cell phones and then other tribe members interpreted what they said into Portuguese. As Tembé has no written language, experts can **turn it into** a set of symbols to represent sounds, but this takes one hour for every minute of speech!

3 The Pirahã tribe also lives in the Amazon region of Brazil. Daniel Everett's research into their language has surprised many people because some things about it are completely different from any other language. For example, Pirahã has no words for colors and no way to count.

4 Perhaps most interesting of all, there is no way to talk about the past. Everett's explanation is that jungle life **relies on** understanding and noticing everything around you at all times, so it is a waste of time thinking about the past.

5 Globally, there are around 470 languages with fewer than 100 speakers, including one Mexican language with only two, and unfortunately, they refuse to talk to one another! The loss of so many languages means that we could **end up** with only a few languages left. That would be sad because languages are an important part of who we are. When they disappear, so do our traditions and culture.

3 **Are the sentences *T* (true) or *F* (false)?**

1 Experts believe we will lose many languages this century. T
2 The Tembé speakers wrote down examples of their language. ___
3 The Pirahã language is similar to other languages in the Amazon region. ___
4 The Pirahã tribe uses special words to talk about the past. ___
5 By protecting our languages we protect our beliefs. ___

4 **Write the words in bold that mean …**

1 disappear completely. die out
2 finally be in a particular situation. ______
3 needs something in order to exist. ______
4 has taken the place of. ______
5 change it and become something different. ______

Voice It!

5 **Discuss the questions.**

1 According to the article, what is happening to the number of languages?
2 Diversity means there are many ways to be, to live, and to communicate. What is unique and unusual about the Pirahã language?
3 Is it important to keep languages alive? Why?

Explore It!

Guess the correct answer.

The three languages with the most native speakers in the world are Mandarin Chinese, Spanish, and then English. Which is the fourth?

a Arabic
b French
c Hindi
d Portuguese

Find an interesting fact about a language from your country. Then write a question for your partner to answer.

SHAPE IT!

CULTURE PROJECT

A Fact File

A fact file gives information about a topic in a clear and interesting way. In groups, make a fact file about a country and its languages.

Teacher's Resource Bank

3 REVIEW

VOCABULARY

1 Match the sentence beginnings with the endings.

1 In my country, we ☐
2 Julio whispered something ☐
3 My sister posts ☐
4 Mr. Hicks greeted everyone and said, ☐
5 When I visit Italy, ☐

a my friend interprets for me.
b "Welcome to the school."
c shake hands when we meet someone new.
d a lot of messages on social media.
e into his friend's ear.

2 Complete the text with the phrases in the box and *to say* or *to tell*.

hello	jokes	something	stories	the truth	yes	you a secret

My friend is getting married in Mexico. He's asked me to make a speech at his wedding and I [1] ________________, but I hate making speeches. People expect you to [2] ________________ and make them laugh. I can [3] ________________ about when we were in school together, but that's all. He wants me to [4] ________________ funny in Spanish, but can I [5] ________________? I've told him I speak Spanish, but I only know how to [6] ________________! It's always best to [7] ________________.

GRAMMAR IN ACTION

3 Complete the text with the correct form of *can*, *could*, or *will be able to* and a verb from the box.

do	have	learn	live	say	speak	understand

When I first went to Auckland, I [1] ________________ some words in English, but I [2] ________________ a conversation. I thought, "I [3] ________________ here in the future without learning the language." So I practiced and got better.
I [4] ________________ everything yet, but I'm sure that after a few more years I [5] ________________ English really well. When people ask, "What about me? [6] ________________ another language one day?" I tell them, "Work hard, and you [7] ________________ anything."

4 Complete the conversation with the correct form of the present perfect or simple past. Use the verbs in parentheses.

INTERVIEWER How many languages can you speak, Janet?
JANET Three. English, Spanish, and Russian.
INTERVIEWER Excellent. And how long [1] ________________ (work) as a tour guide?
JANET Well, I [2] ________________ (start) in 2008, so I [3] ________________ (be) a guide for over ten years.
INTERVIEWER Can you interpret from and into Russian?
JANET Yes, I can. I [4] ________________ (study) Russian since I was very young, and I [5] ________________ (work) in Moscow for two years.
INTERVIEWER Can you start work next week?
JANET Of course. Thank you – *Spasibo*!

Self-Assessment

I can talk about communicating in English. ☹ 😐 ☺
I can use collocations with *to say* and *to tell*. ☹ 😐 ☺
I can use *can*, *could*, and *will be able to* to talk about ability. ☹ 😐 ☺
I can use the present perfect with *for*, *since*, and *How long …?* ☹ 😐 ☺
I can use the present perfect and simple past. ☹ 😐 ☺

LEARN TO ... RECORD COLLOCATIONS IN DIFFERENT WAYS

When you learn new collocations, record them in your notebook in different ways. If you choose the best way for you, you'll remember them more easily.

1 Complete the collocation box, chart, and spidergram with the correct words and phrases.

appointment cancel doctor's late noise phone school 6 p.m.

Collocation Box for *Appointment*

make an 1 ________ an miss an a 2 ________ / dentist's	appointment

Collocation Chart for *To Make/To Do*

To Make	To Do	
✓		a mistake
	✓	the dishes
	✓	well/badly on an exam
✓		a 3 ________
	✓	your homework
	✓	the housework
✓		the bed
✓		an 4 ________

Collocation Spidergram for *To Leave*

To Leave

Departing
- leave at 5 ________
- leave early / 6 ________
- leave on time

Exiting
- leave home
- leave 7 ________
- leave work

Other Phrases
- leave the TV/ light on
- leave your key/8 ________ at home
- leave a message for someone

2 Play *Beep!* Say a sentence with a collocation from Exercise 1. Don't say the verb – say *beep!* Can your partner guess the missing word?

I want to ***beep!*** *an appointment with Dr. Smith.*

Make! I ***beep!*** *school at four o'clock every day.*

SHAPE IT!

3 Make a collocation box for *friend* and a collocation box for *to take* in your notebook. Write the words and phrases in the correct collocation box.

a close a long time an old a selfie best make a the bus

	friend

take	

4 Copy the spidergram below in your notebook. Then complete it with the words and phrases.

Collocation Spidergram for *To Have*

To Have
- Talking / Speaking
- Food and Drink
- Time / Experience

a chat a conversation a cup of coffee a good/bad time breakfast something to eat the time of your life

5 Make a collocation chart for *to do, to go,* and *to play* in your notebook. Then complete it with the words.

basketball cards exercise jogging karate skiing soccer tennis

4 How can I stay healthy?

LEARNING OUTCOMES

I can ...

- understand texts about exercise in space and staying healthy
- give advice
- write a post on a forum
- understand how to use quantifiers and *should, shouldn't,* and *ought to*
- talk about health, fitness, and healthy eating
- record vocabulary by topic, notice differences in cognates, and check my writing for common mistakes
- write a report

Start It!

1 Look at the photo. Do you think the person is healthy? Why?

2 Before you watch, do you exercise your mind? How?

3 What does emotional intelligence help you do? Watch and check.

4 Are you emotionally intelligent?

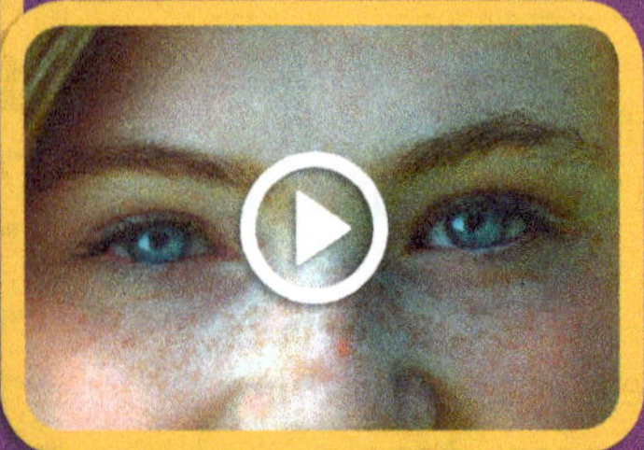

Watch video 4.1

p49

Grammar in Action 4.2

p51

Grammar in Action 4.3

p52

Everyday English 4.4

1

2

3
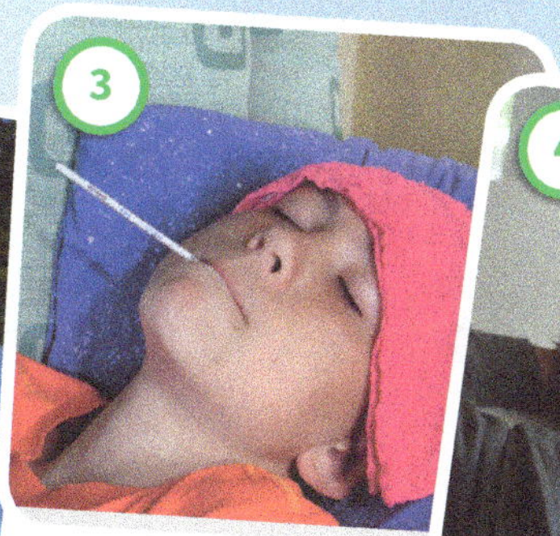
4

5

6

7
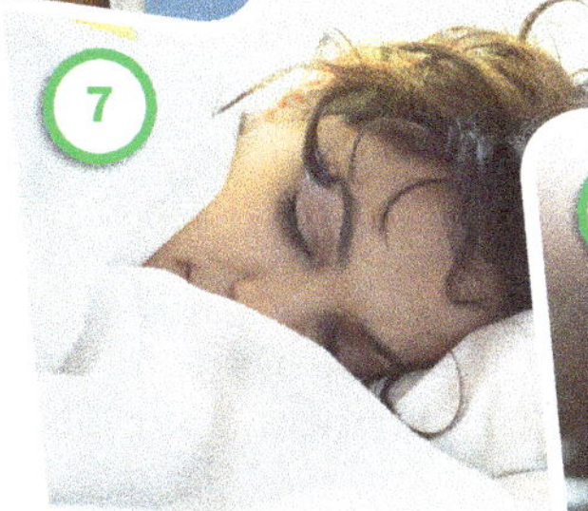
8

9

VOCABULARY

Health and Fitness

4.01 **1 Match the words and phrases with the photos (1–9) and definitions (10–13). Then listen, check, and repeat.**

cough	1	relax	
get better		sneeze	
get enough sleep		sweat	
get sick		train	
get stressed		warm up	
go jogging		work out	
have a fever			

10 to become unwell
11 to exercise gently before doing a sport
12 to stop feeling sick
13 to practice a sport regularly

LEARN TO LEARN

Recording Vocabulary by Topic

Add new words to different pages in your notebook for different topics.

2 Label one page in your notebook "Health" and another "Fitness." Add the phrases from Exercise 1. Think of and add more.

3 Tell your partner your extra phrases. Can they guess if they're about health or fitness?

Use It!

4 Complete the questions with the correct form of words from Exercise 1. Then write two more questions.

1 When was the last time you ___got___ sick?
2 Have you ever ________ a fever?
3 How often do you ________ stressed?
4 Do you ever go ________?
5 ________________
6 ________________

5 Ask and answer the questions in Exercise 4.

When was the last time you got sick?

It was about three months ago.

Explore It!

Guess the correct answer.

Your sneezes can travel at speeds of up to … kilometers per hour.

a 50 b 100 c 160

Find another interesting fact about the human body. Then write a question for your partner to answer.

Frequently Asked Questions

Send us your questions about staying healthy in space.

How many movies have you seen about life in space? It looks fun, right? But is it? Our readers have asked us a lot of questions about life on the International Space Station (ISS). The list is too long to answer all of them, but we've answered four of the best ones.

1 **Q** ☐
A They do a lot! They go on space walks, repair things, do experiments, and communicate with Earth. But too much work isn't good for anyone, and we all need a little fun! Astronauts play games, watch movies, and listen to music. If they get stressed, they relax by enjoying the incredible views of our beautiful planet from space.

2 **Q** ☐
A Yes, it does. Gravity is very weak, so everything floats – imagine sneezing in space! This means it's easy to lift things. Astronauts train a lot on Earth, but if they don't do enough exercise in space, their muscles and hearts lose strength and their bones get weaker, and this can happen in just a few weeks! These are only a few examples of the problems astronauts can have. Sometimes, when they get back to Earth, they're not strong enough to walk! The answer is exercise, and not just a little exercise – a lot!

3 **Q** ☐
A Well, quite a lot. Take Japanese astronaut Koichi Wakata, for example. He lived on the ISS for 188 days and worked out for at least two hours every day. Some astronauts go jogging! One astronaut, Chris Hadfield, even ran a marathon in space!

4 **Q** ☐
A Good question. We all need to get enough sleep, but in space, with 16 sunrises and 16 sunsets every 24 hours, that's not easy. Too many changes from day to night make it difficult to know when to sleep, so astronauts have very strict routines and wear special blindfolds to block out the sunlight.

READING
Online FAQs

1 Guess the answers to the questions.

a How much exercise do astronauts do?
b How and what do astronauts eat?
c What do astronauts do on the International Space Station every day?
d Does the body change in space?
e When and how do astronauts sleep?

4.02 **2** EXAM **Read the text. Match the questions (a–e) from Exercise 1 with the answers (1–4) in the text.**
Which question is not answered? ☐

3 Find words in the text that mean …

1 the force that makes objects fall to the ground (answer 2). ____________
2 the noun from the adjective "strong" (answer 2). ____________
3 a very long race (answer 3). ____________
4 times when the sun appears in the morning (answer 4). ____________

Voice It!

4 Discuss the questions.

1 How do you think astronauts train before going into space?
2 Would you like to live on the ISS? Why / Why not?

Finished? p121 Ex. 1

Watch video 4.2
How many hours of sleep do teenagers need?
What is she going to practice?

GRAMMAR IN ACTION

Quantifiers

With Adjectives	With Countable Nouns	With Uncountable Nouns
The list is **too long**.	[2] ______ **many changes** from day to night …	[4] ______ **much work** isn't good for anyone.
Are you **old enough** to be an astronaut? They're **not strong** [1] enough .	We have **enough chairs**.	We all need to get [5] ______ **sleep**.
	This can happen in just [3] ______ **few weeks**.	We all need [6] ______ **little fun**.

1 **Complete the examples in the chart above. Use the text on page 48 to help you.**

2 **Replace the underlined words in the sentences with *a few* or *a little*.**

1 I have some time to do my homework but not much.
a little

2 I do some exercises to warm up. ______

3 The team has three or four good players.
______

4 I only got four hours of sleep! ______

3 **Write sentences about the situations with *not enough* or *too* and the words in parentheses.**

1 There are 12 students in the class but only 11 chairs. (be / chairs)
There aren't enough chairs.

2 Jo was wearing shorts and a T-shirt in the cold weather. Now she's sick. (wear / clothes)
______

3 Jake is 16. He wants a car, but he can't drive until he's 18. (young / drive)
______

4 I want to go out, but I'm coughing and sneezing and have a fever. (sick / go out)
______

Get It Right!

Too does not mean the same as **very**. We use **too** to mean "more than enough." We use **very** to make an adjective or adverb stronger.

I'm very happy. Let's celebrate.

NOT ~~*I'm too happy. Let's celebrate.*~~

4.03 **4** **Complete the conversation with the correct quantifiers. Then listen and check.**

A Hey, how was the game?

B We lost. The other team was just [1] too strong. We weren't even good [2] ______ to score one goal! We spent too [3] ______ time defending and not [4] ______ time attacking.

A Maybe you aren't doing [5] ______ training. You always lose!

B No, we don't. We've won a [6] ______ games this season.

A But if you lose too [7] ______ games, you'll be out of the tournament.

B I know! We need a [8] ______ luck!

Use It!

5 **Complete the sentences about you. Then compare with a partner.**

1 Yesterday, I ate too many ______.

2 Last week, I didn't get enough ______.

3 Last summer, I saw a few ______.

4 Last night, I watched a little ______.

5 My parents don't have enough ______.

6 I usually have too much ______.

Finished? p121 Ex. 2

VOCABULARY AND LISTENING

Healthy Eating

4.04 **1** **Complete the health facts with the words in the box. Then listen, check, and repeat.**

a balanced diet calories ~~carbohydrates~~ dairy products fat fiber nutrition protein vitamins

1. *Carbohydrates* give the body most of its ENERGY.
2. ______ helps the body grow and be STRONG.
3. CHEESE, CHOCOLATE, and BUTTER contain a lot of ______.
4. ______ is in foods such as FRUIT. It helps food pass through the body.
5. ______ include MILK and foods made from milk.
6. ______ (A, B, C, etc.) are natural substances that keep the body HEALTHY. A B C
7. The number of ______ tells us how much ENERGY is in food.
8. ______ is a healthy mixture of DIFFERENT types of food.
9. ______ is about the food you EAT and how it affects your HEALTH.

LEARN TO LEARN

Cognates

Food and nutrition words are often similar in different languages. There are sometimes small differences in spelling or pronunciation.

2 **Which of the words from Exercise 1 are similar in your language?**

3 **Say a word to your partner. They spell the word correctly. Then swap.**

Use It!

4 **Work in pairs. Use the words from Exercise 1 to talk about the foods below.**

Bananas have a lot of vitamins.

An Interview

4.05 **5** **Read the health advice. Do you agree or disagree? Listen and check.**

1. Chocolate is bad for you.
2. It's important to drink eight glasses of water a day.
3. Waking up during the night is bad for your health.
4. Stress is always bad.
5. A little exercise every day is better than a lot of exercise once a week.

4.05 **6** **Copy the chart in your notebook. Listen again and complete the professor's advice.**

It's a good idea to …	It's a bad idea to …
eat a lot of fruit and vegetables.	*count calories.*

Voice It!

7 **Discuss the questions.**

1. Can you think of any other advice?
2. Are people in your country today healthier than 50 years ago? Why / Why not?

GRAMMAR IN ACTION

Should, Shouldn't, and Ought To

Watch video 4.3 What advice did his coach give him? Does he think it was good advice?

+	We **should** eat the right things. A balanced diet **ought** [1] ______ include some fat.
–	We **shouldn't** eat too many bad carbohydrates.
?	What [2] ______ we do to be healthy?

Pronunciation p141

1 **Complete the examples in the chart above.**

2 **Match the problems with the advice. Then use the prompts to write sentences with *should*, *shouldn't,* and *ought to*.**

1. I have a fever. [c] *You should stay in bed and you shouldn't go to school.*
2. My eyes are tired. [ ] ______
3. My team loses every game! [ ] ______
4. I sneeze a lot in the summer. [ ] ______

a train harder
b not walk in the country
c ~~stay in bed and not go to school~~
d not look at your phone before bed

3 **Use the prompts to write questions with *should*. Then ask and answer with a partner.**

1. I / do / improve my English
   What should I do to improve my English?
   You should watch movies in English.
2. people / do to be happy
   ______
3. people / do to be healthier
   ______

4.09 **4** **Complete the ultra-marathon advice with *should*, *shouldn't*, or *ought*. Then listen and check.**

NEW TO ULTRA-MARATHONS?

Here are our top five tips.

1 Well, you [1] *shouldn't* try the 100 k – it's too difficult. You [2] ______ to start with the 50 k.

2 You [3] ______ to train most days, but you [4] ______ also rest one day a week. On training days, you [5] ______ run too much – a few hours is fine! Add a few extra kilometers each time.

3 You [6] ______ eat well in the morning and, during the marathon itself, drink a lot of water (but you definitely [7] ______ drink too much – that's dangerous).

4 If there are a few hills, it's OK to walk up them. You [8] ______ to save your energy for the end of the ultra-marathon.

5 Finally, you [9] ______ stay positive. In 2015, 70-year-old Bob Becker ran 469 km! If he can do it, you can!

Use It!

5 **Read the silly opinions and think of reasons to support them. Write the sentences in your notebook.**

1. Students should wear hats in class.
   Students should wear hats in class because there isn't time to do our hair in the morning.
2. Pokémon ought to be an Olympic sport.
3. Teachers shouldn't give homework on Tuesdays.
4. Everybody should have a snake as a pet.
5. People shouldn't eat dessert on the weekend.

6 **Compare your ideas from Exercise 5.**

Finished? p121 Ex. 3

SPEAKING

Giving Advice

4.10 **1 Look at the photo. Why do you think the girl is so tired? Listen and check.**

ROBBY Hey, Nicole, are you feeling OK? You look exhausted!

NICOLE I'm really stressed. I have too many exams this week and not enough time to study.

ROBBY You really ought to get more sleep. You can't do anything well without enough sleep.

NICOLE Tell me about it! I always get stressed before exams. Do you have any advice?

ROBBY [1] How about going jogging? Exercise always [2] ____________!

NICOLE Jogging isn't really my thing.

ROBBY [3] ____________ go for a walk. You definitely shouldn't study all night.

NICOLE Hmm, I guess I could try.

ROBBY: And drink a lot of water. It improves your memory.

NICOLE Seriously? I didn't know that.

ROBBY [4] ____________ is to listen to music with my eyes closed. It helps me relax. But [5] ____________ listen to something gentle.

NICOLE OK, thanks. I'll give it a try.

4.10 **2 Complete the conversation with the phrases from the *Useful Language* box. Then listen again and check.**

Useful Language

~~How about … (+ *ing*)?~~

Make sure you …

Something else I find useful …

… works for me.

You could just …

3 Match the phrases (1–4) with the words and phrases in the *Everyday English* box.

1 Are you joking?

2 I know exactly what you mean.

3 I'll have a go at it.

4 I don't really like …

Watch video 4.4
Everyday English

I'll give it a try.	☐	… isn't really my thing.	☐
Seriously?	☐	Tell me about it!	☐

PLAN

4 Think of some advice for these problems. Write notes.

1 I want to make new friends, but I'm too shy.

____

____

____

____

2 I can't sleep because I'm worried about school.

____

____

____

____

5 Work in pairs. Choose one of the problems and compare your advice. Plan a conversation.

SPEAK

6 Practice a conversation. Remember to use *should*, *shouldn't*, *ought to*, and words and phrases from the *Useful Language* and *Everyday English* boxes.

CHECK

7 Work with another pair. Listen to their conversation. Do you agree with the advice?

Forum: **What Should I Do?**

Posts:

Jo17: Help! I play too many online games and don't get enough sleep.

Chad: I eat a lot of unhealthy snacks between classes, but what can I do? I get so hungry!

Sally16: I post 250 photos online every day. It's too many!

AdviceGirl: Hi! Thanks for telling us about your problem. A lot of us eat too many snacks, so you're not alone. We all know what the problem is – many snacks are full of fat and sugar and aren't good for us, and that's why we shouldn't eat too many. Have you tried making healthy snacks at home? That's what I do. I used to buy a lot of chips and candy, but now I make healthy sandwiches and take them to school. Why don't you look online for some ideas? You could always ask your mom or dad to help you. Also, I recommend always having enough fruit in the house. That way, you can just take some as you leave the house. Finally, you shouldn't let your friends influence you. If they offer you an unhealthy snack, offer them a piece of your orange! Hope it all goes well!

WRITING

A Post on a Forum

1 **Read AdviceGirl's post on a forum. Which problem is she answering?**

____

2 **Which things does AdviceGirl include?**

1 reasons ☐
2 thanks ☐
3 formal language ☐
4 a greeting ☐
5 a title ☐
6 advice ☐
7 paragraphs ☐

3 **Do you agree with AdviceGirl? Why / Why not?**

4 **Complete the phrases in the *Useful Language* box. Then check in AdviceGirl's post.**

Useful Language

Have you [1] ______________ (+ -*ing*)?
I [2] ______________ (+ -*ing*)
That [3] ______________, you can [4] ____________ …
Why [5] ______________ you … ?
You [6] ______________ always …

PLAN

5 **Write your own post on a forum. Choose one of the other problems on the forum. Write notes giving advice.**

Greeting: Hello!

Thanks: Thank you for ______________________

Advice: I think you should ______________________

____

____

____

Reasons: That's why ______________________

____

____

____

6 **Decide what language you need to use. Use the information in Exercise 2 to help you.**

WRITE

7 **Write your post. Remember to use *should*, *shouldn't*, *ought to*, quantifiers, and phrases from the *Useful Language* box.**

CHECK

8 **Do you …**

- have a greeting?
- give advice with reasons?
- use an informal style?

Finished? p121 Ex. 4

PE PROJECT

A Report

1 **Read the text. Do you think your school should help you become healthier? Why / Why not?**

....

Scientists are discovering more about our mental and physical health all the time. A healthy mind and a healthy body go together. We spend a lot of time at school, so it is important for schools to take care of students' health.

2 **Read Fiona and Sanjay's report. Match the problems (1–6) with their suggestions (a–f).**

How to Do a Survey

3 **Read the tips a–f below. Do you agree or disagree with each tip? Why?**

a Explain what the survey is about.
b Use a long list of questions.
c Use simple language.
d Use *Yes/No* questions if possible.
e Ask for extra information.
f Interview one or two people.

We interviewed 100 students to find out how our school can help us be healthier and happier. The students talked about six main problems.

Problems

1 There are too many exams in the same week. This is stressful for everyone. [f]
2 Classes are too long – three hours without a break. It's difficult to concentrate. [ ]
3 There aren't enough computers in the library. Students without computers get stressed because they can't do their work. [ ]
4 The gym is not open enough – only a few hours every day. [ ]
5 There is too much fast food in the cafeteria and there aren't enough healthy meals. [ ]
6 There aren't enough sports facilities. Other schools have tennis or basketball courts or a soccer field. [ ]

Our Suggestions

a Every class should have a short break in the middle.
b The cafeteria shouldn't sell fast food. It should offer healthy food, like salads.
c The gym ought to be open all day.
d There should be enough computers for everyone and free Wi-Fi in all the buildings.
e The school should use the empty field next to the library for sports.
f There should be a mixture of exams and project work, and exams shouldn't all happen in the same week.

SHAPE IT!

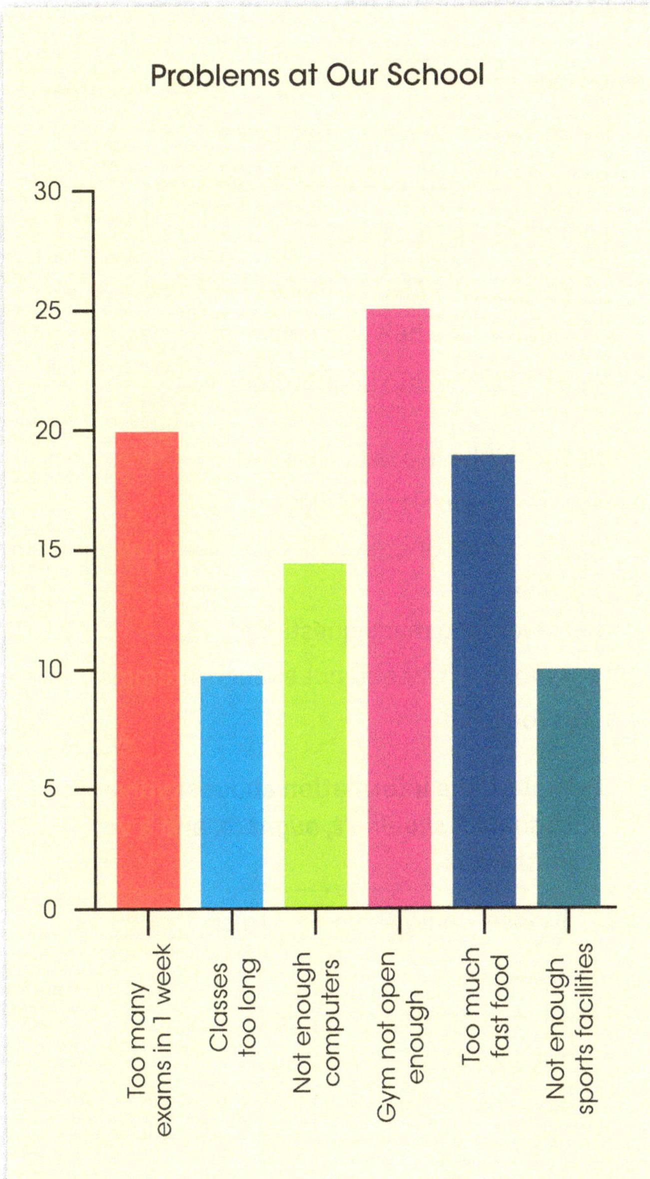

PLAN

4 Work in pairs to write a report about your school. Find out how your school could improve students' health.

- Write questions for your classmates. Use the ideas to help you.

break times	exams	food and drink	homework	sports facilities

Do you think there are enough / too much / too many . . . ?

Do we need more / less . . . ?

Do you think your school should / ought to . . . ?

- Interview your classmates and take notes on their answers.
- Think of ideas to solve the problems your classmates talked about.
- Prepare your report.
- Decide with your partner who will talk about what.

PRESENT

5 Present your report to your classmates and answer their questions. Remember to include quantifiers, *should*, *shouldn't*, *ought to,* and vocabulary from this unit.

CHECK

6 Listen to your classmates' reports. What problems did they talk about? Which idea was the best?

4 REVIEW

VOCABULARY

1 Complete the conversation with the correct form of the words and phrases in the box.

cough	get better	get sick	get stressed	go jogging	have a fever	relax	sneeze	sweat	train

TANIA Doctor, I [1] ________________ in the park yesterday and felt fine, but now I think I'm [2] ________________. Look at my red nose! I'm [3] ________________ all the time.

DOCTOR Does your chest hurt? You're [4] ________________ a lot.

TANIA It does. And I'm [5] ________________ all the time, but I feel cold.

DOCTOR Well, let's take your temperature. Hmm, 39 degrees. You [6] ________________. Here's some medicine. You need a week in bed.

TANIA This is terrible! My basketball team needs me. We're [7] ________________ for a big game next Saturday.

DOCTOR [8] ________________! Don't [9] ________________. Your health is more important than a basketball game.

TANIA But it's the championship!

DOCTOR You want to [10] ________________, don't you? Rest first, eat well – a balanced diet of protein, carbohydrates, dairy products, vitamins, and fiber – basketball later. Doctor's orders!

GRAMMAR IN ACTION

2 Match the sentence beginnings with the endings.

1 I didn't finish the exam because ☐
2 We canceled the soccer game because ☐
3 I'm unhealthy because ☐
4 I didn't go out with my friends because ☐
5 His doctor says he's sick because ☐
6 Paula is strong and healthy because ☐

a he doesn't have a balanced diet.
b we didn't have enough players.
c she does a lot of exercise and is careful about what she eats.
d there were too many questions.
e I eat too much fat and not enough vitamins.
f I was too tired.

3 Complete the information about skydiving with *should*, *shouldn't*, *ought to*, and a verb from the box.

close	enjoy	panic	trust	try

1 Everyone ________________ skydiving. It's an incredible sport.
2 It's OK to scream but you ________________.
You ________________ your instructor.
3 You ________________ your eyes.
You ________________ every second of the experience.

Self-Assessment

I can talk about health and fitness in English. ☹ 😐 ☺
I can talk about healthy eating. ☹ 😐 ☺
I can use quantifiers. ☹ 😐 ☺
I can use *should*, *shouldn't*, and *ought to*. ☹ 😐 ☺

LEARN TO … CHECK YOUR WRITING FOR COMMON MISTAKES

It is good to make mistakes because you can learn from them. If you make a list of your mistakes, you can remember not to make them again and your English will improve.

1 After you've done a piece of writing, how often do you …

1 check that you've spelled everything correctly?

2 check that you haven't made any grammar mistakes?

3 write it again and make improvements (more details, extra ideas, etc.)?

2 **Beatriz keeps a list of her common mistakes. Complete the chart with the correct words.**

Let me see …
Have I added "s" to verbs after "he" and "she"? I always forget that!

	My Common Mistakes	My Corrections
a	he ~~like~~, she ~~want~~	he [1] ________, she [2] ________
b	she ~~don't~~ have	she [3] ________ have
c	he/she/it ~~have~~	he/she/it [4] ________
d	depend ~~of~~ something, ~~on~~ July, more ~~off~~	prepositions: depend [5] ________ something, [6] ________ July, more [7] ________
e	~~hoter~~, ~~planed~~, ~~siting~~	double letters before *-er*, *-ed*, and *-ing*: hotter, [8] ________, [9] ________
f	easyest, fryed, happyer	*-y* to *-i*: easiest, [10] ________, [11] ________
g	whith	with
h	~~much~~ photos, ~~many~~ time	*many* + countable, *much* + uncountable: [12] ________ photos, [13] ________ time
i	~~do~~ sure	[14] ________ sure

3 **Read AdviceGirl's answer to Sally16's post on page 53. Which of the common mistakes (a–i) from Exercise 2 does she make? What other common mistake does she make?**

____

____

Hi Sally16. Thanks [1]of ________ sharing your problem [2]whith ________ us. Many young people love posting photos online. My blog [3]have ________ thousands. However, 250 a day is too many. You probably don't have [4]many ________ time for other things. Have you [5]tryed ________ [6]seting ________ a limit every day? For example, tomorrow, [7]do ________ sure you don't post more [8]off ________ 200. The next day, don't post more [9]off ________ 150. [10]that ________ way, you can make sure the photos are all excellent. If that [11]don't ________ work, ask a friend to help you. The friend [12]check ________ your social media and [13]tell ________ you if you post too [14]much ________ photos. Good luck!

4 **Use the chart in Exercise 2 to correct the mistakes (1–14) in AdviceGirl's answer.**

SHAPE IT!

5 **Make a list of your common mistakes in your notebook.**

6 **Use the list to check and correct the writing you do in Units 5–9. Add more common mistakes to your list when you make them.**

5 How can we save our planet?

LEARNING OUTCOMES

I can ...

- understand texts about saving our planet
- give an opinion in a discussion
- write an opinion essay
- understand how to use conditionals
- talk about planet Earth and natural environments
- use techniques to remember vocabulary and understand how I learn
- use reference words

Start It!

1 Look at the photo. Do you like it? Why?
2 Before you watch, which animals are in danger of dying out? Why?
3 Choose an animal from the video. What has happened to it? Watch and check.
4 What can we do to help these animals?

Watch video 5.1

p61

Grammar in Action 5.2

p63

Grammar in Action 5.3

p64

Everyday English 5.4

p66

Globetrotters 5.5

VOCABULARY

Planet Earth

5.01 **1 Match the words with the icons (1–12). Then listen, check, and repeat.**

carbon dioxide	☐	pollution	☐
climate change	☐	solar power	☐
endangered species	☐	the environment	☐
energy	☐	the planet	☐
marine life	☐	waste	☐
oxygen	☐	wildlife	1

LEARN TO LEARN

Look, Cover, Remember

Use the look, cover, remember technique to help you learn new vocabulary.

2 Look at the words in Exercise 1 for one minute. Then close your book. Write the words you can remember. Compare with a partner.

3 Match the words from Exercise 1 with the verbs to make collocations.

produce: waste [P]
______ ☐
______ ☐
______ ☐
______ ☐
______ ☐

protect: wildlife [S]
______ ☐
______ ☐
______ ☐
______ ☐

reduce: pollution ☐
______ ☐
______ ☐
______ ☐

destroy: the planet ☐
______ ☐
______ ☐
______ ☐
______ ☐

4 Which of your collocations in Exercise 3 are problems and which are solutions? Write *P* (problems) or *S* (solutions) after the collocations.

Use It!

5 Tell your partner a problem from Exercise 3. Can they think of a solution?

Explore It!

Guess the correct answer.

We cut down … trees each day so that we can have toilet paper!

a 27,000 b 5,000 c 100,000

Find another interesting fact about planet Earth. Then write a question for your partner to answer.

READING

A News Story

1 **Look at the photos and the title of the news story. What problems do we have with our oceans?**

5.02 2 **Read the news story and check.**

3 **Complete the news story with the phrases.**

a giant floating islands of waste
b fish, sea birds, and other marine life eat them
c ~~bags, bottles, and straws~~
d if we collect all the plastic
e the plastic from the ocean and recycle it
f it takes around 450 years for a plastic bottle to disappear

4 **What do these numbers in the news story refer to?**

1 22,000 species of fish in the ocean
2 5.25 trillion ______
3 five ______
4 2050 ______
5 16 ______
6 2.6 million ______

5 **Find words in the text (including the missing phrases) that mean ...**

1 movements of water. ______
2 thin pieces of plastic you drink through. ______
3 very big. ______ , ______
4 objects that stop things or people from going somewhere. ______

Voice It!

6 **Discuss the questions.**

1 What do you think of Boyan's project?
2 What other problems could plastic in the ocean cause?
3 Can you think of any solutions?

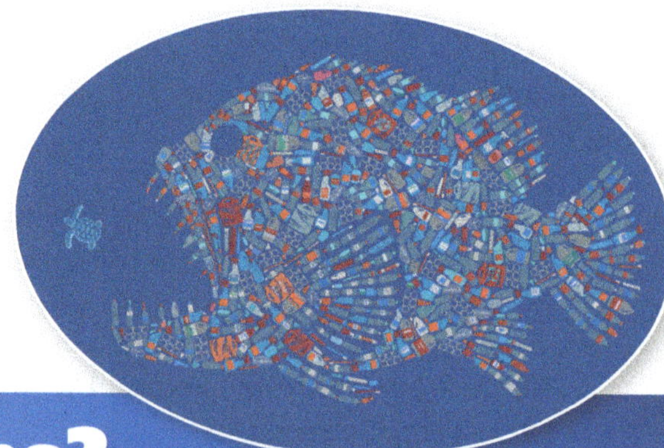

Can We Save Our Oceans?

Did you know there are over 22,000 species of fish and around two million whales in our oceans? However, something terrible is happening, and if it doesn't stop soon, it may destroy our oceans forever. Our oceans are filling up with plastic: [1] c . There are over 5.25 trillion pieces! The plastic moves from rivers into the ocean; then ocean currents push it together to make [2] ___ . There are five enormous areas of plastic pollution, called garbage patches. One in the Pacific Ocean is twice the size of France! The main problem is that the plastic takes an extremely long time to disappear. Did you know that [3] ___ ? Scientists predict that unless we do something to reduce the waste, by 2050 there could be more plastic in the ocean than fish. This is because the plastic breaks into smaller pieces and then [4] ___ and die.

But maybe Boyan Slat has the answer. When he was 16, he went on vacation to Greece and was shocked when he saw more plastic bags than fish in the ocean. Back in the Netherlands, Boyan started a school project to reduce ocean pollution and explained that [5] ___ , we might be able to protect our oceans. He shared his ideas on YouTube and got over 2.6 million views. In 2013 he started "The Ocean CleanUp," a program to collect [6] ___ . Long barriers float in the ocean and catch all the waste and then boats take it back to land to recycle it. Nobody is sure if Boyan's project will be successful, but we'll destroy our beautiful oceans if we don't do something now!

Finished? p122 Ex. 1

GRAMMAR IN ACTION

The First Conditional

Watch video 5.2
How many species of sea turtles are in danger?
Why may people put signs up on the beach?

If- Clause	Main Clause
If it **doesn't** [1] stop soon,	it **may** destroy our oceans forever.
Unless we [2] ______ something to reduce the waste,	by 2050 there **could** be more plastic in the ocean than fish.
[3] ______ we **collect** all the plastic,	we **might** be able to protect our oceans.
Main Clause	***If*- Clause**
We [4] ______ **destroy** our beautiful oceans	**if** we **don't do** something now.

Pronunciation p142

1 **Complete the examples in the chart above. Use the news story on page 60 to help you.**

2 **Match the sentence beginnings with the endings.**

1 If I have enough money,
2 Unless we meet before 8 p.m.,
3 Mario might not come to the party
4 They could lose the game next month
5 You will be cold

a if you don't wear a jacket.
b if they don't start training.
c we won't have time to buy tickets.
d if he doesn't finish work on time.
e I might go on vacation.

Get It Right!

We use **may**, **might**, and **could** when we are less sure of the result.

If I go to college, I might study biology, but I'm not sure.

3 **Put the words in the correct order to make sentences.**

1 we recycle / we might / our plastic, / If / reduce pollution
If we recycle our plastic, we might reduce pollution.

2 the planet / stop climate change, / If / we / won't get hotter and hotter
______

3 if we / We / collect plastic in the ocean / could reduce the enormous plastic garbage patches
______

4 unless we / Many animals / take care of our planet / will die
______

4 5.05 **Complete the conversation with the correct form of the verbs in parentheses. Then listen and check.**

DJ Thank you for coming to tell us how we can help save our planet. What [1] will happen (happen) if climate change [2] ______ (not slow down)?

JEN Well, we know that the ice in the polar regions is melting, so if Arctic animals like polar bears [3] ______ (lose) their homes, they [4] ______ possibly ______ (die out).

DJ No polar bears? Oh, no!

JEN And unless we [5] ______ (stop) throwing away plastic, it is possible that a lot of marine life [6] ______ (disappear), too.

DJ That's very sad.

JEN Yes, but if we [7] ______ (not use) plastic bottles, we [8] ______ (help) reduce plastic waste. Unless we [9] ______ (reduce) pollution now, we [10] ______ (destroy) our beautiful planet for sure.

Use It!

5 **Complete the sentences about you. Then compare with a partner.**

1 If I have some free time this week, …
2 If I don't finish all my homework, …

Finished? p122 Ex. 2

VOCABULARY AND LISTENING

Natural Environments

5.06 **1** **Match the words with the photos (1–10). Then listen, check, and repeat.**

bay	☐	iceberg	☐	volcano	☐
cave	☐	rainforest	☐	waterfall	☐
cliff	☐	stream	☐		
coast	1	valley	☐		

5.07 **2** **Listen and write the places you hear from Exercise 1 in your notebook.**

1 waterfall

LEARN TO LEARN

Drawing Pictures

Drawing pictures of new words can help you remember them.

3 **Work in small groups. Take turns drawing pictures of the words from Exercise 1. Who can guess the word first?**

Use It!

4 **Which words from Exercise 1 ...**

1 are near where you live?
2 have you visited?

A Class Discussion

5.08 **5** **Listen to a class talking about ways to protect the environment and number the words in the order you hear them.**

blankets	☐	clouds	☐	sunglasses	1
caves	☐	showers	☐	worms	☐

5.08 **6** **Copy the chart in your notebook. Listen again and complete the notes.**

Object(s)	Idea	How It Protects the Environment
sunglasses	Reflect the sun's rays away from the Earth.	reduces the Earth's temperature

Voice It!

7 **Discuss the questions.**

1 Which idea do you like the best? Why?
2 Which idea do you think is the craziest?

8 EXAM **Ask and answer the questions with a partner.**

Student A:
What natural environments is your country famous for?
Which natural environment would you like to see or explore?

Student B:
What is your favorite natural environment?
Which natural environment would you like to know more about?

Watch video 5.3
Which natural environment words does she mention? What transportation would people use if she ruled the world?

GRAMMAR IN ACTION

The Second Conditional

	If- Clause	Main Clause
+	[1] ________ we **lived** in caves,	we **would reduce** the energy we use.
	Main Clause	***If*- Clause**
–	We [2] ________ **use** so much water	**if** we **took** shorter showers.
?	What **would happen**	if we [3] ________ more clouds?
?	[4] ________ we **reduce** waste Yes, we **would**. / No, we [5] ________.	if we **kept** worms in the kitchen?

1 Complete the examples in the chart above.

2 Circle the correct words.

1. If we (made) / *would make* houses from recycled materials, we *reduce* / *'d reduce* waste.
2. If we *would have* / *had* more electric cars, we *'d produce* / *produce* less carbon dioxide.
3. What *would happen* / *happened* if people *wouldn't use* / *didn't use* plastic bottles?

5.09 **3 Complete the conversation with the correct form of the verbs. Then listen and check.**

be (x2)	can	~~do~~	drive	have
listen	not be	not have	work	

RITA So, what [1] would you do if you [2] ________ change anything in the world?

OSCAR Well, the first thing to go would be all exams and homework. Can you imagine how good school [3] ________ if we [4] ________ exams or homework?

RITA Ha ha! Great idea! Well, I'd make all cars electric. If we only [5] ________ electric cars, there [6] ________ so much pollution.

OSCAR Well, I'd give people more free time because if people [7] ________ more free time, they [8] ________ harder at school.

RITA Yeah, and I'd play music on the street. If we all [9] ________ to more music, we [10] ________ much happier.

4 Write second conditional sentences.

1. The Internet exists. I send messages to my friends and family all the time.
   If the Internet didn't exist, I wouldn't send messages to my friends and family all the time.
2. I go to school every day. I don't play a lot of video games. If I didn't ________
3. I get up early to go to school. I don't sleep for a long time. ________
4. I have a computer. I can watch movies and TV shows every day. ________

Use It!

5 Put the words in the correct order to make questions. Then ask and answer with a partner.

1. lived forever / the world be like / What would / if people / ? ________
2. How would / people could fly / if / life be different / ? ________
3. would happen / if we / memories / What / didn't have / ? ________
4. if you / What would / you do / were invisible / ? ________

Finished? p122 Ex. 3

SPEAKING
Giving Your Opinion

5.10 **1 Listen to the conversation. What do Josie and Marc think about zoos and marine parks?**

JOSIE I'm off to see my cousins. We're going to the park or the zoo, I think. Wanna join us?

MARC Well, if you go to the zoo, I'll have to pass. I don't like the idea of huge animals like elephants in small spaces. It's not cool.

JOSIE They have enough space. And don't forget that if we didn't have zoos, a lot of animals would disappear. They protect endangered species.

MARC Yes, maybe you're right, but have you ever thought about how the animals feel?

JOSIE Yeah, but remember that zoos take care of animals. And kids learn tons about them from visiting zoos.

MARC But marine parks aren't educational. They're just for entertainment. It would be much kinder to animals if we closed them!

JOSIE If we didn't have marine parks, some kids would never get to see animals such as dolphins or killer whales.

MARC I see your point, Josie, but let's agree to disagree.

2 Match the uses (1–3) with the phrases in the *Useful Language* box.

1 trying to get someone to change their opinion
2 showing you agree a little
3 showing you disagree

Useful Language

- Don't forget that … ☐
- I see your point, but … ☐
- Let's agree to disagree. ☐
- Maybe you're right, but … ☐
- Remember that … ☐

3 Match the uses (1–4) with the phrases in the *Everyday English* box.

When you …

1 want to invite someone somewhere
2 don't want to go somewhere with someone
3 are going somewhere
4 don't like something

Watch video 5.4
Everyday English

I'll have to pass.	☐	I'm off to …	☐
It's not cool.	☐	Wanna join us?	☐

PLAN

4 Do you agree or disagree with these ideas? Write notes.

1 We shouldn't keep wild animals as pets.

____

2 Plastic should be banned.

____

3 All transportation should be electric.

____

4 It's OK to cut down rainforests.

____

5 Work in pairs. Compare your opinions. Plan a conversation.

SPEAK

6 Practice a conversation. Remember to use the first and second conditional and phrases from the *Useful Language* and *Everyday English* boxes.

CHECK

7 Work with another pair. Listen to their conversation and decide what idea they are talking about. Do you agree with their opinions?

WRITING

An Opinion Essay

Who Should Protect the Planet?

1 ☐ Earth is a beautiful planet with amazing coasts, rainforests, and icebergs. However, we are not taking care of it, and unless we act now, we might destroy it forever. But who should protect our planet?

2 ☐ Some people believe that governments and big organizations should stop climate change. However, the planet belongs to everyone, and in my view, we should all reduce, reuse, and recycle. Did you know that people have made clothes, roads, and even houses from old plastic bottles? Furthermore, we should refuse to buy any more plastic bottles or bags.

3 ☐ In addition, we should use cleaner energy. For instance, if cars had solar panels, they would produce clean energy and reduce pollution.

4 ☐ In summary, in my opinion, if we all do small things to help every day, we will reduce climate change and protect our beautiful planet for the children of the future.

1 **Read Camila's essay. Which of her ideas do you like? Why?**

2 **Match information a–d with paragraphs 1–4.**

a her main idea and examples to support her opinion

b an introduction with a question for you to think about

c a conclusion to summarize her opinion

d a second idea to support her main opinion

3 **Match the uses (1–4) with the words and phrases in the *Useful Language* box.**

To introduce …

1 an opinion

2 a new idea

3 a conclusion

4 a contrast

Useful Language

Furthermore, …	☐	However, …	☐
In addition, …	☐	In my opinion, …	☐
In my view, …	☐	In summary, …	☐
Some people believe that …	☐		

PLAN

4 **Write your own opinion essay. Choose a topic. Think of two ideas to support your opinion. Write notes.**

pollution and its effect on the environment
how to protect the planet

Idea 1 ______________________

Idea 2 ______________________

5 **Decide what information to include in each paragraph. Use the information in Exercise 2 to help you.**

WRITE

6 **Write your opinion essay. Remember to include four paragraphs, the first and second conditional, and words and phrases from the *Useful Language* box.**

CHECK

7 **Do you …**

- have an introduction with a question for the reader to think about?
- have ideas and examples to support your opinions?
- have a conclusion to summarize your opinion?

Finished? p122 Ex. 4

AROUND THE WORLD

READING

A Journal

Globetrotters

Watch video 5.5
Take Action Now!

- What is the problem in the Congo Basin?
- Which organization helps animals?
- How is the Mexican government helping?

1 Look at the photo and answer the questions.

1 Where do you think the person is?
2 What type of natural environment is it?
3 What is difficult about her lifestyle?

5.11 **2 Read the journal and check.**

3 Complete the spidergram.

Nenets and Their Reindeer

Where They Travel
The reindeer lead the Nenets to either the north or south of Siberia to look for food.

When They Travel

How Far They Travel

Clothes

Food and Drink

Houses

Wednesday, October 24 – Snowstorm!

Today we only walked a few kilometers because of the snowstorm. It's amazing how the reindeer know which direction to go in and don't get lost, even in a storm! The Nenets are **nomads** and follow the reindeer on their 1,000 km journey twice a year. In the summer they travel to the north of Siberia and in the winter to the forests in the south to look for food.

I don't think the Nenets would be able to survive without their reindeer. They provide them with everything: their clothes, their food, their tools, their transportation and even their houses. The Nenets use around 120 reindeer skins, or **hides**, to make each house, and they're so warm! Well, they have to be, I guess! If they didn't use reindeer hide for their clothes and houses, they wouldn't be able to survive when it's –50 °C.

We arrived here this evening and set up camp in the dark. My job was to build a wall of snow around the house to protect us from the **icy** wind. I asked why they travel when it's so cold and dark, and they said that they have to follow the reindeer. If they waited for warm weather and light, they wouldn't move for months. But every three days, they pack up and travel a few more kilometers.

We had dinner in the house around the fire. Raw reindeer meat mixed with reindeer blood and cheese from the reindeer milk. Surprisingly, it was delicious and very **nutritious**, too! The Nenets eat reindeer for every meal. They said that if it's warmer tomorrow, we'll have a picnic outside. By warmer, I think they mean –20 °C!

They tell me that the temperature is getting warmer because of climate change. This is making it more difficult for the reindeer to find enough food. And it also means that traveling is more dangerous. The Nenets walk across a giant frozen river. The river freezes later in the fall, and if it doesn't freeze completely, the ice could break. Unless we try to reduce climate change, it might be difficult one day for the Nenets and their reindeer to live as they have for thousands of years.

4 **Match the words in bold with the definitions.**

1 animal skins ________________

2 people who travel a lot and don't live in the same place for long ________________

3 extremely cold ________________

4 healthy, provides a lot of energy ________________

Voice It!

5 **Discuss the questions.**

1 Being resourceful means being good at finding solutions to problems. Why is this necessary for the Nenets?

2 What problems have the Nenets solved?

3 How can we be more resourceful with challenges in our own environment?

LEARN TO LEARN

Reference Words

We use reference words such as *it*, *they*, *its*, *their*, or *them* to avoid repeating the same noun.

6 **What do the words in bold mean? Look at the journal again to help you.**

a [1]**They** provide [2]**them** with everything; [3]**their** clothes, their food …

b And [4]**they**'re so warm! Well, they have to be, I guess.

c By warmer, I think [5]**they** mean –20 °C!

d If [6]**it** doesn't freeze completely, the ice could break.

1 *reindeer*

2 ________________

3 ________________

4 ________________

5 ________________

6 ________________

Explore It!

Guess the correct answer.

Nenets *use* / *don't use* cell phones.

Find another interesting fact about the Nenets. Then write a question for your partner to answer.

SHAPE IT!

CULTURE PROJECT

A Magazine Article

A magazine article gives interesting and detailed information about a topic. In groups, prepare a magazine article about a tribal nation.

NO FOOD FOR OUR REINDEE

Teacher's Resource Bank

5 REVIEW

VOCABULARY

1 **Circle the noun that we can't use with each verb.**

1 **produce:**
energy carbon dioxide
solar power endangered species

2 **protect:**
wildlife oxygen marine life
the environment

3 **reduce:**
waste climate change the planet
carbon dioxide

2 **Circle six natural environments in the wordsnake.**

eathbayartcliffortericebergfulrainforestionvolcanostwaterfallennew

GRAMMAR IN ACTION

3 **Circle the correct words.**

[1]*If / Unless* you take your own bottle to London's Natural History Museum, you [2]*don't / won't* see plastic water bottles there. If visitors [3]*want / might want* to drink water at the museum, they [4]*will / can* be able to fill their own bottles or drink from water fountains, but they [5]*won't / don't* be able to buy water in a plastic bottle. The museum thinks that if it [6]*stops / will stop* selling plastic water bottles, it [7]*helps / might help* reduce the amount of plastic in the ocean.

4 **Circle the correct words.**

If you [1]____ to protect the planet, what [2]____ you do? Lewis Pugh, the "human polar bear," swims long distances in some of the world's coldest waters to make people think about climate change. Sometimes the water is 0 °C, and he can stay in the water for only 20 minutes. If he [3]____ any longer, his body [4]____ working and he [5]____ probably die. Pugh wants governments to protect our oceans. He says that unless we [6]____ them now, we [7]____ them forever.

	a	b	c
1	want	wanted	would want
2	will	won't	would
3	stay	stayed	would stay
4	stops	stopped	would stop
5	doesn't	will	would
6	protect	will protect	would protect
7	lose	will lose	would lose

5 **Complete the questions for the answers. Then write the questions and answers in the second conditional in your notebook. How does this change the meaning?**

1 What will happen if *we don't reduce pollution*?
If we don't reduce pollution, we will destroy our beautiful oceans.

2 What will happen if ________________ ________________? If we don't protect endangered species, they will disappear.

3 Can we protect the environment if ________________?
If we make new laws, we can protect the environment.

Self-Assessment

I can talk about the planet Earth in English.	☹	😐	☺
I can talk about natural environments.	☹	😐	☺
I can use the first conditional.	☹	😐	☺
I can use the second conditional.	☹	😐	☺

LEARN TO ... UNDERSTAND HOW YOU LEARN

When you know what kind of language learner you are, you can decide how to improve your English.

1 Ask your partner the quiz questions and circle their answers.

Are You a Communicator or a Perfectionist?

Take our quiz to find out!

1 **In class, do you prefer to ...**
a speak in English with a partner?
b read and listen to a text on your own?

2 **If an English-speaking student visited your school, would you ...**
a chat with them to practice your English?
b only say hello to them or ask them simple questions like "How are you?"

3 **How do you feel when you're studying grammar in class?**
a I can't wait to do a different activity.
b I enjoy understanding and practicing the rules. It's my favorite thing!

4 **Your teacher gives you back a piece of written work. What do you do?**
a I quickly look at my grade and then put it in my bag.
b I read all of the corrections and comments carefully. They can help me do better next time.

5 **How do you feel when you make a mistake with your pronunciation?**
a If the person can still understand me, I don't mind.
b Embarrassed. I hate making mistakes.

6 **When you write or speak in English, do you ...**
a try to use new grammar and vocabulary?
b only use grammar and vocabulary you already know?

7 **If you did a presentation in English, would you ...**
a try to speak naturally without memorizing everything?
b memorize the whole presentation first?

2 Ask your partner how many *a* and *b* answers you have. Then read what kind of learner you are.

Mostly *a* answers: You're a communicator. You like speaking and if the other person understands you, you don't worry about making mistakes. This is good because you try to express what you want to say.

Mostly *b* answers: You're a perfectionist. You like to understand the rules of English and you hate making mistakes. This is good because you aim to speak and write correctly.

3 Do you agree with the description of you in Exercise 2? Why / Why not?

4 Which advice is for a communicator? Which is for a perfectionist?

1 You should try to use new language and practice speaking in class as much as possible. If you do, you'll be able to communicate more naturally. ____

2 You should pay more attention to grammar rules and to your teacher's corrections. If you do, you'll be able to speak and write more correctly. ____

5 What are the advantages and disadvantages of being a perfectionist, and of being a communicator?

SHAPE IT!

6 Look at the advice in Exercise 4. Tell your partner one thing you can do to improve your English.

6 How can inventions change our lives?

LEARNING OUTCOMES

I can ...

- understand texts about inventions
- give and follow instructions
- write a review of an invention
- understand how to use the passive
- talk about making things, materials, and containers
- use visualization techniques to remember vocabulary
- use background knowledge to understand texts and improve my speaking with games
- present an idea for an invention

Start It!

1 Look at the machine in the photo. What do you think it does?
2 Before you watch, what inventions are important to you?
3 What did Thomas Edison say when things went wrong? Watch and check.
4 What would you like to invent?

Watch video 6.1

p73

Grammar in Action 6.2

p75

Grammar in Action 6.3

p76

Everyday English 6.4

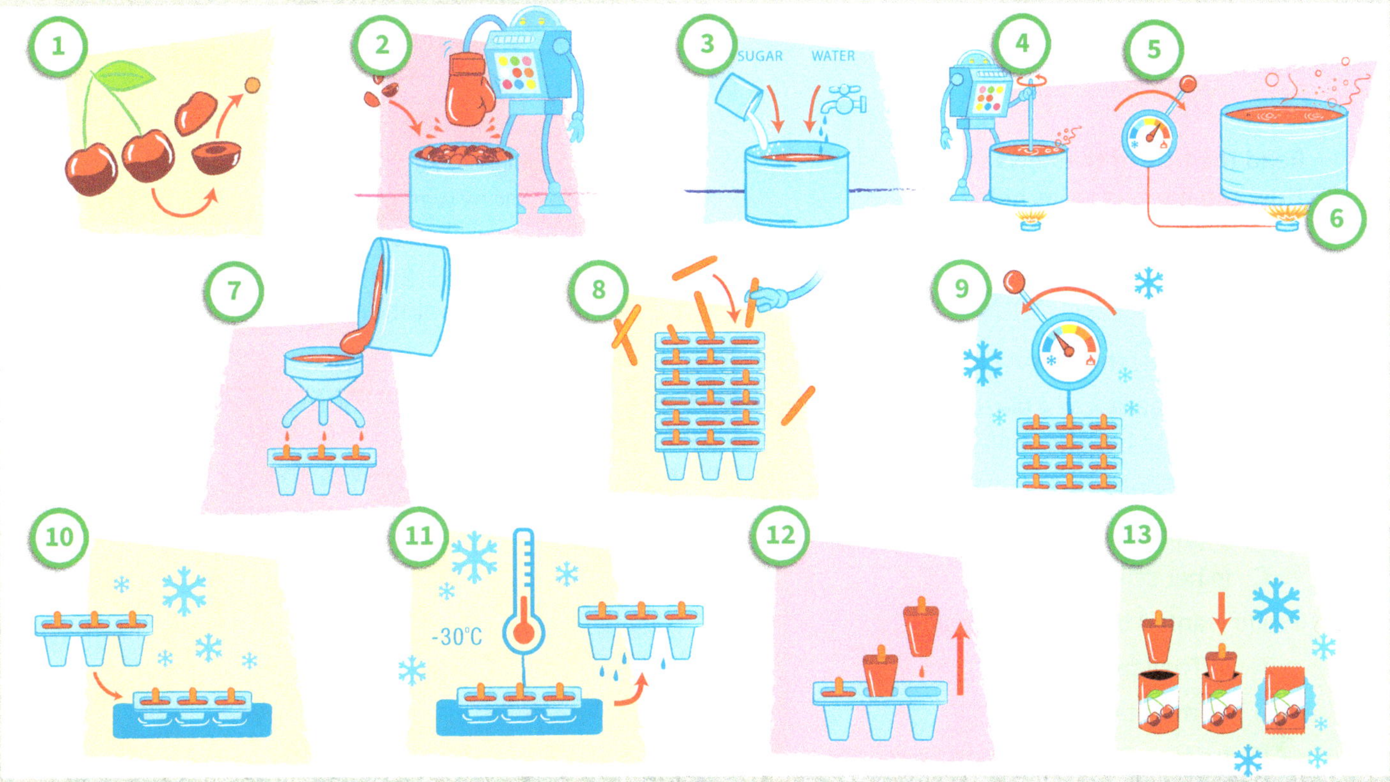

VOCABULARY

Making Things

6.01 **1 Listen to how you make an ice pop. Match the verbs with the pictures.**

add	☐	freeze	☐	pull	☐
boil	☐	increase	☐	reduce	☐
cover	☐	place	☐	remove	1
dip	☐	pour	☐	stir	☐
		press	☐		

6.02 **2 Listen again, check your answers to Exercise 1, and repeat.**

Pronunciation p142

LEARN TO LEARN

Visualizing

Thinking of an image to go with new words can help you remember their meaning.

3 Think of a strange or funny image for each of the verbs in Exercise 1. Tell your partner your ideas.

Use It!

4 Choose one of the things in the box and write how to make it in your notebook.

a candle a cup of coffee ice cream
perfume a smoothie soup

5 Tell your partner what to do. Can they guess what you are making?

First, you boil the water. Then you pour some milk into a cup and add some sugar ...

Are you making a cup of coffee?

Explore It!

Guess the correct answer.

An ... invented the ice pop in 1905.

a 11-year-old American boy
b 80-year-old Mexican man
c 18-year-old Spanish girl

Find another interesting fact about ice pops. Then write a question for your partner to answer.

READING

A News Story

1 **Read the title of the news story. How can banana skins help the environment?**

6.06 **2** **Read the news story and check.**

3 EXAM **Circle the correct answers.**

1 Elif saw there was a plastic pollution problem in her city while she was …
   A at school.
   B walking by the Bosphorus.
   C in her science class.

2 Elif wanted to make bioplastic …
   A in Thailand.
   B from potatoes.
   C from something we don't eat.

3 Elif chose banana skins because …
   A they contain starch.
   B they're yellow.
   C she couldn't find enough potatoes.

4 Elif made bioplastic …
   A in her first experiment.
   B when she was 14.
   C from banana skins and some liquids.

4 **Match the words in bold with the meanings.**

1 did ______
2 put in the trash can ______
3 stop trying ______
4 getting older ______
5 search for ______

Voice It!

5 **Discuss the questions.**

1 What do you think of Elif's invention?
2 Can you think of anything else we throw away that could be used again?

Finished? p123 Ex. 1

Teen's Banana Skin Invention

Growing up in Istanbul, Elif Bilgin used to enjoy walking beside the Bosphorus. However, Elif noticed that there was more and more pollution, like plastic bags, in the river. The 14-year-old decided to **look for** a solution.

At school, Elif learned that bioplastics are more environmentally friendly than normal plastics because they are made from starch. Starch is found in foods like potatoes and bananas. However, she wanted to use an organic material that isn't eaten. Then she learned that in Thailand, over 200 tons of banana skins are **thrown away** every day, and that's when she got her idea!

The teen inventor spent two years developing her idea. She did a lot of research online and at the library and **carried out** 12 experiments at school and in her kitchen. Not all the experiments were successful, but Elif didn't **give up**, and finally, she produced a bioplastic from banana skins. At 16, she won the Science in Action Award and the Inspired Idea Award at the Google Science Fair. Her invention could help make rivers, lakes, and oceans clean again. Since then, Elif has traveled the world telling people about her invention and has studied science in college so she can continue to make a difference in our world.

How is Elif's bioplastic made?

1 The banana skin is dipped in a special liquid.
2 The banana skin is placed in a glass and is heated for 30 minutes.
3 The banana skin is dried and is pressed into a paste.
4 Different liquids are added to the paste and the mixture is stirred.
5 The mixture is cooked in an oven and it is made into plastic.

Watch video 6.2
What does she use nail polish for?
How does she clean her keyboard?

GRAMMAR IN ACTION

Simple Present Passive

	Singular	Plural
+	The mixture [1] _______ **cooked** in an oven.	Different liquids **are added** to the paste.
–	She wanted to use an organic material that [2] _______ **eaten**.	Plastic bags **aren't recycled**.
?	How **is** Elif's bioplastic [3] _______?	How many banana skins **are thrown** away in Thailand every day?

1 Complete the examples the chart above. Use the news story on page 72 to help you.

2 Put the words in the correct order to make sentences.

1 found / starch / Where / is / ?
Where is starch found?

2 aren't / Most students / taught / to make bioplastic at school _______

3 every day / experiments / How many / carried out / are / ? _______

4 always / full of plastic bottles / The river / is _______

3 6.07 Complete the text with the correct form of the verbs in parentheses. Then listen and check.

So, how [1] is a cell phone made (make)? Well, first the case [2] _______ (create) and then the circuit board [3] _______ (make). This is the most important part of the cell phone, as it runs the whole system. If the circuit board [4] _______ (not design) correctly, the phone won't work. Once the circuit board [5] _______ (finish), it [6] _______ (place) inside the case, and other parts, such as the screen, keypad, microphone, and speakers, [7] _______ (add). Finally, the phone [8] _______ (test) to check that it works before it [9] _______ (sell).

Use It!

4 Write questions in the simple present passive. Then answer them with a partner.

1 What ingredients / use / to make pasta?
What ingredients are used to make pasta?

2 Where / Arabic / speak?

3 In which countries / insects / eat?

4 What / make / from paper?

5 Which places / visit / by tourists in your country?

5 Work in pairs. Write two more questions in the simple present passive. Ask another pair.

Finished? p123 Ex. 2

VOCABULARY AND LISTENING

Materials and Containers

1 6.08 **Use a word from each box to describe the photos (1–6). Then listen, check, and repeat.**

Materials
cardboard glass leather rubber ~~silk~~ tin
Containers
~~bag~~ box can case jar tube

1 

a silk bag

4 

2 

5 

3 

6 

Use It!

2 Work in small groups. Use the words from Exercise 1 to write things you can see in your classroom.

A Quiz Show

LEARN TO LEARN

Using Background Knowledge

Before you listen, think about what you already know about a topic. This helps you understand what you will hear.

3 Tell your partner everything you know about two of the things in the photos.

bagpipes

boomerang

piñata

chewing gum

4 6.09 **Guess and circle the answers. Then listen and check.**

1. Where do bagpipes originally come from?
   a the U.S.A. b Europe c the Middle East
2. Where is the oldest boomerang from?
   a Australia b Poland c Brazil
3. Where do piñatas originally come from?
   a Argentina b Mexico c China
4. Which one of these inventions was an accident?
   a the ballpoint pen b the can opener c chewing gum

5 6.09 **Listen again and complete the sentences.**

1. Anton thinks the first bagpipes came from ______.
2. The oldest boomerang is around ______ years old.
3. Marco Polo introduced ______ to Italy.
4. Thomas Adams wanted to make ______ from chicle.

Voice It!

6 Discuss the questions.

1. What information is the most surprising?
2. Which invention is the most useful? Why?

Watch video 6.3
Who created chocolate chip cookies?
What was Ruth given?

GRAMMAR IN ACTION

Simple Past Passive

	Singular	Plural
+	A boomerang **was discovered** in Poland.	Ice cream and pasta **were brought** to Italy from China [2] ______ Marco Polo.
–	The musical instrument [1] ______ **invented** in Europe.	Bagpipes **weren't found** in Europe first.
?	Where **was** the oldest boomerang **found**?	What objects [3] ______ **invented** by accident?

1 **Read the information below. Then complete the examples in the chart above.**

Get It Right!

We use **by** to show who or what is doing the action in passive sentences.

The students are taught by Ms. Goodall.

We do not use **by** when it's not important to know who or what is doing the action.

The newspaper is delivered every morning ~~by the newspaper carrier~~.

6.10 **2** **Circle the correct form of the verb. Then listen and check.**

Easter Island, or Rapa Nui, [1]*(is)* / *was* located in the Pacific Ocean, about 3,500 km from Chile. The small island [2]*first inhabited* / *was first inhabited* around 1,000 years ago. In 1722, the island [3]*discovered* / *was discovered* by a Dutch explorer. He [4]*found* / *was found* a small population of about 3,000 people and nearly 900 mysterious statues around the island. The giant head statues, or Moai, [5]*built* / *were built* from volcanic stone and [6]*placed* / *were placed* along the coast with their backs to the ocean. But how [7]*were* / *did* these enormous statues moved around the island 1,000 years ago?

3 **Rewrite the sentences in the simple past passive.**

1 Isaac Newton invented the cat door.
The cat door was invented by Isaac Newton.

2 A dentist invented cotton candy.
Cotton candy ______.

3 Ernö Rubik didn't design the Rubik's Cube to be a toy.
The Rubik's Cube ______.

4 People in Norway didn't eat bananas until 1905.
Bananas ______.

Use It!

4 **Work in pairs. Write questions in the simple past passive about your country 50 years ago.**

1 music / listen to / by teenagers?
What music was listened to by teenagers in your country 50 years ago?

2 sports / play / at school? ______

3 shows / watch / on TV? ______

4 special days / celebrate / at home? ______

5 subjects / study / at school? ______

Finished? p123 Ex. 3

SPEAKING

Giving and Following Instructions

6.11 **1 Listen to the conversation. What does Alicia make?**

ALICIA Hey Juan, I saw a video the other day of a great invention that was made from a balloon. Do you want me to show you how to make it?

JUAN Yeah, go for it!

ALICIA Well, [1] first of all, take a balloon, any old balloon, any color you want.

JUAN OK. [2] ____________________?

ALICIA Then blow up the balloon and hold it tightly so that the air doesn't escape.

JUAN OK, that's easy.

ALICIA [3] ____________________ the balloon's inflated, place it on a table in front of you and place your phone on the balloon with the screen facing upward.

JUAN OK, I get it. [4] ____________________?

ALICIA [5] ____________________ kind of tricky. Press the phone down on the balloon. Don't let go of the balloon and don't let the air out too quickly. In the video, the air came out really slowly.

JUAN Hang on a sec! [6] ____________________. So, push down carefully until all the air is removed.

ALICIA Exactly. [7] ____________________! A cell phone case!

JUAN [8] ____________________. Hey, that's so cool!

6.11 **2 Complete the conversation with the phrases from the *Useful Language* box. Then listen again and check.**

Useful Language

Giving Instructions	Following Instructions
And there you have it!	Let me get this straight.
~~First of all, ...~~	Oh, I see.
Once (something is done), ...	Then what?
The next part's ...	What's next?

3 Match the words and phrases (1–5) with the phrases in the *Everyday English* box.

1 Wait a minute!
2 difficult
3 I understand.
4 Do it!
5 any (informal)

Watch video 6.4
Everyday English

any old ... ☐
Hang on a sec! ☐
kind of tricky ☐
Go for it! ☐
I get it. ☐

PLAN

4 Read the conversation again. Complete Alicia's notes about how to make something from a balloon.

What you need: ____________________
What you do first: ____________________
What you do next: ____________________
What you do last: ____________________
What happens in the end: ____________________

5 Work in pairs. Plan a conversation about how to do something. Use the ideas below or your own.

cook some food make a paper plane play a sport

SPEAK

6 Practice a conversation. Remember to use the simple present passive and phrases from the *Useful Language* and *Everyday English* boxes.

CHECK

7 Work with another pair. Listen to their conversation and decide what they are talking about.

HOME | STORIES | PHOTOS

BRINGING COLOR TO A GRAY WORLD

Millions of people around the world are color blind. They can't see some colors, such as red, green, or blue. Some people who are color blind can't see any colors at all, so the world looks very different. But now there are special glasses to help color-blind people.

The glasses look like normal glasses, but the lenses are made from special glass or plastic. The glasses separate colors, such as red and green, so that people can see them. When they are worn by color-blind people, they can see colors they have never seen before.

What I like about them is that they look really cool. There are sunglasses, glasses for children, and sports sunglasses. However, I should point out that the glasses are really expensive. Overall, I think they are an amazing invention that can help millions of people see our beautiful world.

WRITING

A Review

1 **Look at the photo. What do the glasses do? Read the review and check.**

2 **Put a–f in the order they appear in the review.**

a ☐ a description of the invention

b ☐ how the invention works

c ☐ a disadvantage

d ☐ the reviewer's general opinion

e ☐ what the reviewer likes

f [1] who the invention is for

3 **Cover the review and complete the sentences in the *Useful Language* box. Then read it again and check.**

Useful Language

The glasses look like [1] ________________, but the lenses are made from [2] ________________.

What I like about them is [3] ________________ ________________.

However, I should point out that [4] ________________ ________________.

Overall, I think they are [5] ________________ ________________.

PLAN

4 **Write your own review of an amazing invention. Think of the invention. Write notes.**

Who the invention is for: ________________

How it works: ________________

The advantages: ________________

One disadvantage: ________________

Your opinion: ________________

5 **Decide what information to include. Use the information in Exercise 2 to help you.**

WRITE

6 **Write your review. Remember to include the parts of the review from Exercise 2, the passive, and phrases from the *Useful Language* box.**

CHECK

7 **Do you …**

- describe the invention and who it's for?
- say what the advantages and disadvantages are?
- give your general opinion?

Finished? p123 Ex. 4

TECHNOLOGY PROJECT

A Presentation

6.12 **1 Match the headings (a–d) with the slides (1–4). Then listen to the presentation and check.**

a A Problem and Some Solutions
b How Our Invention Works
c Problems at Our School
d Our Design

2 Discuss the questions.

1 What is the invention called? Why?
2 What problem does it solve?
3 What is the invention made from?
4 How does it work?
5 Is it a good idea? Why / Why not?

How to Brainstorm

3 Put the stages in order.

a Compare ideas in a group. ☐
b Have a time limit. ☐
c Make a list of as many ideas as possible. ☐
d Put two ideas together if necessary. ☐
e Think of ideas on your own. ☐
f Use your imagination and creativity to think of ideas. ☐
g Write down or draw your ideas. ☐

6.13 **4 Listen again to the students presenting the first two slides and check your answers. Which stage is not mentioned?** ________

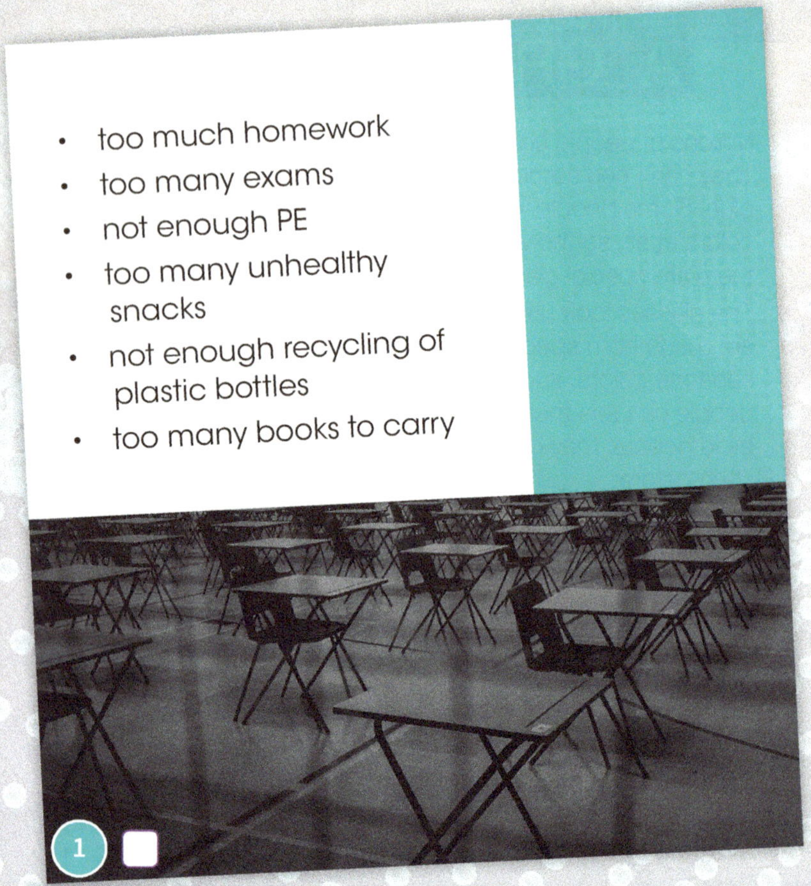

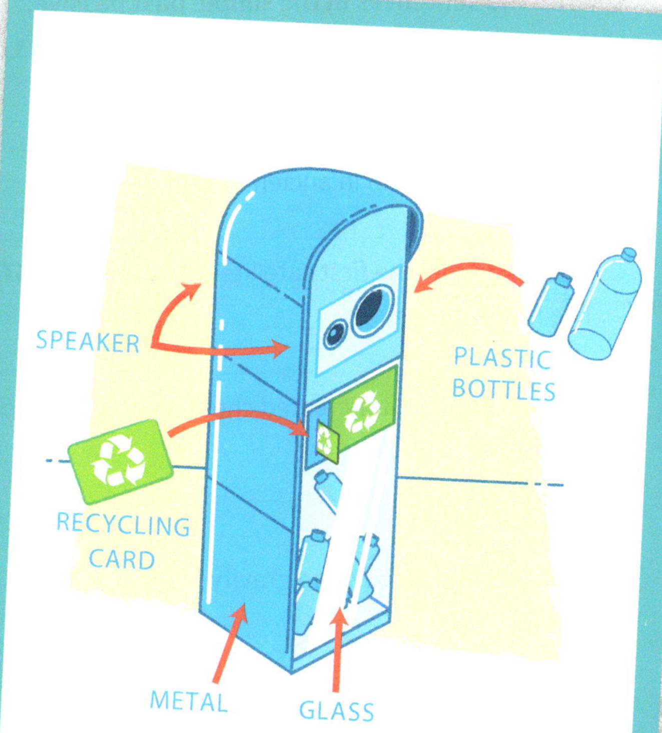

3

4

PLAN

5 Work in groups. Complete the steps. Use the stages from Exercise 3.

- Make a list of problems people have at school or at home.
- Choose one problem and think of a lot of solutions.
- Choose one solution and create an invention. Use Exercise 2 to help you.
- Draw the design. What materials are used? How does it work?
- Make four slides to present your invention.
- Decide who presents each slide.
- Listen to everyone in the group practice their slide and help them improve.

PRESENT

6 Present your slides to the class. Remember to say how the invention solves a problem and how it works.

CHECK

7 Listen to your classmates' presentations. Do they include all the information from Exercise 2?

6 REVIEW

VOCABULARY

1 Match the verbs with the definitions.

dip increase place reduce remove stir

1 put something in a position ________
2 put something in a liquid ________
3 make a temperature higher ________
4 make something less ________
5 take something away ________
6 move a liquid with a spoon ________

2 Write the letters in the correct order to make words for materials and containers.

1 gba ________
2 drbdrcraoa ________
3 nit ________
4 slsag ________
5 xob ________
6 thealre ________
7 brbreu ________
8 lkis ________
9 nac ________
10 scae ________
11 raj ________
12 bute ________

GRAMMAR IN ACTION

3 Complete the text with the simple present passive form of the verbs in parentheses.

Street festivals and celebrations are fun, but they also create a lot of trash, which [1] ________ (not put) in trash cans, but [2] ________ just ________ (throw) on the floor. One inventor in Portugal has solved this problem with his Garbage Jukebox – a trash can that plays music. The machine [3] ________ (not power) by electricity, but by trash, so when a drink can or bottle [4] ________ (place) in the machine, music [5] ________ (play) – 30 seconds for each can and one minute for each bottle. What a great idea!

4 Rewrite the sentences in the simple past passive.

1 Someone discovered unique fingerprints in 1823.
Unique fingerprints ________________________.

2 People spoke Latin in ancient Rome.
Latin ________________________.

3 Scientists sent the first satellite into space in 1957.
The first satellite ________________________.

4 A comic book writer created chess boxing in one of his stories.
Chess boxing ________________________.

5 Isaac Newton discovered gravity in 1664.
Gravity ________________________.

6 People built the largest Egyptian pyramid in Giza, near Cairo.
The largest Egyptian pyramid ________________________.

Self-Assessment

I can talk about making things in English.
I can talk about materials and containers.
I can use the simple present passive.
I can use the simple past passive.

LEARN TO ... IMPROVE YOUR SPEAKING WITH GAMES

When you play speaking games, you can relax and use English in different situations.

1 Which of the situations below is the most difficult for you? Why?

a describing something in English when you don't know the word

b asking questions in the past, present, active, and passive

c speaking in English without thinking in your language first

2 Play *Forbidden Words* in pairs. Take turns describing each word in bold without using the other words on the card.

box
put
cardboard
keep
open

soccer
sport
play
ball
team

phone
call
screen
number
app

school
study
student
teacher
learn

This is an object. It's usually square. It's often made of, err, a kind of stiff paper.

Is it a box?

Yes! Your turn.

3 Work with a partner and make eight *Forbidden Words* cards like the ones in Exercise 2. Swap your cards with another pair. Then read the rules and play the game.

1 Put the cards face down.

2 Take four cards each. Don't show your partner.

3 Describe the word on the card without using the forbidden words.

4 Your partner gets one point if they guess the word in less than one minute.

5 The player with the most points at the end of the game wins.

4 Stefan and Anne are playing *Guess Who?* Stefan is thinking of someone. Anne has two minutes to guess the person. She can only ask *Yes/No* questions. Write the person.

ANNE Is this person a man?
STEFAN No, it isn't.
ANNE Is it a woman?
STEFAN Hmm … not a woman, no.
ANNE Is it a girl then?
STEFAN Yes.
ANNE Have I met her?
STEFAN I don't think so!
ANNE Have we studied her in this book?
STEFAN Yes, we have.
ANNE Did she invent something to help clean rivers?
STEFAN Yes, she did.
ANNE Was her invention made from banana skins?
STEFAN Yes, it was.
ANNE I know! Is it ____________________ ____________________?

5 Play *Guess Who?* with a partner. Take turns thinking of a person.

SHAPE IT!

6 Discuss with a partner. Look again at Exercise 1 and answer the questions.

1 Which things a–c have you practiced in *Forbidden Words*? __________

2 Which things a–c have you practiced in *Guess Who?* __________

7 What do you celebrate?

LEARNING OUTCOMES

I can ...

- understand texts about a folktale and festivals
- invite someone to a party
- write an email to a friend
- understand how to use the past perfect and reported speech
- talk about festivals and live music
- mark word stress, predict information, identify and understand prefixes and suffixes , and challenge yourself to do more in class

Start It!

1 Look at the photo. Would you like to go to this festival?
2 Before you watch, what kind of things do people celebrate at festivals?
3 When was the first Snowbombing Festival? Watch and check.
4 What is your favorite festival? Describe it.

Watch video 7.1

p85

Grammar in Action 7.2

p87

Grammar in Action 7.3

p88

Everyday English 7.4

p90

Globetrotters 7.5

VOCABULARY

Festivals

7.01 **1 Match the words with the photos (1–9) and definitions (10–12). Then listen, check, and repeat.**

atmosphere	☐	fireworks	☐
ceremony	☐	float	☐
costume	1	lantern	☐
crowd	☐	parade	☐
decoration	☐	program	☐
fair	☐	stall	☐

10 the feeling in a place or situation
11 an event that happens on important occasions
12 a large group of people in one place

LEARN TO LEARN

Stress Patterns

Knowing the stress pattern of a word can help you pronounce it and hear it when people say it.

7.02 **2 Complete the chart with words from Exercise 1 according to their stress pattern. Then listen, check, and repeat.**

1	oO	parade
2	Oo	______, ______, ______, ______
3	Ooo	______
4	Oooo	______
5	ooOo	______

Pronunciation p142

7.05 **3 Listen to the conversation and (circle) the words in Exercise 1 that you hear. Then work in pairs to describe the festival.**

The Caribbean Parade and Festival is a celebration of Caribbean culture in Montreal, Canada ...

Use It!

4 Write sentences in your notebook about a festival using words from Exercise 1. Then read your sentences to a partner.

In my town, there's a parade every year. Everyone wears costumes and there are decorations in the streets.

Explore It!

Guess the correct answer.

The biggest parade and festival in the world is held in …

a Venice. b Rio de Janeiro. c New Orleans.

Find another interesting fact about a festival. Then write a question for your partner to answer.

READING
A Folktale

A Princess, a Farmer, and a Bridge of Birds

Throughout history, different cultures have looked up at the stars in the night sky and told stories about them. The ancient Greeks told stories about heroes, and the Native Americans about bears and fishermen. In Japan, people still tell the story of Altair and Vega, two very special stars.

Once upon a time, there was a princess named Orihime. She made beautiful clothes for her father, the Sky King, while she sat on the **bank** of the *Amanogawa River* (the Milky Way). Orihime had always loved her work, but she wanted to find a husband, so her father introduced her to a farmer named Hikoboshi. Hikoboshi took care of cows on the other side of the river. The princess and the farmer fell in love and got married. However, they hadn't been together long when Orihime stopped making clothes and Hikoboshi forgot about his cows.

The Sky King was **furious**. "You will never meet again," he told them, and he sent them to opposite sides of the river. But when he saw how **heartbroken** his daughter had become, he changed his mind. "If you do your jobs well," he said, "you can meet once a year, on the seventh day of the seventh month." However, the first time the couple tried to meet, they couldn't cross the river. "I want to see him!" cried Orihime. Almost immediately, a **flock** of magpies came and made a bridge with their wings. Now people say if it rains on July 7, the magpies can't come and Orihime and Hikoboshi have to wait another year.

Every year, this story is celebrated in Japan as the *Tanabata* – the Star Festival. There are parades, fireworks, lanterns, and stalls with traditional food, and people write their wishes on *tanzaku* (pieces of colorful paper), remembering how Orihime's wish had come true.

1 **Look at the title and the pictures. What do you think happens in the story?**

7.06 **2** **Read the folktale and check.**

3 **Are the sentences *T* (true) or *F* (false)?**

1 All cultures have told the same stories about the stars. F
2 The Sky King wanted Orihime to get married. ___
3 After Orihime and Hikoboshi married, Orihime continued making clothes for her father. ___
4 Orihime and Hikoboshi try to meet every year. ___
5 During *Tanabata*, Japanese people say what they hope will happen in the future. ___

4 **Match the words in bold with the definitions.**

1 the land at the side of a river ___
2 a group of birds ___
3 very angry ___
4 very, very sad ___

Voice It!

5 **Discuss the questions.**

1 Do you think the king was fair to his daughter?
2 Why are folktales important?
3 Are there similar festivals in your country?

Finished? p124 Ex. 1

GRAMMAR IN ACTION

Past Perfect

Watch video 7.2
What's another name for Yuri's night?
Why was the DJ still able to play music?

+	When he saw how heartbroken his daughter [1] ______ **become**,	he **changed** his mind.
–	They **hadn't** [2] ______ together long	when Orihime **stopped** making clothes.
?	**Had** the parade already **started**	when you **arrived**?

1 **Complete the examples in the chart above. Use the folktale on page 84 to help you.**

2 **Match the sentence beginnings with the endings.**

1 I'd studied German before I went to Germany, [c]
2 I was very hungry when I got home from soccer, [ ]
3 She was cold [ ]
4 He didn't come to see the new movie [ ]

a because she hadn't brought her jacket.
b because he'd already seen it.
c but I learned more while I was there.
d so I was pleased that my dad had cooked dinner.

3 **Complete the sentences with the correct form of the past perfect.**

1 When we got to the park, (the fireworks / finish).
When we got to the park, the fireworks had finished.
2 (Jaime / never / go) to a music festival, so he was really excited.
______
3 (you / hear) about the Caribbean Parade before you came to Montreal?
______
4 After (she / buy) some food at a stall, she went to watch the parade.
______
5 It was nine o'clock, but (the event / not / start) yet.
______

4 7.07 **Complete the text with the correct form of the verbs in parentheses. Then listen and check.**

Today was almost a disaster. My friends and I were going to the Albuquerque International Balloon Fiesta, but when we [1] *got* (get) there, I [2] ______ (realize) I [3] ______ (not bring) my ticket. I [4] ______ (leave) it at home. At first, I [5] ______ (not know) what to do, but then I [6] ______ (call) my mom. Luckily, she [7] ______ (not leave) the house to go to work yet, so she [8] ______ (find) the ticket, [9] ______ (take) a photo of it, and [10] ______ (send) me the photo. Anyway, it [11] ______ (be) an amazing event. I [12] ______ (never see) so many balloons before. The sky was full of them!

Use It!

5 **Write questions about what you knew before you started this book. Ask and answer.**

1 … (hear) of the *Tanabata* festival?
Before you started this book, had you heard of the Tanabata festival?
2 … (study) the past perfect?
______
3 … (read) about color-blind glasses?
______
4 … (think) about how astronauts exercise?
______

Finished? p124 Ex. 2

VOCABULARY AND LISTENING

Music Festivals and Live Music

7.08 **1 Match the words with the definitions. Then listen, check, and repeat.**

band members ☐	headliner ☐	tent 1
campsite ☐	stage ☐	track ☐
encore ☐	supporting act ☐	venue ☐
gig ☐		

1 something you sleep in outdoors
2 where a special event happens
3 the main band at a festival
4 a song or piece of music
5 the musicians in a group
6 an extra song at the end of a show
7 where musicians perform
8 where people can stay in tents
9 a music performance
10 not the main artist

2 EXAM **Write the correct answer in the gap. Write one or two words from Exercise 1.**

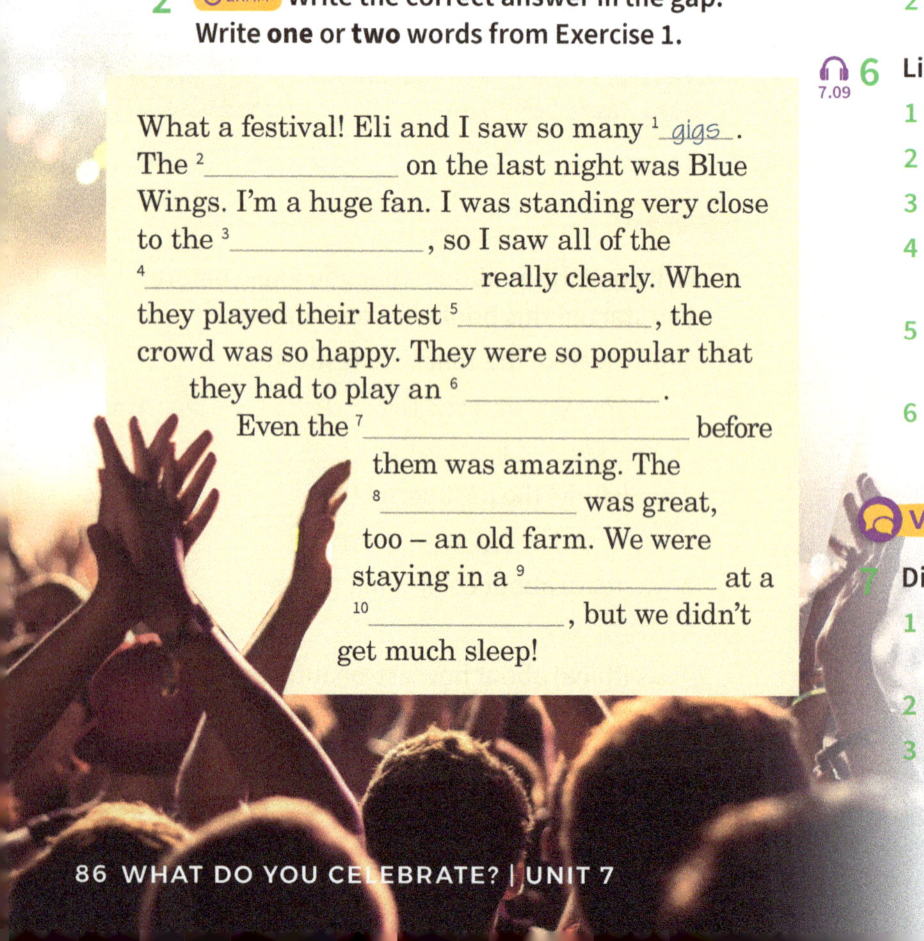

What a festival! Eli and I saw so many [1] gigs. The [2] ________ on the last night was Blue Wings. I'm a huge fan. I was standing very close to the [3] ________, so I saw all of the [4] ________ really clearly. When they played their latest [5] ________, the crowd was so happy. They were so popular that they had to play an [6] ________. Even the [7] ________ before them was amazing. The [8] ________ was great, too – an old farm. We were staying in a [9] ________ at a [10] ________, but we didn't get much sleep!

Use It!

3 Imagine you went to a music festival recently. Write notes about it using the vocabulary from Exercise 1. Tell your partner.

____
____
____
____

A Conversation

7.09 **4 Listen to the conversation. What are Daryl and Jackie going to do in the summer?**

LEARN TO LEARN

Predicting Information

Skim the questions before you listen and try to predict what kind of information you need.

5 Look at Exercise 6. What kind of information is missing from each of the sentences?

a an object   b a place   c a number

1 c   3 ___   5 ___
2 ___   4 ___   6 ___

7.09 **6 Listen again and complete the sentences.**

1 Daryl's cousin went to Morocco two years ago.
2 Gemma sold ________ at a stall.
3 There are ________ main stages at *SumFun*.
4 Last year more than ________ people were at the festival.
5 Jackie can only remember the name of ________ band.
6 *SumFun* has always taken place at a venue in the ________.

Voice It!

7 Discuss the questions.

1 Are there any famous music festivals in your country? Where are they?
2 What other jobs do volunteers do at a festival?
3 Which jobs would you most like to do? Why?

Watch video 7.3
Where was the rock festival that her neighbor went to? What advice did the neighbor give her?

GRAMMAR IN ACTION

Reported Statements

	Direct Speech	Reported Speech
Simple Present	"The people [1] _are_ ______ really friendly."	He said the people **were** really friendly.
Present Continuous	"I[2] ______________ about volunteering."	She said she **was thinking** about volunteering.
Simple Past	"I [3] __________ Blue Wings."	She said she **had seen** Blue Wings.
Present Perfect	"I[4] ______________________ really hard."	She told me she **had worked** really hard.

1 **Complete the examples in the chart above.**

2 7.10 **Circle the correct answers. Then listen and check.**

Mark told me he [1]*was going / had gone* to Thailand next week. He said he [2]*has been / was* really excited and that it [3]*will be / was* the only thing he [4]*can / could* think about. He told me he [5]*had bought / bought* his ticket last week and he [6]*'d downloaded / 's downloaded* an app to learn Thai yesterday. He said he [7]*packed / 'd packed* his suitcase this morning and that he [8]*was / 'd be* in Bangkok next Monday. He said he [9]*went / was going* to meet his sister there. He told me he [10]*had written / 'd write* and tell us all about it.

Get It Right!

We use words like *me*, *he*, *her* after **tell**, but not after **say**.

He told me he couldn't.

He said he couldn't.

NOT ~~He said me he couldn't.~~

3 **Rewrite the sentences as reported speech.**

1 "I went to an incredible festival." She told me _she'd been to an incredible festival_ .

2 "I don't have a costume." He said ______________________ .

3 "I'm waiting for the parade to start." She told me ______________________ .

4 "I can't see the stage because there are too many people." He said ______________________ .

5 "Don't forget to send me some photos." He said ______________________ .

4 **Rewrite the reported speech as direct speech. Then check in the story on page 84.**

1 He told them they would never meet again.
____

2 He said that if they did their jobs well, they could meet once a year.
____

3 She said she wanted to see him.
____

Use It!

5 **Work in pairs. Ask and answer the questions.**

1 What sports do you like?
2 What did you do last weekend?
3 What have you eaten today?

6 **Work in different pairs. Report what your partner said in Exercise 5.**

Finished? p124 Ex. 3

SPEAKING
Inviting a Friend to a Party

7.11 **1 Listen to the conversation. What does Ryan think he's doing on Saturday?**

JOSH Hey, Lara! [1]What are you up to on Saturday?
LARA Why? Is something happening?
JOSH It's Ryan's 17th. We're organizing a little celebration for him. Why don't you join us?
LARA Sure, [2]__________. I'd forgotten it was his birthday. Where is it?
JOSH It's at my place, but don't say anything to him. It's a surprise.
LARA A surprise party? Really?
JOSH Yeah, he told me once he'd never had one before, so I thought, why not? He thinks we're going to a gig.
LARA OK. I won't say a word. [3]__________________________?
JOSH It kicks off at six, but you can come when you like.
LARA OK, [4]__________ around seven. [5]__________________________?
JOSH Why don't you bring some snacks?
LARA OK. What about a present? Should I get him something?
JOSH He said he wanted a new backpack. We can buy him one together if you like.
LARA Sure. Count me in.
JOSH Great! See you there, then! And tell your brother to come. The more the merrier!

7.11 **2 Complete the conversation with the phrases from the *Useful Language* box. Then listen again and check.**

Useful Language

I'd love to.	I'll be there (at/around) …
Should I bring anything?	~~What are you up to … ?~~
What time should I be there?	

3 Complete the sentences with the phrases in the *Everyday English* box.

1 __________________________ I'm good at keeping secrets.
2 Of course I want to come with you. __________________________
3 Invite everyone you know – __________________________.
4 Why don't we meet __________________________?
5 __________________________ ten o'clock.

Watch video 7.4
Everyday English

at my place	Count me in.
It kicks off at …	I won't say a word.
The more the merrier.	

PLAN

4 Read the conversation in Exercise 1 again. Write notes about the party.

What type of party is it? __________________________

Where and when is it? __________________________

What should people bring? __________________________

5 Work in pairs. Plan a conversation about a party. Use the ideas from Exercise 4.

SPEAK

6 Practice a conversation. Remember to use the past perfect, reported speech, and phrases from the *Useful Language* and *Everyday English* boxes.

CHECK

7 Work with another pair. Listen to their conversation and answer the questions from Exercise 4.

WRITING

An Email to a Friend

To: Mason

Hi Mason,

Thanks for your email. It was great to hear from you!

Yesterday was my sister's graduation. I'd never been to a graduation before. It was a little different from what I'd expected! The ceremony took place at the University of Venice in Italy. Everyone was wearing formal clothes and there were some really long speeches. Then the students went up to the stage to collect their certificates. I was so proud of Sally when she got hers!

Later there was a party by one of the canals. All the students had put on crowns, an ancient symbol of victory. The craziest thing was that everyone was throwing eggs at each other. Sally said it was a tradition from Venice. I told her it felt more like a festival than a graduation!

Anyway, that's all from me. Write back soon!

Bye for now,

Gloria

1 **Look at the photo. What is the girl wearing? Read Gloria's email and check.**

2 **Put a–e in the order they appear in Gloria's email.**

a ☐ goodbye

b ☐ thanks for writing

c ☐ greeting

d ☐ description of the ceremony

e ☐ request for a reply

3 **Look at the phrases in the *Useful Language* box. Are they opening or closing phrases? Write *O* (opening) or *C* (closing).**

Useful Language

a Anyway, that's all from me. ___

b Bye for now, ___

c It was great to hear from you! ___

d Thanks for your email. ___

e Write back soon! ___

PLAN

4 **Write an email about a ceremony. Think of a ceremony you have been to. Write notes.**

What was it for? ____________

Where was it? ____________

What did people wear? ____________

What did people do? ____________

5 **Decide what information to include. Use the information in Exercise 2 to help you.**

WRITE

6 **Write your email. Remember to include the structure from Exercise 2, the past perfect, reported speech, and phrases from the *Useful Language* box.**

CHECK

7 **Do you ...**

- have a greeting and a goodbye?
- describe the ceremony?
- request a reply?

Finished? p124 Ex. 4

AROUND THE WORLD

READING

A Travel Blog

1 **Look at the photo of the lanterns. What do you know about Chinese festivals?**

7.12 2 **Read and match the photo with one of the festivals in the blog.** ______________________

Globetrotters

Watch video 7.5
A Monkey Buffet

- Can you think of any festivals with animals?
- When does the Monkey Buffet Festival take place?
- Do you agree that this is a good reason to celebrate? Why / Why not?

Ollie in China

Chinese people love to celebrate, so they have a lot of festivals throughout the year. Here are my top three.

1

Harbin Ice and Snow Sculpture Festival

When I was a kid, I used to think my snowy creations were excellent, but they were nothing compared to what I saw at the Harbin International Ice and Snow Sculpture Festival. Artists from around the world come to the event and compete to build the most beautiful sculptures from snow and ice. Many were covered in colorful lights. In 2007, a group of Canadian artists made a sculpture of Niagara Falls that was 250 meters long and used 13,000 m^3 of snow. Nobody had ever made such a huge snow sculpture before!

2

Chinese New Year

Did you know that about 20 percent of the world's population celebrates Chinese New Year? But it doesn't take place on January 1, it starts just before spring. It's a time when families pay respects to their ancestors and exchange gifts. In China, red is a lucky color, so there are red decorations everywhere, red lanterns in the street, and poems in bright red paint on the doors of houses. People also enjoy traditional food. *Tangyuan*, the sweet rice balls I tried in Beijing, were one of the most delicious things I'd ever eaten.

3

Dragon Boat Festival

When my Chinese friends told me they wanted to take me to see a dragon boat race in Hong Kong, I thought, dragons in boats?! But no – I'd misunderstood! The boats are wooden and decorated as dragons. They're about 25–30 meters long and look awesome. Each boat has a team of up to 60 powerful rowers. People have celebrated the festival since 273 BCE! They say that good luck and happiness come to the winners. While we were watching, I ate *zongzi*, a traditional dish made of rice and bamboo leaves. It was really good!

3 **Write the name of the festival(s).**

1 People give presents. Chinese New Year

2 You can take part in a competition.

____

____

3 People celebrate with food.

____

____

4 It is over 1,700 years old.

____

____

4 **What do these numbers in the blog refer to?**

a 20 The percentage of the world's population that celebrates Chinese New Year.

b 250 ______________________

____

c 25–30 ______________________

____

d 60 ______________________

____

e 13,000 m^3 ______________________

____

Voice It!

5 Discuss the questions.

1 During Chinese New Year, families pay respects to their ancestors. Why is this important?
2 In what ways do people show respect to others?
3 Who do you most respect in your life?

LEARN TO LEARN

Suffixes

Suffixes can help expand your vocabulary.

6 Find the adjectives from nouns 1–5 in the blog and underline the suffixes. Then use the suffixes to make adjectives from nouns 6–10.

1 beauty *beautiful*
2 color ______
3 luck ______
4 power ______
5 snow ______
6 care ______
7 dirt ______
8 health ______
9 hope ______
10 thought ______

Explore It!

Guess the correct answer.

In the Chinese zodiac, every New Year is represented by an animal. Which of these animals is not in the zodiac?

a lion b monkey c snake

Find another interesting fact about China. Then write a question for your partner to answer.

SHAPE IT!

CULTURE PROJECT

A Travel Blog

A travel blog has short texts about one or more locations.
In groups, write a travel blog post about a festival.

Teacher's Resource Bank

7 REVIEW

VOCABULARY

1 Complete the sentences with the words in the box.

ceremony fireworks floats parade

Did you know ...

1 The world's biggest ______________ takes place in Manhattan in November. It is famous for its huge balloons.

2 The word for ______________ in Japanese means "fire-flower."

3 During the opening ______________ of the Olympic Games, Greek athletes always enter the stadium first.

4 During the Bloemencorso Parade in the Netherlands, ______________ decorated with eight million flowers drive through the streets.

2 Match the parts of the poster with the words.

band members ☐ gig ☐ headliner ☐
supporting acts ☐ venue ☐

GRAMMAR IN ACTION

3 Answer the questions with the past perfect.

1 Why was Cheng so happy? (his team / win / the match)

____

2 Why didn't Freddy buy a sandwich? (leave / his money / at home)

____

3 Why did they come home late? (miss / the bus)

____

4 Why was Lisa bored? (see / the movie / before)

____

4 Rewrite the sentences as reported speech.

1 "There's a festival in the park," Jacob told me.

____

2 "Don't touch my things!" Nellie told her brother.

____

3 "I've never been to a festival before," said Mike.

____

4 "You can watch the fireworks with my family," said Chloe.

____

5 "I'll visit Grandma on the weekend," said Claire.

____

Self-Assessment

I can talk about festivals in English.

I can talk about music festivals and live music.

I can use the past perfect.

I can use reported statements.

LEARN TO ... CHALLENGE YOURSELF TO DO MORE IN CLASS

You can feel more positive about learning by challenging yourself to do more. When you make an effort, you get better results.

1 **Charlotte and Gael finish a project before their classmates. How can they use their time well? Why?**

a do their homework for another subject
b do extra English activities together or alone
c chat in their language

2 **Charlotte and Gael decide to play *Blank!* to practice vocabulary. Read how to play. Write the *Blank!* words.**

How to Play *Blank!*

- Choose a text you've read in this book.
- **Player A:** Read the first half of the text to Player B but say "*blank*" instead of some words.
- **Player B:** Try to remember the missing words.
- Swap roles.

OK, Gael, the Japanese folktale. Throughout Blank!, different cultures ...

History!

That's right. ... different cultures have looked up at the Blank! [1] ______________ in the night sky and told Blank! [2] ______________ about them.

3 **Nathan and Rita finish a speaking activity before their classmates. How can they use the extra minutes well? Why?**

a ask each other some more questions in English
b clean up their desks
c listen to the other pairs

4 **Student A: talk for one minute about a topic from the box. Student B: when your partner finishes, ask three questions about the topic. Then swap roles.**

a folktale I know an interesting festival I have been to my favorite TV show

5 **George finishes the last activity of the class before his classmates. He makes a mini-plan for the next class. Complete his plan with the words in the box.**

grammar practice vocabulary

Mini-Plan
In the next class, I want to ...
use this [1] ______________ : past perfect
use this [2] ______________ : program, atmosphere, crowd
and [3] ______________ : asking questions

SHAPE IT!

6 **Choose a reading text from Units 1–7 and play *Blank!***

7 **Make a mini-plan for the next class like the one in Exercise 5. Use and practice these things in the next class.**

8 What is education?

LEARNING OUTCOMES

I can ...

- understand texts about dangerous journeys to school and school rules
- explain and ask about rules
- write an essay about rules at school
- talk about obligation, permission, and prohibition
- talk about school, behavior, and attitude
- personalize vocabulary, think about content before listening, and ask for help when you don't understand.
- design a school brochure

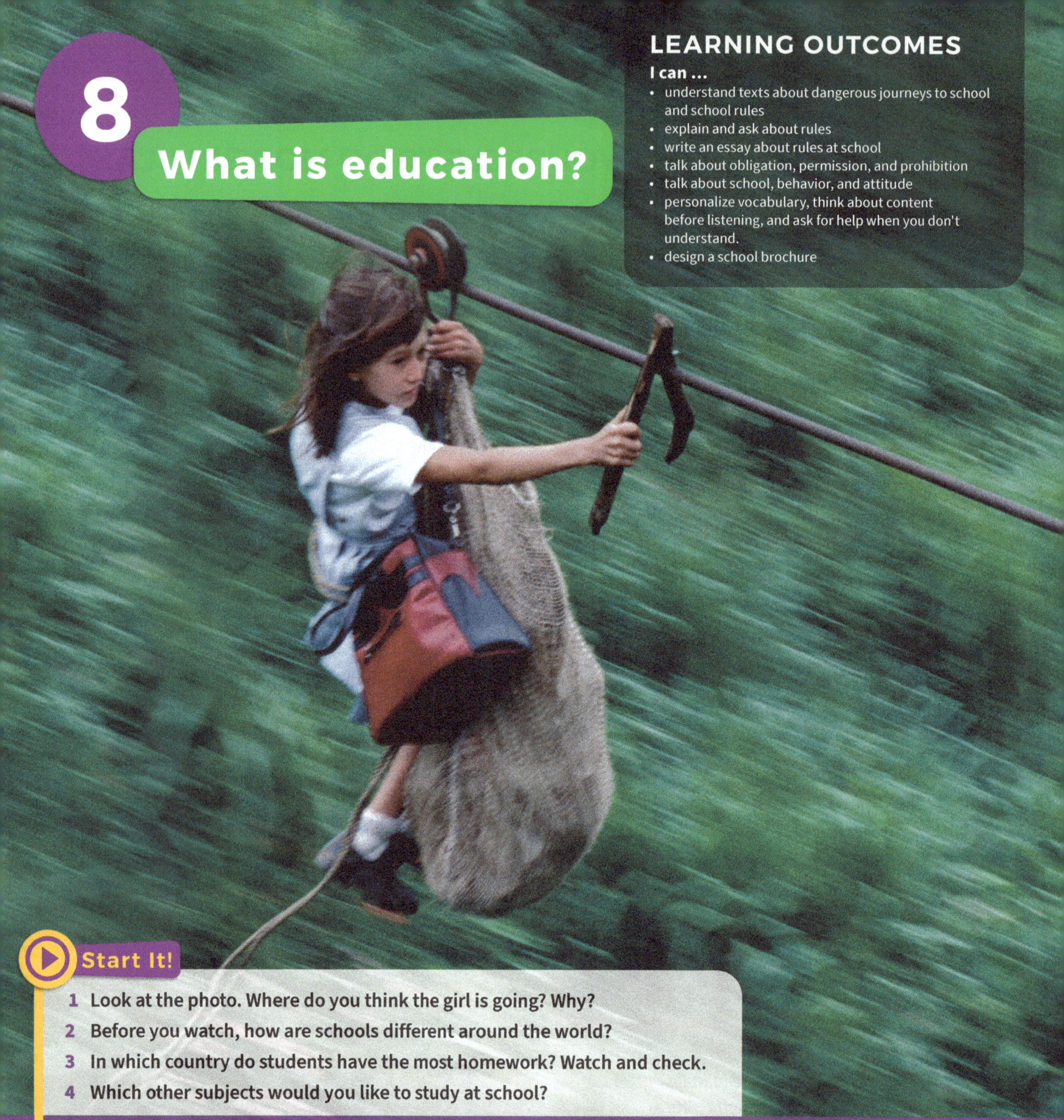

Start It!

1 Look at the photo. Where do you think the girl is going? Why?

2 Before you watch, how are schools different around the world?

3 In which country do students have the most homework? Watch and check.

4 Which other subjects would you like to study at school?

Watch video 8.1

p97

Grammar in Action 8.2

p99

Grammar in Action 8.3

p100

Everyday English 8.4

VOCABULARY
School

8.01 1 Match the phrases with the photos (1–11). Then listen, check, and repeat.

cheat on a test	☐	pass an exam	☐
fail an exam	☐	pay attention to the teacher	☐
get detention	☐	study for a test	☐
get good grades	☐	take an exam	☐
give somebody a talk	☐	write an essay	☐
hand in homework	1		

Pronunciation p142

8.04 2 Listen and write the phrases you hear from Exercise 1. Then use the phrases to tell your partner what you remember.

1 get detention
2 ______
3 ______
4 ______
5 ______
6 ______
7 ______
8 ______

LEARN TO LEARN
Personalizing Vocabulary

Using new words to talk about your life helps you remember them.

3 Write true and false sentences about you with phrases from Exercise 1. Tell your partner your sentences. Can they guess which are false?

I always hand in my homework on time.

Use It!

4 Read the questions and write two more. Then ask and answer with a partner.

1 Is it better to study alone or with friends?
2 What should happen to students who cheat?
3 What are the good and bad things about exams?

______

______

Explore It!

Guess the correct answer.

How many students does the biggest school in the world have?

a between 25,000 and 35,000
b between 35,000 and 45,000
c more than 45,000

Find another interesting fact about a school. Then write a question for your partner to answer.

READING

A Report

1 **How many ways of getting to school can you think of?**

8.05 2 **Read the report. Does it mention your ideas?**

3 **Match the headings (a–d) with the paragraphs (1–4).**

a A Suggestion for the Future
b Why Can't Every Child Go to School?
c A Risk, but an Essential One
d Introduction to My Report

4 **Circle the correct answers.**

1 What does the writer say about parents?
  a Their children shouldn't make dangerous journeys.
  b They care about their children's education.
  c They think it's difficult for children to get an education.
2 What does the writer think about online education?
  a It's more expensive than building bridges.
  b It could help more children learn.
  c It's a good idea if children have computers.

5 **Find words in the text that mean ...**

1 looking for information (paragraph 1).

____

2 go regularly to a place (paragraph 2).

____

3 dangerous (paragraph 3).

____

Voice It!

6 **Discuss the statements.**

1 The children in the text are brave.
2 We need more online education for children.
3 Education is the most important thing for a happy, successful future.

Dangerous Journeys to School

1 ☐

This report looks at the problem of dangerous journeys to school. I have been researching this for my school project on education around the world. Here, I give some examples of these journeys and suggest one way to change the situation.

2 ☐

Children in many countries attend both elementary and secondary school. However, in some countries, school is too expensive or there aren't enough spots for everyone. In others, boys can go to school but girls can't. Some children aren't allowed to go to school because their parents need their help at home. In many cases, school is free and all children can attend, but some students make dangerous journeys to get there.

3 ☐

In Indonesia, for example, children from Batu Busuk village walk along a rope nine meters above a river and then walk 11 kilometers through a forest to get to school. They have been doing this since a bridge was destroyed in a rainstorm two years ago. In Los Pinos, Colombia, children cross the Rio Negro on an 800-meter rope because walking to school the long way takes four hours. In China, the children of Atuler village climb mountains to get to school. Children are allowed to make these risky journeys because education is important to parents and children everywhere.

4 ☐

Online education could be one answer to the problem. A teacher can give classes by video, and students can hand in homework by email and take exams online. Of course, electricity, a computer, and an internet connection are all necessary, but these things are cheaper to provide than roads and bridges. It is not a perfect solution, but if we spent money on these things, then children in remote places would have a basic education, and dangerous journeys to school would be a thing of the past.

Finished? p125 Ex. 1

GRAMMAR IN ACTION

Can/Can't

Watch video 8.2
What are boys not allowed to have in school?
What is Wu Yan allowed to do at school?

1 **Complete the sentences with *can* or *can't*. Do they express permission, prohibition, or ability? Write *PE* (permission), *PR* (prohibition), or *A* (ability).**

1. Students ___can___ borrow two books from the library. (✓) ___PE___
2. You ________ use a dictionary in the French exam. (✗) ________
3. Tom ________ play soccer very well. (✗) ________
4. Students ________ stay in the classroom when it's raining. (✓) ________
5. My sister ________ speak English better than me. (✓) ________

To Be Allowed To

+	The student **is allowed to** hand in homework by email.
–	Some children **aren't** [1]________ **to** go to school.
?	[2]________ you **allowed to** take your phone to school? Yes, I **am**. No, I'**m** [3]________.

2 **Complete the examples in the chart above.**

3 **Rewrite the sentences with *to be allowed to*.**

1. We can use a calculator in the exam.
   We're allowed to use a calculator in the exam.
2. My sister and I can't watch TV.
   ____
3. Can you choose the subjects you want to study?
   ____
4. Students at Luke's school can go home for lunch if they live near the school.
   ____
   ____

8.06 **4** **Complete the text with the correct form of the words in the box. Then listen and check.**

can / come ~~can / play~~ can / wear
not allow / give not allow / tell
not allow / wear

Every year, we have a big party on the last day of the school. We [1]___can play___ games or listen to music in class and the teachers [2]________ us any work! We [3]________ our own clothes instead of our uniform (although we [4]________ any jewelry – that's always against the rules). We [5]________ even ________ in costumes if we want to. There's a competition for the best costume, but the teachers [6]________ us what the prize is – it's a surprise.

Use It!

5 **Use the ideas to write questions with *to be allowed to* in your notebook.**

have posters in your bedroom
~~play video games before dinner~~ stay out late
use your phone when you want

Are you allowed to play video games before dinner?

6 **Ask and answer the questions in Exercise 5.**

Are you allowed to play video games before dinner?

If I've finished all my homework.

Finished? p125 Ex. 2

VOCABULARY AND LISTENING

A Phone Call

1 Look at the photo. Why do you think the two students are cleaning the windows?

LEARN TO LEARN

Preparing to Listen

Deciding what you want to know about the topic before you listen helps you prepare.

2 You will hear Harry talking about his Japanese exchange trip. Write three questions you want to know the answer to.

____

____

____

8.07 3 Listen to the conversation. Then tell your partner which of your questions from Exercise 2 were answered.

8.07 4 Listen again and circle the correct answers.

1 How do Harry and Denise know each other?
   a They're brother and sister. b They're friends.

2 When do the students clean the school?
   a in the morning b at the end of the day

3 How well does Harry speak Japanese?
   a not at all b not perfectly

Attitude and Behavior

8.08 5 Complete the chart with the opposite adjectives. Then listen, check, and repeat.

~~careful~~ ~~careless~~ disobedient disorganized immature mature organized polite rude well-behaved

Positive	Negative
careful	*careless*

6 Complete the school reports with the words from Exercise 5.

Andy used to be very [1] *disobedient* – never paying attention and always talking – but recently, I haven't had to give him a talk because he's been very [2] _______. However, he's still very [3] _______, especially with his books and papers. He should be more [4] _______ and keep his things in order.

Last year, Lizzy was very [5] _______ with her work and she made a lot of mistakes, but this year she has spent more time doing her homework and has been much more [6] _______. She also used to be [7] _______ and silly in class, always making jokes, but she has grown up a lot, and now she is much more [8] _______.

Use It!

7 Put the words from Exercise 5 in order from most positive (1) to least positive (10). Then compare with a partner.

I think "polite" is the most positive because ...

GRAMMAR IN ACTION

To Have To, Must, and *To Need To*

Watch video 8.3
What don't the students have to carry with them? Why doesn't Anna need to study?

	To Have To	*Must*	*To Need To*
+	The students **have to** wear a uniform.	All students **must** attend orientation.	You **need to** make mistakes.
–	They **don't have to** do it.	Students **must not** (mustn't) use cell phones during the exam.	You **don't** [2] ________ tell me that.
?	**Do** you [1] ________ clean, too?		What [3] ________ we ________ do?

1 Complete the examples in the chart above.

2 Complete the sentences with the correct form of *to have to*.

1. You don't have to work in pairs. You can work alone if you want.
2. ________ you ________ wear a uniform?
3. Sam's teacher says she ________ study harder if she wants to pass her exams.
4. I ________ pay for guitar lessons. My best friend is teaching me!
5. ________ your parents ________ meet with your teachers once a year?

Get It Right!

The phrase **must not** means it's important not to do something. We use **don't have to** to express that an action is not necessary.

Visitors must not enter the school without permission

NOT ~~Visitors don't have to enter the school without permission.~~

3 Rewrite the sentences with *to have to*, *must*, or *to need to*.

1. It isn't necessary for us to wear a uniform.
   We don't need/have to wear a uniform.
2. It's obligatory for all students to take the exam.
   All students ________.
3. Is it necessary for me to buy the book?
   Do I ________?
4. It's against the rules for students to be late.
   Students ________.
5. Joining an after-school club is optional. Students ________.

4 Write sentences about the signs with the phrases below and *to have to*, *must*, or *to need to*.

be quiet ~~make an appointment~~ run wear formal clothes

1 Student Counselor's Office
Hours: 9:30 to 2:00
Monday to Friday
No appointment necessary

2 NO RUNNING IN THE HALLWAYS

3 Silence during the exam, please.

4 Graduation party: July 23 at 6 p.m. Formal clothes optional

1. You don't need/have to make an appointment.
2. ________
3. ________
4. ________

Use It!

5 Complete the rules for your dream school.

1. We don't have to study ________.
2. Teachers must not ________.
3. We don't need to ________.

6 EXAM Ask and answer the questions with a partner.

Student A:
What rules does your school have?
What would you change about your school's rules?

Student B:
What signs are in your school?
What rules do most people follow? What rules do they break?

Finished? p125 Ex. 3

SPEAKING

Explaining and Asking about Rules

8.09 **1 Listen to the conversation. How is Javier feeling about going on an exchange program?**

WILL So, how are you feeling, Javier? Excited?

JAVIER Kind of. I'm a little nervous, to be honest, Will.

WILL Don't be. Everyone's really friendly and polite. But our rules might be a bit different from yours – for example, we have to wear a uniform, but that's no big deal. You'll love it!

JAVIER Yeah, right! [1] What are the rules about phones?

WILL You're not allowed to bring one to school.

JAVIER How come? [2] ____________________

WILL You get detention.

JAVIER Really? In my school you're not allowed to use them in class, but we can use them during breaks. What about lunch? Do you have to eat in the cafeteria?

WILL You don't have to. You can bring your own food if you want.

JAVIER OK. [3] ____________________

WILL Um, we have to wait outside the classroom for the teacher.

JAVIER [4] ____________________

WILL Because the teacher tells us where to sit as we go in the classroom.

JAVIER It's a lot to remember.

WILL Don't worry, you'll be fine!

8.09 **2 Complete the conversation with the phrases from the *Useful Language* box. Then listen again and check.**

Useful Language

Anything else I need to know?	~~What are the rules about … ?~~
What happens if you do?	Why's that?

3 Match the meanings (1–4) with the phrases in the *Everyday English* box.

1. A little bit.
2. Why?
3. I don't believe you!
4. That's not a big problem.

Watch video 8.4
Everyday English

How come? ☐	Kind of. ☐
That's no big deal. ☐	Yeah, right! ☐

PLAN

4 Plan your own conversation. Read the conversation in Exercise 1 again. Take notes about the three school rules Will and Javier talk about.

Phones: ____________________

Lunch: ____________________

Teachers: ____________________

5 Work in pairs. In your notebook, write notes on three rules in your school.

6 Plan a conversation to explain the rules to a friend from another country.

SPEAK

7 Practice a conversation. Remember to use *can/can't, to be allowed to, to have to, must, to need to,* and phrases from the *Useful Language* and *Everyday English* boxes.

CHECK

8 Work with another pair. Listen to their conversation. Which school rules did they talk about?

WRITING

An Essay

1 **Make a list of good and bad things about school uniforms. Then read the essay. Does it have your ideas?**

Should Students Have to Wear a Uniform?

For many students, a uniform is a part of daily life and they must wear it. But some students don't have to follow any rules about what to wear.
[1] ______________________ some advantages and disadvantages of uniforms.

People have strong views about uniforms. [2] ______________, wearing a uniform is preparation for the future. Many people have to wear one, such as firefighters, doctors, and nurses. [3] ______________ a uniform shows the world that you belong to an important group.

[4] ______________, you don't need to wear a uniform to get good grades. [5] ______________ youth is an important time to discover who you are. If students aren't allowed to be creative, they lose the opportunity to show their identity.

In summary, I think students should be able to choose what they wear. Uniforms are not necessary for success, and students might not have the freedom to be creative with their clothes when they start work.

2 **Put the parts of the essay in the correct order.**

- a a conclusion with the writer's opinion ☐
- b good things about school uniforms ☐
- c an introduction to the topic ☐
- d bad things about school uniforms ☐

3 **Complete the essay with the phrases from the *Useful Language* box.**

Useful Language

In this essay, I outline …
On the other hand, …
Some say that …
On the one hand, …
Others argue that …

PLAN

4 **Write your own essay. Think of two good things and two bad things about using phones in schools. Write notes.**

Good Things: ______________________

____

Bad Things: ______________________

____

5 **Look at the essay question below. Write notes on your opinion. Decide what to include. Use the information in Exercise 2 to help you.**

Can phones help students learn in class?

____

____

____

WRITE

6 **Write your essay. Remember to include *can/can't, to be allowed to, to have to, must, to need to,* and the phrases from the *Useful Language* box.**

CHECK

7 **Do you …**

- have an introduction and conclusion?
- write about good things and bad things?

Finished? p125 Ex. 4

CITIZENSHIP PROJECT

A School Brochure

1 **Read the brochure for Unity Hill School. What is special about this school?**

2 **Write down the things you like and don't like about Unity Hill. Then compare your answers.**

I like that every student can suggest a new rule, and every student has the right to vote on it.

How to Make Decisions in a Group

8.10

3 **Put the stages of decision-making in order. Then listen to the students from Unity Hill. Do they follow the same order?**

a Find the best solution. ☐
b Check the group is ready to vote. ☐
c Present the problem. 1
d Vote on the decision. ☐
e Ask for suggestions. ☐
f Discuss the pros and cons of each idea. ☐

Unity Hill School

Introduction

Are you organized? Do you want to get good grades and develop skills to succeed in our modern world? Then come to Unity Hill – one of the most exciting schools of the 21st century.

What Makes Unity Hill Unique?

We believe our students should be responsible for their school, so at Unity Hill the students make the rules. Every student can suggest a new rule, and every student can vote on it.

Rules Students Have Decided

- Students must respect other students and staff.
- Students don't have to wear a uniform. However, if students decide to have a uniform in the future, they will design it.
- Students have to study seven subjects, but they can choose which ones. One of the subjects must be a language.
- Students have to do PE twice a week, but they don't have to do the same sport every time.
- Students must not use their phones in class, but they can use them during lunch.
- Students don't have to do homework on the weekend.

Responsibilities

- Students can vote yes or no on new rules, but after a new rule has been decided, students must follow it, even if they voted no.
- Students can use any of the facilities, but they have to keep everything clean.
- Students don't have to eat the school lunch, but if they do, they have to help clean up.

PLAN

4 Work in groups to design a school brochure. Complete the steps.

- Decide why your school is special.
- Choose a school name.
- Suggest some school rules.
- Discuss and vote on the rules.
- Decide what responsibilities students will have.
- Decide who prepares each part of the brochure.

PRESENT

5 Present your brochure to the class. Remember to include an introduction and explain why your school is special, the rules, and the responsibilities.

CHECK

6 Read your classmates' brochures. What rules do they have? Which school do you like?

8 REVIEW

VOCABULARY

1 Complete the text.

cheat on tests grades pass studied take

Sometimes I used to [1] ______ by copying my classmates because I hadn't [2] ______ at all. These days I'm different. Next year I have to [3] ______ some important exams and I really want to [4] ______ them and get good [5] ______.

2 Write two adjectives to describe each student.

careful disobedient immature organized polite rude

1 Sometimes Lilly is silly in class and says bad things to her classmates.

______

______

2 Gareth speaks nicely to everyone and plans his work well.

______

______

3 Ben behaves very badly at school, but he pays a lot of attention to his homework.

______

______

GRAMMAR IN ACTION

3 Complete the texts with the correct form of *to be allowed to* and the verbs in the box.

bring study use

EduTV

Should students [1] ______ the subjects they want? We want to hear from you for our new documentary: *Should We Choose Our Education?*

Home Inbox Sent New

Dear Parents,

We are writing to remind you that students [2] ______ their phones to school, but they [3] ______ them in class. Please do not call students during classes.

Sincerely,

The Principal

4 Circle the correct options.

1 Ben *needs to / doesn't have to / must not* study Spanish if he doesn't want to. He can choose Arabic instead.

2 Students *need to / don't have to / must not* play games on school computers.

3 We *need to / don't have to / must not* wear a uniform at school. We can wear what we want.

4 Toni *needs to / doesn't have to / must not* pay more attention in class – she never listens!

Self-Assessment

I can talk about school in English.

I can talk about attitude and behavior.

I can use *can/can't* and *to be allowed to*.

I can use *to have to*, *must*, and *to need to*.

LEARN TO ... ASK FOR HELP WHEN YOU DON'T UNDERSTAND

There are different ways to ask English speakers for help and check if you understand what they've said.

1 Have you ever had any of these problems? How did you solve them?

Problems Understanding Someone in English

a The other person speaks too fast.
b The person uses a lot of words I don't know.
c I understand, more or less, but I don't understand all of the details.
d I think I understand, but I'm not 100 percent sure.
e I'm too shy to say that I don't understand.

2 Match situations a–d with conversations 1–4.

a ☐ explaining the rules of a game
b ☐ at the train station
c ☐ asking directions
d ☐ studying in class

1
A OK, everybody, why are infographics useful online?
B Teacher, [1]___.
A Which word? Infographic?
B Yes.
A OK, an infographic is …

2
A If you land on a blue square, you have to take a card, but you must not show it to anyone. But if you …
B [2]___. I don't understand very well.
A Sorry! I always speak too fast when I'm excited. OK, if you land …

3
A Excuse me, how do I get to the museum?
B Go straight down this road, cross the bridge, and it's on the corner.
A Sorry. [3]___.
B Sure, go straight down this road, cross the bridge, …

4
A Excuse me, I'm trying to get to the airport.
B You need to take the blue line to Airport Station. Then from the station take the shuttle bus.
A OK, [4]___. I take the blue line to Airport Station?
B That's right.
A And then the shuttle bus?
B Exactly.
A Thanks.

3 Complete the conversations in Exercise 2 with these phrases. Write a–d in the gaps.

a Could you speak more slowly, please
b I don't understand what that word means
c Let me check I've got this right
d Could you say that again, please

SHAPE IT!

4 Work in pairs. Take turns talking about one of the topics below. Use the phrases in Exercise 3 to help you understand.

how to get from your school to your house
how to make and use the past perfect
how to use a social media app
the rules of a club you are in
the rules of a sport

9 Where would you go?

LEARNING OUTCOMES

I can ...

- understand texts about vacations in the future and vacation situations
- talk about a future trip
- write an email
- use *to be going to*, the present continuous, the future continuous, relative pronouns, and relative clauses
- talk about travel and use phrasal verbs
- make verb and noun collocations, record phrasal verbs by preposition, make adjectives from nouns, and use technology to practice English

Start It!

1 Look at the photo. Would you like to be in this place? Why / Why not?

2 Before you watch, do you think we'll be able to go to the moon on vacation soon?

3 How long is a day on the moon? Watch and check.

4 Would you like to go to space? Why / Why not?

Watch video 9.1

p109

Grammar in Action 9.2

p111

Grammar in Action 9.3

p112

Everyday English 9.4

p114

Globetrotters 9.5

1

2

3

4

5

6

7

8

VOCABULARY

Travel

9.01 **1 Match the words with the photos (1–8) and definitions (9–12). Then listen, check, and repeat.**

abroad	☐	journey	☐
accommodation	1	resort	☐
backpacking	☐	sightseeing	☐
book	☐	tour	☐
cruise ship	☐	tourist attraction	☐
destination	☐	trip	☐

9 a visit to and around a place, often with a guide
10 in or to a foreign country
11 a (usually short) visit to another place
12 the act of traveling to a place (usually long distance)

Pronunciation p142

9.04 **2 Listen and circle the correct words.**

1 *trip / accommodation*
2 *tourist attraction / cruise ship*
3 *tour / abroad*
4 *book / backpacking*
5 *destination / journey*

LEARN TO LEARN

Learning Collocations

When you learn new words, write which verbs they can be used with.

3 Complete the chart with words from Exercise 1. Add *a* if necessary.

Go	abroad, ______, ______
Book	______, ______, ______
Go on	______, ______, ______, ______
Visit	______, ______
Arrive at	______, ______

Use It!

4 In your notebook, write questions with the collocations from Exercise 3 and the ideas in the box.

Have you ever … ?
When was the last time you … ?
Do you like … ? Would you like to … ?

Have you ever been on a cruise ship?

5 Ask and answer your questions from Exercise 4.

Have you ever been on a cruise ship?

Yes, I went on a cruise ship around the Caribbean last year.

Explore It!

Guess the correct answer.

Which country has the most tourists each year?

a the U.S.A. b Spain c France

Find another interesting fact about a tourist destination. Then write a question for your partner to answer.

READING

A Magazine Interview

1 **Look at the picture. How do you think vacations will be different in 2030?**

9.05 **2** **Read the magazine interview. Does it mention any of your ideas?**

3 EXAM **Complete the interview with the sentences. There are three extra sentences.**

A No, or on trains, in hotels, or at tourist attractions either.

B Tourists will travel by robot horse.

C The trip used to take six hours.

~~D One of the main changes will be where people go on vacation.~~

E People will go on many more vacations.

F Space tourism will be a lot of fun.

G More passengers will be traveling by high-speed train than by plane.

H Mars will be a favorite tourist resort.

4 **Complete the chart with words from the interview.**

Noun	Adjective Form
[1] ______ or tourist	touristy
adventure	[2] ______
smell	[3] ______
pilot	[4] ______

Voice It!

5 **Discuss the questions.**

1 Do you agree with Chen's predictions? Why / Why not?

2 What surprises you most about vacations in the future?

3 Which vacation from the interview would you most like to go on? Why?

VACATIONS OF THE FUTURE

Katya What is going to be the biggest change in tourism in the future?

Chen [1] D . In 2030, for example, we won't be staying at campsites. People will be sleeping in far more exciting accommodations, like floating resorts and hotels under the sea. Imagine waking up face-to-face with a shark! And if that's not adventurous enough, how about relaxing at a space hotel in zero gravity and going on day trips to the moon? [2] ___ . However, it might be a little smelly, as space tourists won't be able to take a shower!

Katya Ugh! So, in 2030, will tourists still be traveling to the same destinations as now?

Chen Yes, they will, but they'll be using virtual reality to test them first. Tourists will be able to experience resorts before they book their trip to help them choose the perfect destination.

Katya And how will tourists travel there?

Chen Good question. We won't be teleporting for a while, but some experts predict that the way people travel will change. [3] ___ . Next week, I'm traveling from Beijing to Shanghai by high-speed train in just four and a half hours, and that journey is predicted to get even shorter in the future. [4] ___ . Airplanes aren't going to disappear, but the whole flying experience is going to change. Flights will be quicker, and by 2040, passengers will even be flying on pilotless planes, looking up at the sky through a clear roof while enjoying a meal served by a robot.

Katya So, won't there be any humans working on planes?

Chen [5] ___ .

Finished? p126 Ex. 1

GRAMMAR IN ACTION

To Be Going To and Present Continuous for Future

Watch video 9.2
What does Matt predict he'll be doing by 2022?
What will everybody be doing this summer?

The whole flying experience **is going to change**.
Next week **I'm traveling** from Beijing to Shanghai.

1 **Look at the examples above and complete the sentences with *to be going to* or the present continuous. Use the verbs in parentheses. Which are arrangements? Which are predictions?**

1. Next week I'm going (go) to Turkey on vacation. arrangement
2. Technology ______ (change) our ideas about space tourism. ______
3. Robots ______ (do) more jobs on planes and in hotels. ______
4. Tomorrow I ______ (travel) to Istanbul by high-speed train. ______
5. We ______ (meet) her at the airport two hours before the flight departs. ______

Use It!

2 **In your notebook, write three arrangements and three predictions about next weekend with *to be going to* and the present continuous.**

I'm having lunch with my friends on Saturday.
I'm going to have a great time with my friends.

Future Continuous

+	By 2040, passengers [1] will even **be flying** on pilotless planes.
–	In 2030, we [2] ______ **be staying** at campsites.
?	In 2030, **will** tourists still [3] ______ to the same destinations as now? Yes, they [4] ______. / No, they **won't**.

3 **Complete the examples in the chart above. Use the magazine interview on page 108 to help you.**

4 **In your notebook, write sentences in the future continuous.**

1. In the future, tourists / stay / on the moon
   In the future, tourists will be staying on the moon.
2. By this time next week I / camp / in Greece
3. Where / you / live / when you're 30 / ?
4. Humans / not work / in hotels in the future

9.06 **5** **Circle the correct options to complete the conversation. Then listen and check.**

KATYA Look at this article! It says that soon passports [1] *are going to disappear* / *are disappearing*! By 2030, we [2] *aren't showing* / *won't be showing* passports to people at the airport; robots [3] *will be checking* / *are checking* people's identity instead.

FABIO Yeah, technology [4] *'s going to change* / *'s changing* everything in the future. I think it [5] *'s going to make* / *'ll be making* everything quicker and safer.

KATYA I guess so, but in a few years' time, robots [6] *are doing* / *will be doing* most jobs, so there [7] *aren't being* / *aren't going to be* any jobs for us!

FABIO Ha ha! We [8] *'ll be sitting* / *'re sitting* at home while the robots do all the work!

Use It!

6 **In your notebook, write predictions about vacations and travel in the future.**

By 2050, we'll be traveling by air taxi.

Finished? p126 Ex. 2

VOCABULARY AND LISTENING

Travel Phrasal Verbs

9.07 **1 Match the phrasal verbs with the underlined phrases and then write the correct form of the phrasal verbs. Listen, check, and repeat.**

check in check out get away get back
get in ~~go away~~ look around
set off take off

1 go away 4 ____ 7 ____
2 ____ 5 ____ 8 ____
3 ____ 6 ____ 9 ____

Hello!

We're on vacation! Dad said he wanted to [1]leave on vacation because he was stressed and that now would be a great time to [2]escape somewhere, so we booked it!

We haven't had time to [3]explore yet because we didn't [4]arrive until 8 p.m. Our plane was delayed, so we didn't [5]start flying until 2:30 p.m.! We [6]started our journey at 6 a.m., so we're all really tired. We've just [7]arrived at the hotel and we're going out to dinner in a minute.

We have to [8]leave the hotel by noon next Friday, so we'll [9]come home at about 9 p.m.

See you then!

Lauren Rogers
15 Castle Street
Newcastle, WA 98056

LEARN TO LEARN

Phrasal Verbs

When you learn a new phrasal verb, write it down with other phrasal verbs that have the same preposition.

2 Complete the chart with the phrasal verbs from Exercise 1.

around	away	back	in	off	out
look					

Use It!

3 Complete the questions with the phrasal verbs from Exercise 1. Then ask and answer the questions with a partner.

1 When was the last time you went away?
2 What documents do you need when you ____ in at a hotel or airport?
3 Do you enjoy looking ____ new places?
4 What time do you usually ____ off in the morning?
5 How do you feel when you get ____ from a vacation?
6 What time did you ____ in last night?

I went away to Peru last summer with my parents.

Conversations

9.08 **4 Listen and match the conversations (1–4) with the photos (a–d).**

a 

b 

c 

d 

9.08 **5 Listen again. Are the sentences *T* (true) or *F* (false)?**

1 Alfie prefers his dad's vacation plans. ___
2 Peter wanted to set off earlier. ___
3 Isla would like to go on a trip to space. ___
4 Tim doesn't believe there will be floating hotels in the future. ___

Voice It!

6 Discuss the questions.

1 What's your favorite type of vacation? Why?
2 Would you fly on a plane with a robot pilot?

Watch video 9.3
Name one place where she wants to go one day. At what point in the future does she imagine she travels to?

GRAMMAR IN ACTION
Relative Pronouns and Relative Clauses

Person	She's the type of person **who** just wants to spend her vacation swimming.
Thing	It's a system [1] that uses virtual reality.
Place	Dad wants to go to a place [2] ________ he can go sightseeing.
Time	We already live in a time [3] ________ people want to go away on exciting vacations.
Reason	This is [4] ________ I told you we needed to set off earlier.
Possession	The girl in our class **whose** dad works for a technology company …

1 Complete the examples in the chart above.

2 Circle the correct words.

1. The tent *that* / *whose* I bought is broken!
2. I'm the person *whose* / *who* sent you the message.
3. That's the boy *whose* / *who* grandparents went on vacation to Greece.
4. July is the month *when* / *who* most people go on vacation.
5. Jon is very confident. That's *why* / *when* he's so good at languages.
6. A destination is the place *when* / *where* you travel to.

3 Complete the text. Then listen and check. 9.09

The other day I met a guy [1] whose cousin is training to be an astronaut. He told me that the place [2] ________ she is training is looking for people [3] ________ want to go into space as tourists and she is going to go. She says the reason [4] ________ she wants to go is to show people that space travel is something [5] ________ anyone can do if they complete the training. She's not sure [6] ________ she is leaving, but the training [7] ________ she has done so far means she is ready to set off any day now!

Get It Right!

The relative pronoun replaces the subject pronoun in a relative clause.

A vacation that ~~it~~ cost $500.

The tourists who ~~they~~ are staying in my hotel.

4 Circle the correct words. Then complete the sentences with your own ideas.

1. My favorite vacation destination is a place *who* / *where* I can go skiing.
2. I prefer to stay in accommodations *that* / *when* ________________.
3. A friend is someone *who* / *why* ________________.
4. School is the reason *where* / *why* ________________.
5. My favorite store is the one *that* / *when* ________________.

Use It!

5 Think of two words for each of the categories in the box. Then write a sentence with a relative clause to describe each word in your notebook.

animals	famous people	places	things

Paris: It's a place where you can see the Eiffel Tower.

Finished? p126 Ex. 3

SPEAKING

Talking About a Future Trip

9.10 **1 Listen to the conversation. What is Gemma going to do on her trip?**

BEN Hey Gemma! So, when are you off to New York?

GEMMA Hey, Ben! Hang on a sec. I'll be with you in a minute. Hey, Sandy. I'll talk to you later. Bye. Sorry, that was my sister on the phone. What were you saying?

BEN I was asking you when you're going to New York.

GEMMA We're going [1] *in two weeks*. I can't wait!

BEN I'm so jealous! New York's on my bucket list. [2] ______________________

GEMMA We're staying in a hotel. It's right in the middle of Manhattan!

BEN Wow! And [3] ______________________

GEMMA Oh, you know, all the usual stuff, so tons of sightseeing. [4] ______________________ seeing the Empire State Building, Statue of Liberty, Times Square, and so on. [5] ______________________ get tickets to see a show. Mom wants to see *The Lion King*, but I'd rather see *Hamilton*.

BEN [6] ______________________

GEMMA Just a week.

BEN It's not fair! While you're jetting off to New York, think of us back home. We'll all be studying for our exams!

GEMMA Ah, poor you! I'll send you some photos!

9.10 **2 Complete the conversation with the phrases from the *Useful Language* box. Then listen again and check.**

Useful Language

How long are you going for?
I'm really looking forward to (+ *-ing*)
~~… in two weeks~~
We're going to try to …
What are you planning on doing?
Where will you be staying?

3 Match the meanings (1–5) with the phrases in the *Everyday English* box.

1 exactly in the center of
2 What were you talking about?
3 together with other similar things
4 list of things to do before you die
5 things

Watch video 9.4
Everyday English

… and so on
… right in the middle of …
What were you saying?
bucket list
the usual stuff

PLAN

4 Read the conversation in Exercise 1 again. Write notes about Gemma's plans.

Going where? ______________________
When? ______________________
Staying where? ______________________
____
Going to do what? ______________________
____

5 Work in pairs. Plan a conversation about visiting a place. Use the ideas from Exercise 4.

SPEAK

6 Practice a conversation. Remember to use *to be going to*, the present continuous, the future continuous, relative pronouns, and phrases from the *Useful Language* and *Everyday English* boxes.

CHECK

7 Work with another pair. Listen to their conversation and answer the questions from Exercise 4.

WRITING

An Email to a Host Family

1 **Look at the photo. Where is it? Why do you think Kerem is going there? Read his email and check.**

From: kerem29@mymail.com
Subject: Next month

Dear Mr. and Mrs. O'Reilly,

I'm writing to introduce myself, as I'm coming to stay with you in San Francisco next month. My name is Kerem. I'm 14 years old and I'm from Bursa in Turkey. Do you know Turkey?

I'm very excited about visiting San Francisco. It'll be my first visit to the United States, so I wanted to ask you some questions about my trip. My friends and I are taking a bus from the airport. Is someone going to meet us there when we arrive? Also, do you know how many hours of English we will be studying every day? I know we'll be sightseeing in the afternoons, but do you know which places we'll be visiting? What's the weather going to be like? What clothes do you think I should bring?

Thank you very much for inviting me to stay with you. I'm really looking forward to meeting you!

Best wishes,

Kerem

2 **Put a–e in the order they appear in Kerem's email.**

a ☐ goodbye
b ☐ questions about the trip
c ☐ greeting
d ☐ reason for writing
e ☐ thanks

3 **Match the phrases from Exercise 2 (a–e) with the phrases in the *Useful Language* box.**

Useful Language

Best wishes, ☐
Dear Mr. and Mrs. … ☐
Do you know … ? ☐
I'm writing to … ☐
Thank you very much for (+ *-ing*) ☐

PLAN

4 **Write your own email to a host family. Think of questions to ask them about these things.**

Your Travel Plans and When You Arrive

____

____

Activities While You are There

____

____

The Weather and Clothes to Bring

____

____

5 **Decide what information to include. Use the information in Exercise 2 to help you.**

WRITE

6 **Write your email. Remember to use *to be going to*, the present continuous, the future continuous, and phrases from the *Useful Language* box.**

CHECK

7 **Do you …**

- use a greeting at the beginning and say goodbye at the end?
- say why you are writing?
- say thank you?

Finished? p126 Ex. 4

AROUND THE WORLD

READING

A Webpage

1 Look at the photos. What do you know about Costa Rica? Discuss with a partner.

2 Read the webpage. Does it mention any of your ideas?

9.11

Globetrotters

Watch video 9.5
One World, One Culture?

- What makes culture? Think of three things.
- How many H&M shops are there around the world?
- What are the advantages and disadvantages of a global culture?

1 Why visit Costa Rica?

Costa Rica is a fascinating, tropical country in Central America. It is also one of the happiest countries in the world because of its relaxed way of life. When you ask someone "How are you?" they answer "pura vida." That means "pure life" or "life is great." Although it's only a small country, it is home to 5 percent of the world's plant and animal species! Over 25 percent of the country is protected, as it is made up of **outstanding** nature reserves. Here you can find more than 1,000 butterflies, 9,000 different types of plants, 20,000 species of spider, and 34,000 varieties of insects! Costa Rica has **spectacular** volcanoes, beaches, jungles, rainforests, and magical cloud forests!

2 Why is conservation so important in Costa Rica?

It's a destination that has always been popular for tourism, and many tourists go back year after year. In fact, tourism is the main reason why conservation is so important. Costa Ricans are proud of their country and they work hard to take care of its **unique** natural beauty. Ecotourism in Costa Rica helps protect the natural environment, benefit local communities, and also educate tourists about the importance of its natural resources.

3 What will I be doing?

Volunteers stay in a coastal town and work on environmental projects. You'll be keeping the beaches clean and safe to protect turtle eggs, and you'll count the baby turtles before they return to the ocean. You'll be helping with wildlife research and will also be working on community projects where you'll be doing some gardening, as well as helping build schools and community centers.

4 Am I going to have any free time?

Yes, you'll be able to get away in your free time to go sightseeing or on day trips to the capital, San José. You can also look around the **stunning** Tortuguero or Manuel Antonio national parks.

What better way to see and explore Costa Rica while making a difference for the local wildlife! So, what are you waiting for? Volunteer now and make a difference!

3 Write the adjectives in **bold** that describe Costa Rica's ...

1 nature reserves. ________________
2 geographical features. ________________
3 natural beauty. ________________
4 national parks. ________________

Voice It!

4 **Discuss the questions.**

1 Why is volunteering and helping others important?
2 Volunteering is one way to make a difference in the world around you. How do people volunteer in your country?
3 How can you make a difference in your everyday life?

LEARN TO LEARN

Making Adjectives from Nouns

When you read a text, try to find different forms of words you already know.

5 **Find adjectives in the webpage for the nouns (1–6).**

1 tropics _tropical_
2 center ________________
3 magic ________________
4 nature ________________
5 coast ________________
6 environment ________________

Explore It!

Guess the correct answer.

Costa Ricans have at least 12 different words for ...

a rain. b butterflies. c volcanoes.

Find another interesting fact about Costa Rica. Then write a question for your partner to answer.

SHAPE IT!

CULTURE PROJECT

A Poster

A poster gives information about a topic in an attractive visual way. In groups, make a poster about a volunteer program.

Teacher's Resource Bank

9 REVIEW

VOCABULARY

1 Complete the text with the words in the box.

abroad | accommodation | backpacking | cruise ship | destination | journey | resort | tourist attractions

Going on a [1] __________ is exciting, especially if you're going [2] __________ to explore another country, but there's a lot to do before you go. First, you need to decide where to go: a popular [3] __________ with a hotel and pool or a less well-known [4] __________ with fewer tourists? Then there's the [5] __________ to think about. Are you going to stay in a hotel or an apartment? Or perhaps you prefer to go [6] __________ around several cities, visiting all the famous [7] __________ or sailing to different places on a [8] __________. Whatever you decide, enjoy it!

2 Add prepositions to the sentences.

1. It's too hot in my town in the summer, so we like to get ________. We usually go to the beach.
2. Let's set ________ at 9 a.m. Then we can check ________ to the hotel and take a look ________ the city.
3. What time does your flight get ________? I'll come and meet you at the airport.

GRAMMAR IN ACTION

3 Circle the correct form of the verbs.

This time next week, I [1] *fly / 'll be flying* to Munich. I [2] *'m going / 'll be going* on a school exchange program, but I'm a little nervous. I know I [3] *won't be enjoying / 'm not going to enjoy* the flight because I hate flying. When we get there, our host families [4] *are waiting / will be waiting* for us at the airport. I think I [5] *'ll be missing / 'm going to miss* my friends.

4 Complete the text with relative pronouns.

The reason [1] ________ many big tourist destinations are next to the ocean is because the ocean provides food. Nowadays, many are overcrowded, and we need to find new places [2] ________ people can stay. One solution is to build resorts [3] ________ float on the water. In the future, people will make big floating areas [4] ________ will support hotels, campsites, and other accommodations. In summer, [5] ________ it gets hot, the floating areas will move further out to sea to keep the city cool.

Self-Assessment

- I can talk about travel in English.
- I can use travel phrasal verbs.
- I can use *to be going to* and the present continuous for future.
- I can use the future continuous.
- I can use relative pronouns and relative clauses.

LEARN TO ... USE TECHNOLOGY TO PRACTICE ENGLISH

When you learn a language, it's important to practice as much as possible. Technology can help you do that.

1 Read what two students say about using technology to practice English. Then complete the chart with *G* (Gorka), *A* (Amanda), or *B* (both).

GORKA

I downloaded a free flash card app for learning vocabulary. You can make your own flash cards and test yourself. Also, I've just changed my phone language and all my social media apps to English. Now I see and read English hundreds of times a day! I also listen to podcasts in English about sports, usually when I'm on the bus to school. I need to start watching videos online as well - my friends tell me that's a great way to learn.

AMANDA

I read a lot of books in English, so I have a dictionary app on my phone to look up new words. Also, there are thousands of videos online for practicing English. Some of them are really funny, and they're free, too! I like to watch them on my phone. What else? Well, once a week I have a video call with my cousin Kylie in Sydney. She doesn't speak any Turkish, so the conversation has to be in English! I really should change my social apps to English, too.

Ways to Use Technology to Practice English	Who Does This?
1 use your phone to practice English	B
2 use an app for learning vocabulary	
3 watch videos in English	
4 listen to podcasts in English	
5 speak face-to-face online with an English speaker	
6 have English as your phone language	
7 have English as the language of your social media	

2 Ask and answer the questions about each of the ways to use technology in Exercise 1.

1 Have you tried this? How easy or difficult was it? How useful was it?

2 If you haven't tried this, would you like to? Why / Why not?

3 Which three ways of using technology to practice English are the most useful? Explain your reasons.

I think podcasts are really useful because you can find ones about a lot of different topics, and it's important to practice listening.

That's true, but I think changing your phone language to English would be more useful because you use your phone all the time.

SHAPE IT!

4 Complete the action plan with three ways to use technology to practice English. Tell your partner. Do you have similar plans?

My action plan for using technology to practice English. I'm going to ...
1
2
3

What are you going to do?

I'm going to download a flash card app to learn and practice new vocabulary.

Good idea. I'm going to ...

1 FINISHED?

1 **Find and write nine more adjectives in your notebook.**

~~amb~~	ible	ful	ca	confi	help	chee	sens	~~itious~~	rful
ac	sensit	talen	able	tive	lm	soci	ted	dent	ive

ambitious

2 **Write sentences with the simple past or past continuous and *when* and *while*. Use the ideas in the circles.**

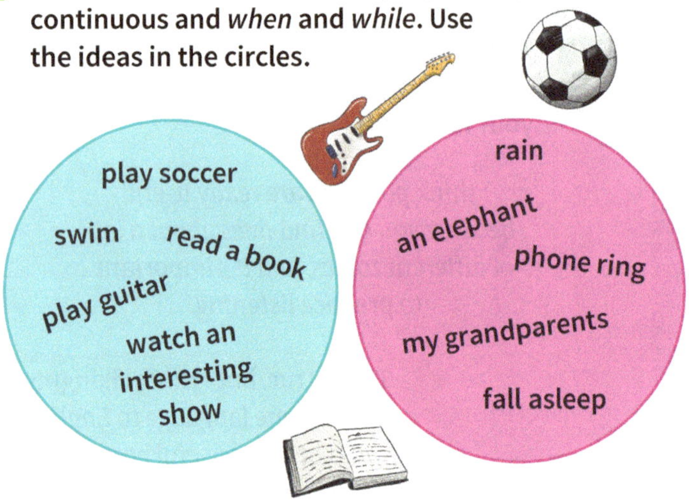

I was playing soccer when an elephant ran onto the field!

3 **Write sentences about what was different in the past with *used* / *didn't use to*.**

People didn't use to have smartphones.

4 **Complete the crossword.**

Across

3 We need to ________ with the problem.

5 I ________ care of my little brother when my parents are away.

6 ________ up! Don't be sad!

Down

1 Don't ________ up when something is hard!

2 I ________ along with Peter very well. We're friends.

3 My sisters are very young, so they ________ on our mom and dad for everything.

4 I really ________ up to my aunt Alicia. She's amazing.

2 FINISHED?

1 Circle eight words connected to art in the wordsnake.

arlogalleryfriarchitecturenchillustrationorperformancerexhibitionhighphotographytofilmakinglispsculpturent

2 Complete the crossword with the past participle forms of the verbs.

Across	Down
1 see	2 eat
7 wear	3 know
8 forget	4 catch
9 go	5 write
10 take	6 do

3 Use the code to write the questions. Then answer them with *already*, *just*, *still*, or *yet*.

A = 1	B = 2	C = 3	D = 4	E = 5	F = 6	G = 7
H = 8	I = 9	J = 10	K = 11	L = 12	M = 13	N = 14
O = 15	P = 16	Q = 17	R = 18	S = 19	T = 20	U = 21
V = 22	W = 23	X = 24	Y = 25	Z = 26		

a 8 1 22 5 25 15 21 8 1 4 12 21 14 3 8 25 5 20 23 18 9 20 20 5 14?
Have you had lunch yet?

b 23 8 1 20 8 1 22 5 25 15 21 10 21 19 20 23 18 9 20 20 5 14?

c 8 1 22 5 25 15 21 1 12 18 5 1 4 25 13 1 4 5 25 15 21 18 2 5 4 20 15 4 1 25?

d 8 1 22 5 25 15 21 8 1 4 12 21 14 3 8?

e 8 1 22 5 25 15 21 1 12 18 5 1 4 25 6 9 14 9 19 8 5 4 25 15 21 18 8 15 13 5 23 15 18 11?

f 8 1 22 5 25 15 21 19 20 9 12 12 14 15 20 2 5 5 14 20 15 16 5 18 21?

4 Complete the puzzle. Write the letters in the correct order to make performing arts words. Then write the letters in the circles in the correct order to make an extra word.

1 hosw
2 edianuce
3 sneil
4 tarp
5 ecnes
6 heasarerl
7 rycsli
8 duisot

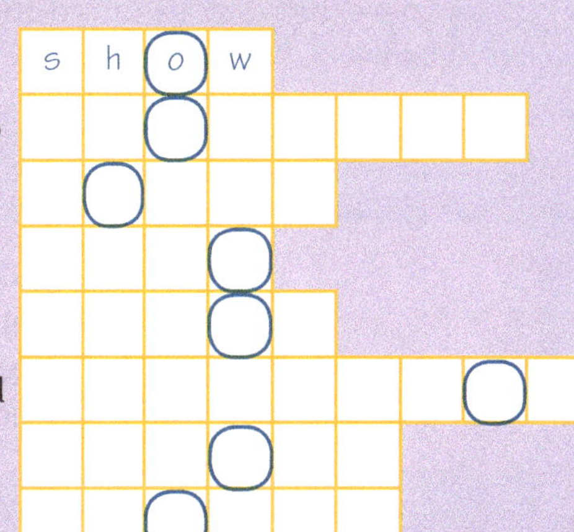

3 FINISHED?

1 **Write the letters in the correct order to make words for communicating.**

1 *egret* greet
2 *entertrip*
3 *vawe*
4 *hutso*
5 *learnstat*
6 *bedsrice*
7 *hakes dsnha*
8 *phewsir*
9 *limes*
10 *greetus*
11 *tops*

2 **Complete the sentences with *can*, *could*, or *able*. Can you answer the questions? Check the answers at the bottom of the page.**

a Now I [1] can walk on two legs. When I was very young, I [2] ________ move on my hands and knees. In the future, I'll be [3] ________ to walk on three legs. What am I?

____

b You [4] ________ hold me in your right hand but not in your left hand. What am I?

____

c In the past, you [5] ________ count me on one finger. I [6] ________ go up, but I will never be [7] ________ to go down. What am I?

____

a I'm a person. (When I was a baby, I couldn't stand up. When I'm older, I'll need a cane!)
b I'm your left hand.
c I'm your age.

3 **Write the phrases in the correct column. Then write the circled letters in the correct order to make the names of two languages.**

~~a century~~ then he was young an hour August a while two months two o'clock three weeks my birthday days last week several years yesterday

For	Since
a century	

________ ________

4 **Find the way through the maze. Match the words and phrases.**

4 FINISHED?

1 Which health and fitness words rhyme with the words?

1 dressed stressed
2 attacks ______
3 freeze ______
4 brain ______
5 off ______
6 weaver ______
7 met ______
8 blogging ______
9 click ______
10 sweater ______

3 Find four more phrases in the chart. Are they things you should or shouldn't do every day? Write sentences.

~~drink~~	relaxing	music
get up	at four	chocolate
eat	more	~~water~~
play	~~enough~~	sports
listen to	a lot of	o'clock

You should drink enough water.

______

______

______

______

2 Look at Emily's list and her shopping cart. Did she get everything she needs? Write sentences with *a few*, *a little*, *too*, and *enough*. What else has she bought that's not on her list?

She has bought a few apples.

She has bought too much chocolate.

______

______

______

______

______

1 carton of milk
1 box of cereal
apples
4 tomatoes
cheese
rice
juice
fish
8 eggs
1 bar of chocolate

4 Write the letters in the correct order to make words for healthy eating.

1 eptorin protein
2 imasvnti ______
3 ferib ______
4 a ablcaned iedt ______
5 fta ______
6 tinntiuro ______
7 syetdrhcabora ______
8 leoscair ______
9 irdya scoputrd ______

5 FINISHED?

1 Circle five more words about planet Earth in the wordsearch.

P	T	O	X	Y	G	E	N
O	H	G	U	T	I	W	Z
L	E	K	Y	U	O	I	W
L	P	Y	S	Y	T	L	A
U	L	I	F	E	O	D	S
T	A	L	G	W	P	L	T
I	N	A	H	E	D	I	E
O	E	Q	J	S	N	F	E
N	T	P	G	H	J	E	R
E	E	N	E	R	G	Y	Q

[OXYGEN is circled in the top row]

2 Match the sentence strips to make six first conditional sentences.

If you go for a walk in the winter,

unless you eat healthy food.

If you go out at night,

You could get sick very quickly

you may be lucky enough to see bats flying.

if they go out in the rain.

They will get wet

I might go for a walk on the beach.

you could fall on some ice.

unless they go on an organized tour.

Tourists cannot go into the castle

If I have time tomorrow,

[A line joins "If you go for a walk in the winter," to "you could fall on some ice."]

3 Complete the story with the missing phrases.

If I had a time machine, I [1]___. If I could do that, I [2]___ when we invented plastic. If I did that, I [3]___. If that happened, we [4]___. If we didn't have that, [5]___. If it was cleaner, [6]___ and people would be happier. But there's a problem! If we didn't have plastic, we [7]___ or bottles or pens or anything! If we didn't have all these things, our lives [8]___. So maybe I wouldn't go back in time! But, wouldn't the world be [9]___ if everyone recycled their waste?

a wouldn't have plastic waste
b could travel back in time
c there would be more animals
d would be very difficult
e would like to travel to the time
f the world would be cleaner
g would stop people from creating plastic
h wouldn't have computers
i a better place

4 Write the letters in the correct order to make words to complete the sentences.

1 You can find sea birds, seals, and crabs on the TSCOA. coast
2 You might see a polar bear standing on an BRGEEIC. ________
3 You can find fish in a MRTEAS. ________
4 Bears sometimes live in a VCEA. ________
5 A lot of different animals live in a TEARSFINRO. ________
6 There are butterflies living in the LLYEVA near where I live. ________

6 FINISHED?

1 **Complete the crossword.**

Across

4 make a liquid move from one place to another
5 make something larger in amount or size
8 heat a liquid to a very high temperature
9 join something to something else
11 make something less

Down

1 put something over something else
2 make something very, very cold
3 move a liquid with a spoon
6 take something away
7 put something in a particular position
10 push something
12 put something into a liquid for a short time

2 **Read the riddles. What are the objects?**

1 *What am I? I am made of glass and metal, plastic, or wood. I am put on the wall or on a shelf. I am looked at by many people. A picture is placed inside me. I am made in different sizes.*
I am a ______________________.

2 *What am I? I am made of wood, metal, or plastic. I am found in the kitchen. I am used to stir liquids.*
I am a ______________________.

3 **Do the quiz. Guess and circle the answers.**

1 When was the first TV program shown?
a 1910 b 1928 c 1935 d 1950

2 When was the first email sent?
a 1971 b 1983 c 1990 d 2001

3 When was the first car invented?
a 1798 b 1832 c 1885 d 1901

4 When was the first chocolate bar made?
a 1655 b 1847 c 1922 d 1940

5 When was the first supermarket opened?
a 1850 b 1900 c 1910 d 1930

6 When was the first smartphone sold?
a 1994 b 1997 c 2010 d 2007

4 **Complete the lists.**

Things in my house made out of:

- cardboard: *boxes*
- glass: ______________________
- leather: ______________________
- rubber: ______________________
- silk: ______________________
- tin: ______________________

Things in my house kept in a:

- bag: ______________________
- box: ______________________
- can: ______________________
- case: ______________________
- jar: ______________________
- tube: ______________________

7 FINISHED?

1 Circle 11 more festival words in the wordsearch.

F	G	P	M	T	C	L	K	D	E	A	E
G	I	G	R	R	V	H	L	R	S	M	P
P	X	R	O	O	F	S	E	A	U	F	C
A	E	W	E	W	G	H	T	T	J	A	E
R	D	K	N	W	P	R	S	A	S	I	R
A	Q	T	L	S	O	O	A	A	L	R	E
D	R	R	O	S	C	R	L	M	X	L	M
E	V	M	Z	Q	G	G	K	Q	H	E	O
I	T	F	L	O	A	T	A	S	F	B	N
A	D	E	C	O	R	A	T	I	O	N	Y
L	A	N	T	E	R	N	T	W	W	U	P
D	O	P	F	R	A	Z	Q	W	P	H	T

2 What had you done by 9 p.m. yesterday? Write as many things as you can remember.

By 9 p.m. yesterday, I'd done all my homework, I'd cleaned my room, I'd read 100 pages of a book, I'd watched a parade, I'd been to a festival ...

3 Guess who said the following. Then rewrite the sentences as reported speech in your notebook.

bass player ~~country music singer~~ jazz musician

1 We are a successful local act, but we hope to play at a big country music festival one day. We want to perform in front of an international audience.

country music singer: The country music singer said they were a ...

2 We are going to play all our latest songs as well as our greatest hits at the event. We hope to sell a lot of albums.

3 We've received an invitation to open the concert for a famous jazz singer on her next European tour. We are going to play at a new concert hall in Spain.

4 Write the letters in the correct order to make words connected to music festivals and live music.

1 igg ______
2 ndab smeebmr ______
3 akcrt ______
4 inpospurtg tac ______
5 lenirehad ______
6 nett ______
7 ectamips ______
8 etasg ______
9 uneev ______
10 recone ______

8 FINISHED?

1 **Circle nine more verbs in the wordsearch. Then use the verbs to complete the phrases about school.**

Q	E	S	V	S	A	O	H	R	S
G	E	T	H	T	W	H	G	M	T
D	A	W	T	U	A	R	R	T	R
E	F	D	I	D	Y	C	I	Z	L
P	A	Y	V	Y	P	I	S	T	L
T	I	H	J	K	E	D	P	P	E
A	L	B	B	C	H	E	A	T	S
F	T	A	L	K	Q	U	S	M	O
H	A	N	D	D	E	C	S	A	E
E	S	P	N	T	A	K	E	M	Q

1. *cheat* on a test
2. ________ / ________ / ________ an exam
3. ________ good grades
4. give somebody a ________
5. ________ in homework
6. ________ attention to the teacher
7. ________ for a test
8. ________ an essay

2 **Read the clues and answer the questions.**

1. You can whisper, but you can't shout. You can take things, but you aren't allowed to keep them. Where am I? *in a library*
2. You can have fun, but you aren't allowed to stand. You can go with your friends, but you aren't allowed to talk to them. Where am I? ____________________
3. You can exercise here, but you can't walk or run. Where am I? ____________________
4. You can buy it and wear it. But you aren't allowed to change it. What is it? ____________________
5. You can sit with a lot of other students, but you aren't allowed to work with them. What am I? ____________________

3 **Invent a sport and its rules. Use *to have to*, *to need to*, and *must* and words from the box.**

ball bat captain catch court field game goal half-time hit kick lose loser net pass player pool team throw point win winner

____

____

____

4 **Four pairs of friends are complete opposites. Follow the lines and match the three other pairs.**

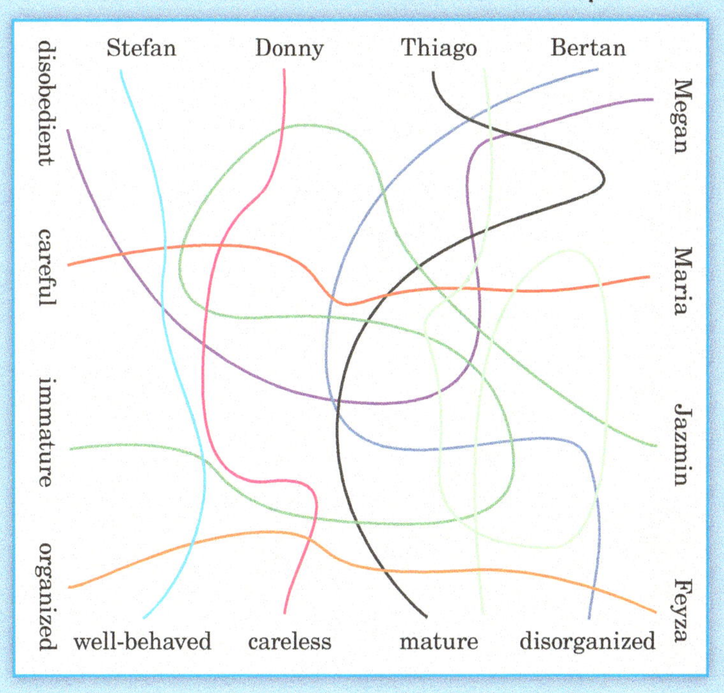

Stefan: well-behaved; Megan: disobedient

____

____

____

9 FINISHED?

1 **Find and write seven more travel words. Each word is in a different color.**

a	b		a			t		i	m	
i			j	a	r	k		p	u	k
p		t	d				a		g	
	c		a	n		b		d		o
g		a	n		s		g		o	
	o		o	t	t	e	i		m	k
n		e	i		i			n	i	
	c		e	y		o			o	i
a		c				r		t	n	
r		h		s			c		o	b
	e		d			o		s	n	

1 purple *accommodation*
2 blue ________
3 dark blue ________
4 red ________
5 orange ________
6 light blue ________
7 yellow ________
8 green ________

2 **Think of a famous person. Imagine you are them and invent three …**

1 arrangements they have for next week with the present continuous.

____
____
____

2 predictions they have about their life with *to be going to*.

____
____
____

3 predictions about next year with the future continuous.

____
____
____

3 **Find five more relative pronouns in the wordsnake. Then complete the sentences with relative clauses so they are true for you.**

tewhosonthatrewhewnhidhatywherenimwhywimwhosewhswhenidal

1 I enjoy things ____.
2 I like people ____.
3 I don't like things ____.
4 I like watching movies ____.
5 I often go to places ____.
6 I want to know ____.

4 **Write the letters in the correct order to make phrasal verbs to complete sentences 1–5. Then write the blue letters in the correct order to make a phrasal verb to complete sentence 6.**

1 We *check in* to the hotel at 6:30 a.m. (chkienc)
2 What time does the plane ____________ ? (kfatofe)
3 It's was a beautiful city, but we didn't have much time to ____________. (laokrnoudo)
4 When you ____________ from your vacation, let's have dinner. (cgeaktb)
5 What time should we ____________ tomorrow to get to the station? (tfosfe)
6 When does their flight ____________ ?

STARTER VOCABULARY BANK

Technology

app	screen
device	social media
emoji	video chat

Feelings

angry	excited
bored	nervous
embarrassed	upset

1 **Write the letters in the correct order to make words to complete the sentences.**

1 I got a new game ________ (pap), but I was soon ________ (drebo) with it.
2 Denise was ________ (cidetxe) about the ________ (dovie tcha) with her cousin.
3 Al was ________ (rabemssarde) about a photo his friend put on ________ (alicos imeda).
4 James used an ________ (jomei) to show he was ________ (gyanr).
5 Sara was ________ (puste) because she broke the ________ (cresen) on her phone.

Music

bass guitar

country

DJ

drums

fans

heavy metal

jazz

keyboard

rap

reggae

2 **Circle eight music words in the wordsearch.**

K	A	D	J	R	I	T	R	C
E	N	I	R	E	G	G	A	E
Y	A	J	G	B	U	N	P	E
B	W	A	S	A	P	O	K	L
O	D	Z	R	F	W	L	K	X
A	E	Z	I	A	R	B	I	V
R	S	Q	U	N	I	K	O	R
D	R	U	M	S	R	E	Y	A
E	F	C	O	U	N	T	R	Y

LEARN TO LEARN

Recording Vocabulary

Writing new words in example sentences can help you remember them.

3 **Match the sentence beginnings with the endings. Then write two sentences with one technology word and one adjective for feelings in each sentence.**

1 ☐ Everyone in my family
2 ☐ Matt plays the
3 ☐ My sister works as
4 ☐ His fans are excited
5 ☐ I find heavy

a drums in a jazz band.
b about his new album.
c metal too loud and boring.
d loves reggae.
e a DJ for a radio station.

____

____

1 VOCABULARY BANK

Describing People

active

ambitious

calm

cheerful

confident

helpful

inspiring

patient

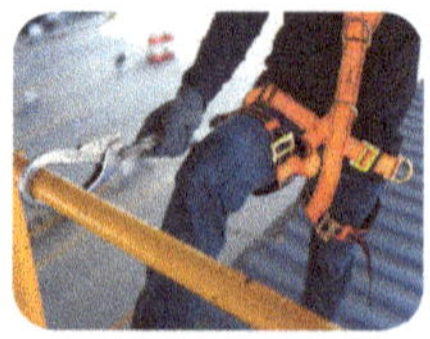
sensible

sensitive

sociable

talented

1 Circle five adjectives for describing people in the wordsnake. Then write them and their opposites.

adrpatientntiolambitiousbrenksensitivedutmsociableweldhelpfulmopert

1 ______ 2 ______ 3 ______ 4 ______ 5 ______

______ ______ ______ ______ ______

Phrasal Verbs

cheer (somebody) up
deal with
depend on
get along with
give up
hang out
look up to
take care of

2 The phrasal verbs in bold are in the wrong sentences. Write the correct phrasal verb in each sentence.

1 Don't be upset! Try to **deal with** ______.
2 Martin and Tom want to succeed and they never **cheer up** ______.
3 I **take care of** ______ my aunt – she's really inspiring!
4 She isn't sensible enough to **look up to** ______ her younger cousin.
5 My parents are always very calm when they **give up** ______ problems.

LEARN TO LEARN

Learning How to Use Phrasal Verbs

Notice the types of words (for example, people or objects) that come after phrasal verbs so that you can use them in a natural way.

I like **taking care of** my grandparents (people ✓), my friends (people ✓), ~~pop music~~ (object ✗).

3 ~~Cross out~~ the incorrect option in each sentence.

1 Mia likes **hanging out** with her *books* / *friends* / *cousins*.
2 James has always **looked up to** his *uncle*/ *new phone* / *older sister*.
3 People often **depend on** their *friends* / *family* / *money* for advice.
4 Everyone has to **deal with** difficult *situations* / *buildings* / *problems* sometimes.
5 Ollie doesn't **get along** with his *brother* / *classmates* / *vacation*.

2 VOCABULARY BANK

Visual and Performing Arts

architecture

contemporary dance

exhibition

fashion design

filmmaking

gallery

illustration

musical theater

performance

photography

sculpture

street art

1 Match the sentence beginnings with the endings.

1 ☐ They went to the gallery
2 ☐ I decided to use a picture of my grandmother
3 ☐ We went to the theater
4 ☐ I looked at the architecture in my city
5 ☐ He loved making clothes and always wanted

a to get ideas for my project about buildings.
b to study fashion design.
c to enter the photography competition.
d to see her new sculpture.
e to see his performance in the play.

Music and Theater

audience, audition, lines, lyrics, orchestra, part, rehearsal, scene, show, studio

2 Are the sentences *T* (true) or *F* (false)?

1 Dancers usually have rehearsals after a show. ___
2 The audience plays music for performances. ___
3 Actors have to learn their lines before a play. ___
4 Performers sing the lyrics in musical theater. ___
5 You go to the theater to see an audition of a play. ___

LEARN TO LEARN

Learning Words in Topic Groups

When you learn a new word, try to learn other words from the same topic group at the same time. This will help you talk about different things connected with the topic.

3 Circle the word that is different in each topic group.

1 orchestra, lyrics, illustration, musical theater

2 exhibition, audition, rehearsal, performance

3 lines, gallery, part, scene

3 VOCABULARY BANK

Communicating

describe

gesture

greet

interpret

post

shake hands

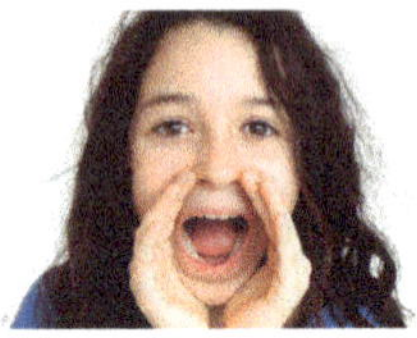
shout

smile

translate

wave

whisper

1 Circle the correct words.

1 Martina *greeted* / *shook hands* us at the door.
2 A woman was *posting* / *interpreting* the president's speech.
3 I asked Luis to *shout* / *describe* the area where he lives.
4 I saw the man *whisper* / *smile* something in Helen's ear.
5 When their guests left, they came outside to *translate* / *wave* goodbye.

Collocations with *To Say* and *To Tell*

Say: hello / something in Italian / sorry / yes/no
Tell: a joke / a lie / a story / someone a secret / the truth

2 Mark (✓) the correct sentence. Change one word in the incorrect sentences to make them correct.

1 ☐ The man told something in French.
2 ☐ Tomas told us a really funny joke.
3 ☐ Come on, say the truth! Where were you yesterday?
4 ☐ I said sorry to Andrea because I said her a lie.
5 ☐ I asked mom to take me to the movies and she told no.

LEARN TO LEARN

Using Flash Cards

When you learn new collocations, make flash cards so you can test yourself on the words.

3 Make flash cards with *say* and *tell* collocations. On one side write a sentence with a blank for the correct form of *to say* or *to tell*. On the other side, write the missing verb.

4 VOCABULARY BANK

Health and Fitness

cough

get better

get enough sleep

get sick

get stressed

go jogging

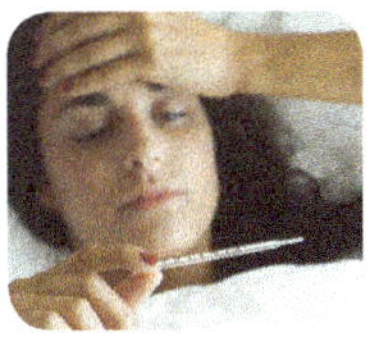
have a fever

relax

sneeze

sweat

train

warm up

work out

1 Complete the sentences with the correct form of the words in the box.

get better get enough sleep
have a fever warm up work out

1 I'm really tired. I didn't ______________ last night.
2 Make sure you ______________ before you go jogging.
3 Lucia is very fit because she ______________ at the gym every day.
4 He's very hot. I'm sure he ______________.
5 I'm sorry you're sick. I hope you ______________ soon.

Healthy Eating

a balanced diet
calories
carbohydrates
dairy products
fat
fiber
nutrition
protein
vitamins

2 Write the letters in the correct order to make words to complete the sentences.

1 You need to eat more ______________ (iesorcal) if you train a lot.
2 I try to eat a ______________ (cedlanba ited) with plenty of protein and fiber.
3 Ben often seems to get sick. I think he needs more ______________ (tanvimis).
4 Her doctor told her not to eat ______________ (yraid ucprdots) such as milk or cheese.
5 Good ______________ (triuninot) is important if you are training for a marathon.

LEARN TO LEARN

Cognates

Food and nutrition words are often similar in different languages. There are sometimes small differences in spelling or pronunciation, so be careful to learn them correctly.

3 What did you eat yesterday? Write a list and compare with your partner. Circle the words that are similar in your language. What nutrients did you get from the food?

Breakfast	
Lunch	soup
Dinner	

5 VOCABULARY BANK

Planet Earth

carbon dioxide	energy	pollution	the planet
climate change	marine life	solar power	waste
endangered species	oxygen	the environment	wildlife

1 **Match the clues with the words.**

1 ☐ We sometimes call Earth this.
2 ☐ Pandas, tigers, elephants, etc.
3 ☐ This is 21 percent of the air we breathe.
4 ☐ We use the sun to make this.
5 ☐ Fish, dolphins, whales, etc.

a marine life
b solar power
c oxygen
d the planet
e endangered species

Natural Environments

bay

cave

cliff

coast

iceberg

rainforest

stream

valley

volcano

waterfall

2 **Complete the puzzle to find the mystery word.**

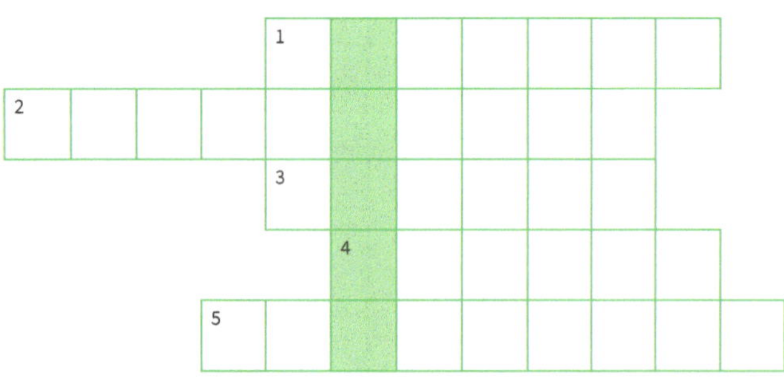

1 a large piece of ice that floats in the sea
2 a hot, wet area with lots of trees
3 a low area between hills or mountains
4 this is smaller than a river
5 water that drops from a high part of a river to a low part

Mystery word ____________

LEARN TO LEARN

Look, Cover, Remember

Use the look, cover, remember technique to help you learn new vocabulary.

3 **Look at the pictures above of natural environments for one minute. Then close your book. Write the words you remember. Compare with a partner.**

6 VOCABULARY BANK

Making Things

add, boil, cover, dip, freeze, increase, place, pour, press, pull, reduce, remove, stir

1 **Are the sentences *T* (true) or *F* (false)?**

1 You usually use a knife to stir things. ___
2 You can cook potatoes by boiling them. ___
3 When you reduce a temperature, you make it higher. ___
4 People often cover food to keep insects off it. ___
5 If you remove something, you add it to something. ___

Materials and Containers

cardboard

glass

leather

rubber

silk

tin

bag

box

can

case

jar

tube

2 **Circle the correct words to complete the sentences.**

1 Remove the printer from its *leather* / *cardboard* / *rubber* box.
2 We should reduce the number of plastic *bags* / *tubes* / *cans* we use.
3 The scarf was made of *tin* / *leather* / *silk*.
4 When the jam is cool, pour it into the *box* / *bag* / *jar*.
5 When you finish your drawing, place the pencils back in their *can* / *case* / *tube*.

LEARN TO LEARN

Visualizing

Thinking of an image to go with new words can help you remember their meaning.

3 **Write two things from the box that you could use to visualize each word (1–4). Write one more thing for each word. Tell your partner your ideas.**

belt   dress   honey   lemonade   olives   shirt   shoes   soup

1 can ______ ______ ______
2 silk ______ ______ ______
3 jar ______ ______ ______
4 leather ______ ______ ______

7 VOCABULARY BANK

Festivals

atmosphere

ceremony

costume

crowd

decoration

fireworks

fair

float

lantern

parade

program

stall

1 Complete the sentences with the correct form of the festivals words.

1 The dancers were all wearing amazing ______________________.
2 There were several ______________________ selling different types of food.
3 We watched the musicians and dancers driving by on a ______________________.
4 Everyone was clapping and singing – the ______________________ in the hall was great!
5 We checked our ______________________ to see what time the band was on.

Music Festivals and Live Music

band member	encore	headliner	supporting act	track
campsite	gig	stage	tent	venue

2 Edwin has been to a festival. What is he talking about? Write the correct music festivals and live music words.

1 "It's a huge field with a stage at one end." ______________
2 "They played for two hours before the main band came on." ______________
3 "In my opinion, it's the best song on their album." ______________
4 "They have a fantastic new guitar player." ______________
5 "It was crowded and the tents were very close together." ______________

LEARN TO LEARN

Stress Patterns

Knowing the stress pattern of a word can help you pronounce it and hear it when people say it.

3 Write the stress pattern for the words 2–6.

O o o
1 band member
2 campsite
3 encore
4 headliner
5 supporting act
6 venue

8 VOCABULARY BANK

School

cheat on a test

fail an exam

get detention

get good grades

give somebody a talk

hand in homework

pass an exam

pay attention to the teacher

study for a test

take an exam

write an essay

1 Match sentences 1–5 with sentences a–e.

1 ☐ She learned some more vocabulary for the topic the evening before.
2 ☐ She listened carefully in class.
3 ☐ Her teacher was angry with her because she was very late for the exam.
4 ☐ She gave her essay to the teacher.
5 ☐ Her grades were good enough to get into college.

a She handed in her homework.
b She passed her exams.
c Her teacher gave her a talk.
d She paid attention to the teacher.
e She studied for a test.

Attitude and Behaviour

careful	disobedient	immature	organized	rude
careless	disorganized	mature	polite	well-behaved

2 Complete the sentences with the words in the box.

careful careless disobedient mature well-behaved

1 You won't pass your exam if you make ________ mistakes.
2 The teacher gave them a talk because they were ________ in class.
3 These are difficult words – be ________ when you spell them.
4 Philip never gets detention because he is so ________.
5 Elif's attitude toward her school work is very ________.

LEARN TO LEARN

Personalizing Vocabulary

Using new words to talk about your life helps you remember them.

3 Look at the attitude and behavior words. Which adjectives are true for you? Choose three and explain why to your partner.

I'm sometimes careless. I make silly mistakes on my homework.

9 VOCABULARY BANK

Travel

abroad

accommodation

backpacking

book

cruise ship

destination

journey

resort

sightseeing

tour

tourist attraction

trip

1 Draw lines to match the three parts of each sentence.

1 When I travel abroad,	I've ever visited is	near the coast.
2 I love going	I usually book	local tour guide.
3 When I arrive at	at a resort	the Grand Canyon.
4 The best tourist attraction	my destination,	I always call my parents.
5 I often stay	sightseeing with a	my accommodations online.

Travel Phrasal Verbs

check in	get back	look around
check out	get in	set off
get away	go away	take off

2 Write the words in the correct order to make sentences.

1 from / do / you / get / when / back / your / trip?

____

2 out / you / check / must / of / your / before / 11 / accommodation

____

3 journey / off / on / their / set / to / the / they / coast

____

4 our / at / gets / in / four / train / o'clock

____

5 looked / we / all / tourist / around / the / attractions

____

LEARN TO LEARN

Remembering New Vocabulary

Using new words in a sentence helps you remember them.

3 Choose four travel phrasal verbs and write sentences. Read them to your partner.

____

____

____

____

We checked in to our accommodation at midnight.

2 ART

Art: Changing Our Lives for the Better

I believe art can bring positive change. First, great art makes us feel and think differently. For example, the *Mona Lisa*, painted by Leonardo da Vinci around 1503, is not just a **portrait**. Look at her face. She follows you with her eyes.

It might make you feel nervous, but it is also **intriguing**. You want to know why she's smiling.

Street art has become a way to inform us about many issues. The street artist Angelina Christina, from Los Angeles, has used her art to spread powerful messages about women. Now she is an Art Ambassador for the Boo2Bullying organization, and she uses her art to organize events to help stop bullying in schools.

Schools have also recognized the health benefits of art and use art projects to help students with stress. As one teenager said, "Doing art is fun; it makes you happier than anything else." Similarly, some children's hospitals have art classes. Being creative allows children to forget about their **treatment** for a while.

Art can therefore change lives. It increases our sense of well-being, makes us think, and sometimes makes us act. Just imagine what a boring place the world would be without it!

1 Discuss the questions.

1. What are your favorite works of art? Why?
2. How can art have a positive effect on our lives?

2.11 **2 Read the text. Check your answer to question 2 from Exercise 1.**

3 Match the causes (1–5) with the effects (a–e).

1. Children have art classes in the hospital.
2. The Mona Lisa's eyes are following you.
3. A painting interests you a lot.
4. Angelina Christina worked as a street artist.
5. Teenagers do art projects at school.

a. You want to learn more about it.
b. They help with their treatment.
c. It could make you feel nervous.
d. It makes them feel good.
e. She started to help children.

4 Complete the sentences with the words in bold in the text.

1. When you are sick, you need ____________.
2. Something is ____________ if it interests you a lot.
3. A ____________ is usually a picture of a person's face.

Explore It!

Guess the correct answer.

The *Mona Lisa* has no eyebrows because …

a. da Vinci did not finish the painting.
b. they disappeared over time.
c. it was the fashion in the 16th century.

Find another interesting fact about a famous painting. Then write a question for your partner to answer.

1 Discuss the questions.

1 How much exercise do you do?

2 How can we use technology to help us exercise more?

2 Read the article. Check your answer to question 2 from Exercise 1.

4.11

3 Complete the chart with information from the article.

Problem: [1] Teens don't get enough exercise and spend too much time on entertainment media.	
Solution: [2]	
Type of Technology	**Positive Results**
3	6
4	7
5	8

4 Complete the sentences with the words in **bold** in the article.

1 One aim of the __________ was to get more people to participate in sports.

2 I always do one __________ workout every week.

3 I want to get fit, so I have set myself weekly exercise __________.

Explore It!

Guess the correct answer.

The average healthy human should walk approximately … steps per day.

a 7,500 b 10,000 c 12,500

Find another interesting fact about physical fitness. Then write a question for your partner to answer.

Technology and Fitness

Developments in technology have changed the way people live. Teenagers spend more time on digital devices than ever before. One recent study found that teens spend, on average, nine hours per day on entertainment media.

Many worry that today's teenagers are becoming too inactive. However, schools could perhaps improve things by using the same technology that teenagers love to attract them to exercise. Here are a few tips.

- Encourage the use of wearable technology. Devices like smartwatches can record calories burned, steps walked, time spent exercising, and the user's heart rate, and users can be responsible for their own progress.

Healthy Heart Rate for 16-Year-Olds	Beats per Minute
at rest	60–90
moderate exercise	102–143
intense exercise	143–173

- Use game-style apps. Some of these apps provide workouts for different types of exercise. They are similar to a personal trainer, and users receive notifications when they reach their daily **targets**.
- Run fitness **campaigns** on social media. Social media is a great way to share advice and information about events. In England, a recent online video for the *This Girl Can* campaign got 23 million views on social media!

Nowadays, sports and exercise have to compete against technology for people's time and energy. We need to think seriously about what would encourage people to exercise more.

6 TECHNOLOGY

WHEN LIONS ATTACK ... GET CREATIVE!

Technology does amazing things for people, and if we get really creative, it can help wildlife, too. That's what Richard Turere discovered after lions attacked his family's **cattle**.

Every year, thousands of cattle in Kenya are killed by lions. This can cost farmers a lot of money, and sometimes they kill the lions to stop the attacks. The situation was serious, until 11-year-old Richard Turere found a clever solution.

He knew the lions never attacked when people were walking around with **flashlights**. This gave him an idea. First, he collected some old flashlights, pulled out the LED lights, and used a long electrical wire to connect them together. Next, he connected an **indicator** box from a motorcycle. This made the lights turn on and off at different times. He put the lights on a fence around the cows. Then he connected an old car battery for power and charged it with a solar panel. When the lights were turned on at night, it looked like someone was moving around with a flashlight.

The lions stopped attacking, so Turere helped set up "lion lights" for many of his neighbors. Lion attacks have dropped 96 percent on farms with the lights.

Sometimes, problems can be solved using a bit of imagination and a few old parts!

1 **Look at the title and the pictures. What do you think the text is about?**

2 **Read the text. Check your answer from Exercise 1.** 6.14

3 **Are the sentences *T* (true) or *F* (false)?**

1. In Kenya, lions kill thousands of cattle each summer. ___
2. Richard had his clever idea when he was a teenager. ___
3. Farms that use the lights have no lion attacks. ___
4. Richard's invention makes the lions think people are present. ___

4 **Put the stages to build lion lights in order.**

a ☐ Connect the wire to a battery.
b ☐ Connect lights to an electrical wire.
c ☐ Turn on the lion lights.
d ☐ Charge the battery with a solar panel.
e ☐ Connect the wire to an indicator box.

5 **Complete the sentences with the words in bold in the text.**

1. We use ______ to see when it's dark.
2. ______ are often used for milk and meat.
3. Drivers use an ______ when they turn.

Explore It!

Guess the correct answer.

What do farmers in Kenya put on their fences to stop elephants from eating their plants?

a chemicals b bees c electricity

Find an interesting fact about another invention. Then write a question for your partner to answer.

8 CITIZENSHIP

1 Discuss the questions.

1. What is a good citizen?
2. What should students learn at school?

8.11 **2 Read the article. Check your answer to question 1 from Exercise 1.**

3 Circle the correct answer.

1. Traditional schools use homework and tests to help students be …
   a positive. b creative. c good. d responsible.
2. Montessori schools allow students to …
   a decide what to study.
   b leave the classroom.
   c teach other students.
   d make the rules.
3. Students at the Green School help grow an organic garden to develop …
   a creativity. b respect for nature. c communication. d independence.

4 Match the words in bold with the definitions.

1. something that is burned to provide heat or power ____________
2. able to work without being told what to do ____________
3. parts of a situation or problem ____________

Explore It!

Guess the correct answer.

One of these people is not a Montessori graduate. Who is it?

a Prince Harry b Jeff Bezos c Kristen Stewart

Find another interesting fact about education. Then write a question for your partner to answer.

GROWING UP AND GIVING BACK

We all need to help make our communities a better place. That is part of being a good citizen. But how do we learn citizenship?

If you go to a traditional school, your days are probably filled with classes, homework, and tests, which teach you how to be responsible for yourself and for the wider community. They also help you develop communication skills to improve the way you share and understand information, which can have a positive impact on all **aspects** of life and relationships.

Montessori schools use a different approach to help children become independent and useful citizens. Students can choose activities that interest them. This encourages them to be **self-motivated**, to think for themselves, and to be creative. Students attend classes with older and younger students, which inspires them to learn from those around them.

At the Green School in Bali, teachers pay special attention to environmental planning so that students grow up to value and care for our planet. The school has an organic garden and saves **fuel** and energy by using solar and hydro power.

Different schools emphasize different types of citizenship. What is important is that students learn how to respect themselves, each other, and the world around them.

PRONUNCIATION

UNIT 1

/t/, /d/, and /ɪd/

1.04 **1 Listen and repeat.**

	Infinitive	Simple Past
/t/	talk	talked
/d/	discover	discovered
/ɪd/	start	started

1.05 **2 Listen and circle the word you hear.**

1 *work / worked*
2 *destroy / destroyed*
3 *want / wanted*
4 *live / lived*
5 *talk / talked*
6 *graduate / graduated*

3 How many syllables do these words have? Circle the one that doesn't fit.

1	walked	1	looked	1	(wanted)	2	climbed	1
2	escaped		decided		rescued		returned	
3	created		ended		visited		reported	

1.06 **4 Listen, check, and repeat.**

5 Take turns saying a word from Exercise 2. Your partner writes the word in their notebook and repeats it.

UNIT 2

Weak and Strong Forms of *To Have*

2.06 **1 Listen and repeat.**

1 **Have** you ever been to Rome?
2 Yes, I **have**.
3 **I've** seen the movie, but I **haven't** read the book.

2 Are the underlined words weak or strong?

A [1]Have you ever eaten shark? ___weak___
B Shark? No, I [2]haven't. ________
A I[3]'ve tried it and it's delicious. ________
What about jellyfish? [4]Have you tried it? ________
B Yes, I [5]have. ________
A Jellyfish! I [6]haven't tried that! ________

2.07 **3 Listen and check.**

4 Practice the conversation in Exercise 2.

UNIT 3

Contractions: *Will*

3.03 **1 Listen and repeat.**

1 I will → I'll
2 You will → You'll
3 He will → He'll
4 She will → She'll
5 We will → We'll
6 They will → They'll

3.04 **2 Listen and circle the option you hear.**

1 *I pass / (I'll pass)* my driving test.
2 *You like / You'll like* this movie.
3 *They play / They'll play* basketball for their country.
4 *We study / We'll study* together.
5 *I go / I'll go* to college.

3 Take turns saying sentences using the different options from Exercise 2. Your partner writes the correct option and repeats the sentence.

UNIT 4

Consonant to Vowel Linking

4.06 **1 Listen and repeat.**

1 Wake_up! It's seven_o'clock!
2 We set_off_early_in the morning.

4.07 **2 Listen and mark the links between consonant and vowel sounds.**

1 They set_off_at ten_o'clock. (3 links)
2 Did you find out what happened at the party? (2 links)
3 Let's look around the town after lunch. (2 links)
4 What time do you wake up on Saturdays? (2 links)

3 Mark the links between consonant and vowel sounds.

1 How do you chill_out? (1 link)
2 Which languages are easy to pick up? (3 links)
3 What time do you get up on the weekend? (2 links)

4.08 **4 Listen, check, and repeat.**

UNIT 5

Stress in First Conditional Sentences

5.03 **1 Listen and repeat.**

1 If you speak good English, you'll get a better job.

2 I'll go to college if I pass my exams.

2 Underline the stressed words.

1 If he doesn't call, I'll send him a message.

2 You'll meet my friends if you get there early.

3 We'll arrive on time if we leave now.

4 She'll help if we have a problem.

5.04 **3 Listen, check, and repeat.**

UNIT 6

/ɪ/ and /iː/

6.03 **1 Listen and repeat.**

1 /ɪ/ sk**i**n c**i**ty 2 /iː/ coff**ee** r**ea**ch

6.04 **2 Listen and circle the option you hear.**

1 *it / eat* 3 *live / leave*

2 *hit / heat* 4 *ship / sheep*

3 Write the words in the correct place according to the pronunciation of the letters in bold.

~~extr**e**me~~ fr**ee** fr**ee**ze g**i**ve l**i**sten s**i**x sw**i**m t**ea**ch w**ee**k

1 /ɪ/ __________

2 /iː/ extreme, __________

6.05 **4 Listen, check, and repeat.**

5 Take turns saying a word from Exercise 2. Your partner says 1 (/ɪ/) or 2 (/iː/) and repeats the word.

UNIT 7

The Letter *U*

7.03 **1 Listen and repeat.**

1 /ʌ/ l**u**ck 2 /uː/ r**u**le 3 /juː/ **u**niform

2 Write the words in the correct place according to the pronunciation of the letters in bold.

~~f**u**n~~ h**u**ge p**u**nctual r**u**de s**u**bject **u**nit

1 /ʌ/ fun, __________

2 /uː/ __________

3 /juː/ __________

7.04 **3 Listen, check, and repeat.**

4 Write two sentences using words from Exercise 2 in your notebook. Then practice saying them.

UNIT 8

/aɪ/ and /eɪ/

8.02 **1 Listen and repeat.**

1 /aɪ/ n**i**ne fl**y** l**igh**t 2 /eɪ/ l**a**ke d**ay** tr**ai**n

2 Write the words in the correct place according to the pronunciation of the letters in bold.

~~afr**ai**d~~ b**i**te fl**igh**t h**a**te m**ay** m**igh**t pl**ay** r**i**de r**igh**t sh**y** sn**a**ke w**ai**t wh**y**

1 /aɪ/ __________

2 /eɪ/ afraid, __________

8.03 **3 Listen, check, and repeat.**

4 Take turns saying a word from Exercise 2. Your partner writes it in their notebook and repeats it.

UNIT 9

Stress in Compound Nouns

9.02 **1 Listen and repeat.**

1 classroom 3 airport 5 cotton T-shirt

2 sunglasses 4 solar energy 6 glass bottle

2 Underline the stressed word in each compound noun.

1 birthday cake 4 plastic chair 7 ice cream

2 swimming pool 5 sunscreen 8 sun hat

3 airplane tickets 6 paper plates

9.03 **3 Listen, check, and repeat.**

4 Describe a party using the compound nouns from Exercise 2. Use the correct stress.

IRREGULAR VERBS

Infinitive	Simple Past	Past Participle
be	was/were	been
beat	beat	beaten
become	became	become
begin	began	begun
bite	bit	bitten
blow	blew	blown
break	broke	broken
bring	brought	brought
build	built	built
buy	bought	bought
catch	caught	caught
choose	chose	chosen
come	came	come
cost	cost	cost
cut	cut	cut
do	did	done
draw	drew	drawn
drink	drank	drunk
drive	drove	driven
eat	ate	eaten
fall	fell	fallen
feel	felt	felt
fight	fought	fought
find	found	found
fly	flew	flown
forget	forgot	forgotten
get	got	gotten
give	gave	given
go	went	gone
grow	grew	grown
hang	hung	hung
have	had	had
hear	heard	heard
hide	hid	hidden
hit	hit	hit
hold	held	held
hurt	hurt	hurt
keep	kept	kept
know	knew	known
leave	left	left
lend	lent	lent

Infinitive	Simple Past	Past Participle
let	let	let
lie	lied	lied
light	lit	lit
lose	lost	lost
make	made	made
mean	meant	meant
meet	met	met
pay	paid	paid
put	put	put
read	read	read
ride	rode	ridden
ring	rang	rung
rise	rose	risen
run	ran	run
say	said	said
see	saw	seen
sell	sold	sold
send	sent	sent
shine	shone	shone
shoot	shot	shot
show	showed	shown
shut	shut	shut
sing	sang	sung
sit	sat	sat
sleep	slept	slept
speak	spoke	spoken
spend	spent	spent
stand	stood	stood
steal	stole	stolen
swim	swam	swum
take	took	taken
teach	taught	taught
tear	tore	torn
tell	told	told
think	thought	thought
throw	threw	thrown
understand	understood	understood
wake	woke	woken
wear	wore	worn
win	won	won
write	wrote	written

ACKNOWLEDGEMENTS

The authors and publishers acknowledge the following sources of copyright material and are grateful for the permissions granted. While every effort has been made, it has not always been possible to identify the sources of all the material used, or to trace all copyright holders. If any omissions are brought to our notice, we will be happy to include the appropriate acknowledgements on reprinting and in the next update to the digital edition, as applicable.

Key: **CLIL** = Content and Language Integrated Learning, **F** = Finished, **SU** = Starter Unit, **U** = Unit, **VB** = Vocabulary Bank

Text

U1: Text about Elvis Ingersoll. Copyright © Elvis Ingersoll Vallejo, Ca. Reproduced with kind permission of Ken Ingersoll; Text about Anoka Primrose Abeyrathne. Copyright © Anoka Primrose; Text about Kelvin Doe. Copyright © Kelvin Doe. Reproduced with permission; **U3:** Text about Pilot Earpiece. Copyright © Waverly Labs. Reproduced with kind permission; Text about Alex Rawlings. Copyright © Alex Rawlings. Reproduced with kind permission; **U6:** Text about Elif Bilgin. Courtesy of Elif Bilgin, reproduced with kind permission of Abdullah Bilgin.

Photography

The following photographs are sourced from Getty Images:

SU: imran kadir photography/Moment; Vertigo3d/E+; Westend61; Thomas Trutschel/Photothek; fotosipsak; FS Productions/Blend Images; Pingebat/iStock/Getty Images Plus; VeroRo39/iStock/Getty Images Plus; Alek_Koltukov/iStock/Getty Images Plus; cougarsan/iStock/Getty Images Plus; Dejan Patic/The Image Bank; Flashpop/DigitalVision; Anze Buh/EyeEm; Lawrence Manning/Corbis; Martin Diebel; Bob Thomas/Corbis Documentary; Tony Hutchings/Photographer's Choice; Fabio Pagani/EyeEm; Ljupco/iStock/Getty Images Plus; Hill Street Studios/Sam Bloomberg-Rissman/Blend Images; Gilbert Carrasquillo/WireImage; andresr/E+; skaman306/Moment; Hill Street Studios LLC/DigitalVision; **U1:** Lost Horizon Images/Image Source; Mark Murphy/DigitalVision Vectors; stockstudioX/E+; Tim Robberts/DigitalVision; Artem Varnitsin/EyeEm; Hero Images; Laurence Mouton/PhotoAlto Agency RF Collections; Yellow Dog Productions/Photodisc; De Agostini Picture Library; Owen Newman/Photodisc; kgtoh/iStock/Getty Images Plus; Natasha Sioss/Moment; Indeed; Comstock/Stockbyte; ithinksky/E+; I just try to tell my emotions and take you around the world/Moment; kosmozoo/DigitalVision Vectors; John Lamparski/WireImage; SolStock/E+; Purestock; **U2:** JeremyRichards/iStock Editorial/Getty Images Plus; Diana Mayfield/onely Planet Images/Getty Images Plus; Neda Krstic/iStock/Getty Images Plus; kckate16/iStock/Getty Images Plus; balipadma/iStock/Getty Images Plus; Hemant Mehta; Eva-Katalin/E+; Daria Botieva/Eyeem; Jim Steinfeldt/Michael Ochs Archive; MarioGuti/E+; papa1266/iStock/Getty Images Plus; Artur Bordalo/Barcroft Media via Getty Images; Ispiyaphong/iStock/Getty Images Plus; Hill Street Studios/Blend Images; AlpamayoPhoto/E+; Vincent van Gogh; VCG Wilson/Corbis via Getty Images; Hoxton/Tom Merton; Maskot; katyau/iStock/Getty Images Plus; David L. Ryan/The Boston Globe; MachineHeadz/iStock/Getty Images Plus; altrendo images; **U3:** Dong Wenjie/Moment; Dan Sipple/Ikon Images/Getty Images Plus; JGI/Blend Images; MarijaRadovic/E+; Charriau Pierre/Photolibrary/Getty Images Plus; portishead1/E+; Flashpop/Stone; swissmediavision/iStock/Getty Images Plus; AndreyPopov/iStock/Getty Images Plus; Dan Sipple/Ikon Images/Getty Images Plus; gyro/iStock/Getty Images Plus; Plume Creative/DigitalVision; BURGER/Canopy; Pakorn Kumruen/EyeEm; Difydave/E+; Nehru Sulejmanovski/EyeEm; INDRANIL MUKHERJEE/AFP; MADDRAT/Creatas Video+; beastfromeast/DigitalVision Vectors; Paulo Amorim/Moment; JulNichols/E+; filipefrazao/iStock/Getty Images Plus; denis_pc/iStock/Getty Images Plus; **U4:** wundervisuals/E+; Brooke Auchincloss/ONOKY; eskaylim/iStock/Getty Images Plus; Colin Hawkins/Cultura; Ben Gingell/iStock/Getty Images Plus; gbh007/iStock/Getty Images Plus; Roberto Machado Noa/LightRocket; Colin Anderson/Blend Images; Geber86/E+; ColorBlind Images/The Image Bank; Alexander Gerst/ESA/Getty Images News; moodboard/Cultura; twomeows/Moment; Ashley Cooper/Corbis Documentary; sturti/E+; Stephen Simpson/DigitalVision; Ekaterina Bedoeva/iStock/Getty Images Plus; Rigel/iStock/Getty Images Plus; Caiaimage/Robert Daly; Yellow Dog Productions/The Image Bank; Carsten Schanter/EyeEm; Jose Luis Pelaez Inc/DigitalVision; kali9/iStock/Getty Images Plus; **U5:** AROON PHUKEED/Moment; Jutta Kuss; John Holcroft/Ikon Images; s0ulsurfing - Jason Swain/Moment; Aolin Li/EyeEm; Yevgen Timashov/Cultura; Photographer who enjoys experimenting with various styles/Moment; MB Photography/Antarctica; sara_winter/iStock/Getty Images Plus; adiartana/iStock/Getty Images Plus; Wild Horizon/Universal Images Group; Peter Lewis/Oxford Scientific/Getty Images Plus; Puripat Lertpunyaroj/Moment; Ben Pruchnie/Getty Images; art-design-photography.com/Moment; Radius Images; VikramRaghuvanshi/iStock/Getty Images Plus; Hype Photography/DigitalVision; Timothy Allen/Barcroft Productions; goir/iStock/Getty Images Plus; CliqueImages/DigitalVision; Terje Eggum/AFP; Andrea Ricordi, Italy/Moment; **U6:** GOSPHOTODESIGN/iStock/Getty Images Plus; Spauln/E+; Ali Kabas/Corbis Documentary; Yann Song Tang/EyeEm; Milkos/iStock/Getty Images Plus; PhasuthornDesign/iStock/Getty Images Plus; hueberto/iStock/Getty Images Plus; puifaiminiiz/iStock/Getty Images Plus; happyfoto/iStock/Getty Images Plus; dmitriymoroz/iStock/Getty Images Plus; DonNichols/E+; Comstock Images/Stockbyte; aldomurillo/E+; novikat/iStock/Getty Images Plus; studiocasper/E+; DarrenMower/iStock/Getty Images Plus; by Chakarin Wattanamongkol/Moment; SasinParaksa/iStock/Getty Images Plus; carloscastilla/iStock/Getty Images Plus; Jerry Leer/iStock/Getty Images Plus; Delpixart/iStock/Getty Images Plus; **U7:** ferrantraite/E+; James Arthur Watulingas/EyeEm; Danita Delimont/Gallo Images/Getty Images Plus; Katsumi Murouchi/Moment; Emportes Jm/The Image Bank; Claudia Weirich/EyeEm; VisitBritain/Ben Selway; Thant Zaw Wai/Moment; Masumi Hamaguchi/EyeEm; Puay Ng/EyeEm; Elles Rijsdijk/EyeEm; Bill Heinsohn/Photographer's Choice/Getty Images Plus; bernardbodo/iStock/Getty Images Plus; watcharit praihirun/Moment; Rob Lewine; Marco Secchi/Getty Images News; © Philippe LEJEANVRE/Moment; Encyclopaedia Britannica/UIG/Getty Images Plus; Gareth Brown/Corbis/Getty Images Plus; Steve Debenport/E+; **U8:** Hill Street Studios/DigitalVision; Image Source/Photodisc; Glow Images; Neustockimages/E+; FatCamera/E+; Jose Luis Pelaez Inc/DigitalVision; AntonioGuillem/iStock/Getty Images Plus; PeopleImages/E+; Prasit photo/Moment; View Stock; Stockbyte; Chen Jie/The Beijing News/Visual China Group; MILATAS; Dexailo/iStock/Getty Images Plus; Paul Bradbury/OJO Images; Con Tanasiuk; Juice Images; monkeybusinessimages/Stock/Getty Images Plus; Sam Bloomberg-Rissman; Nutthaseth Vanchaichana/iStock/Getty Images Plus; Bulat Silvia/iStock/Getty Images Plus; **U9:** Colin Anderson Productions pty ltd/DigitalVision; Trinette Reed/Blend Images; Matteo Colombo/DigitalVision; sturti/E+; JodiJacobson/E+; brittak/E+; Chris Tobin/Photodisc; seb_ra/iStock/Getty Images Plus; Rtimages/iStock/Getty Images Plus; sorbetto/DigitalVision Vectors; Jochen Tack/arabianEye; RomoloTavani/iStock/Getty Images Plus; JIRAROJ PRADITCHAROENKUL/iStock/Getty Images Plus; PhotoAlto/Frederic Cirou; Ascent Xmedia/Taxi; Donald Iain Smith; Westend61; Jonathan Knowles/Corbis/Getty Images Plus; Photo by Scott Dunn/Moment; Rick Gomez; Morsa Images/DigitalVision; Kevin Boutwell/Moment; Kevin Arias Ceciliano/EyeEm; Matteo Colombo/DigitalVision/Getty Images Plus; adam smigielski/iStock/Getty Images Plus; ©Juan Carlos Vindas/Moment; Kevin Arias Ceciliano/EyeEm; jakkapan21/iStock/Getty Images Plus; Burak Karademir/Moment; Fgorgun/E+; Konstantin Trubavin/Indonesia; Jamie Grill; BrianAJackson/iStock/Getty Images Plus; kiszon pascal/Moment; Prykhodov/iStock/Getty Images Plus; Space-kraft/iStock/Getty Images Plus; mrtom-uk/iStock/Getty Images Plus; Pierre-Yves Babelon/Moment; Caiaimage/Sam Edwards; Monty Rakusen/Cultura; Haykal/United Kingdom; Oliver Rossi/The Image Bank; **U1—U9:** mocoo/iStock/Getty Images Plus; **F4:** Carlosgaw/E+; **F5:** JW LTD/Stone/Getty Images Plus; **F7:** Dimedrol68/iStock/Getty Images Plus; **F8:** Ben Pipe Photography/Cultura; Dimedrol68/iStock/Getty Images Plus; **VB0:** Tetra Images; RapidEye/E+; Roberto Westbrook/Image Source; bevrnja/iStock/Getty Images Plus; simonkr/E+; unomat/iStock/Getty Images Plus; AarStudio/iStock/Getty Images Plus; Jac Depczyk/Photographer's Choice RF; mediaphotos/iStock/Getty Images Plus; Lorado/E+; **VB1:** Thomas Barwick/DigitalVision; hadynyah/E+; Westend61; Roberto Westbrook; Caiaimage/Martin Barraud; Steve Hix/Corbis; Sam Edwards/Caiaimage; PT Images; Kittikorn/iStock/Getty Images Plus; kali9/iStock/Getty Images Plus; Hero Images; **VB2:** Mark Nuttall/EyeEm; economica20/iStock Editorial/Getty Images Plus; Matthias Ritzmann/Corbis; SelectStock/Vetta; Caspar Benson; Ghislain & Marie David de Lossy/Photographer's Choice; blackdovfx/iStock/Getty Images Plus; Juanmonino/E+; Hill Street Studios/DigitalVision; Cultura RM Exclusive/Matelly; Oliver Penack/500px; **VB3:** Hero Images; artpipi/E+; gradyreese/E+; Caiaimage/Sam Edwards; Kosamtu/E+; fstop123/E+; Mongkol Chuewong/Moment; Joseph Visaggi/EyeEm; Oko_SwanOmurphy/iStock/Getty Images Plus; asiseeit/E+; B&M Noskowski/E+; **VB4:** andresr/E+; Steve Debenport/E+; Media for Medical/Universal Images Group; PeopleImages/E+; Westend61; PhotoAlto/Frederic Cirou; Stockbyte; Colin Hawkins/Cultura; yellowdog/Cultura; Frank and Helena/Cultura; Mike Harrington/DigitalVision; Caiaimage/Robert Daly; **VB5:** Benjamin Wu/EyeEm; Feng Wei Photography/Moment; Fabian Krause/EyeEm; Arthur Machado/Moment; Eastcott Momatiuk/DigitalVision; Sergiusz Pawlowski/EyeEm; Ippei Naoi/Moment; Stephan Boehme/EyeEm; Antonio Zanghì/Moment; chain45154/Moment; **VB6:** Robert Kneschke/EyeEm; Kessirin Inta/EyeEm; 6381380/iStock/Getty Images Plus; dlerick/E+; Denise Torres/EyeEm; Saravut/

iStock/Getty Images Plus; aopsan/iStock/Getty Images Plus; Fernando Trabanco Fotografía/Moment; Thomas-Soellner/iStock/Getty Images Plus; fotostok_pdv/iStock/Getty Images Plus; Salamatik/iStock/Getty Images Plus; kickstand/E+; **VB7:** Flashpop/DigitalVision; Hill Street Studios/DigitalVision; Zero Creatives/Cultura; Atlantide Phototravel/Corbis Documentary; Pirinal/iStock/Getty Images Plus; C. Colin Houck/EyeEm; Philip Gould/Corbis Documentary; LawrenceSawyer/E+; DigiPub/Moment; HuyThoai/iStock Editorial/Getty Images Plus; whitemay/E+; MarioGuti/iStock/Getty Images Plus; **VB8:** lisegagne/E+; Fuse/Corbis; Echo/Juice Images; Pixsooz/iStock/Getty Images Plus; Hero Images; AntonioGuillem/iStock/Getty Images Plus; Caiaimage/Martin Barraud; Tetra Images; Phil Boorman/Cultura; Fertnig/E+; Zulkhairi Dzulhasnan/iStock/Getty Images Plus; **VB9:** Konstantin Trubavin/Indonesia; **CLIL2:** Fred De Noyelle/GODONG/Corbis Documentary; undefined undefined/iStock/Getty Images Plus; **CLIL4:** FrankRamspott/DigitalVision Vectors; Emma Kim/Cultura; skynesher/E+; songqiuju/iStock/Getty Images Plus; **CLIL6:** Angelika/E+; Peter Von Walter/EyeEm; vlapaev/iStock/Getty Images Plus; **CLIL8:** Michele Falzone/DigitalVision; Nerthuz/iStock/Getty Images Plus; rudchenko/iStock/Getty Images Plus; andreknot/iStock/Getty Images Plus; Hero Images.

The following photographs are sourced from other libraries/sources.s

U1: Copyright © Daniel Kish; Copyright © Elvis Ingersoll Vallejo, Ca; Copyright © Henry Fraser; Copyright © Anoka Primrose; Copyright © Kelvin Doe; **U1–U9:** Carboxylase/Shutterstock; **U2:** Copyright © Kristian Mensa; Courtesy of Shania Mcdonagh; Courtesy of Steve McNicholas; Copyright © Ben Heines, www.benheine.com; Courtesy of Autumn de Forest; **U3:** Courtesy of Waverly Labs; **U6:** Courtesy of Elif Bilgin, reproduced with kind permission of Abdullah Bilgin; **U8:** Copyright © Christoph Otto.

Cover design and illustrations: Collaborate Agency.

Illustration

U1, U3, U4, U5, F1, F4: Amber Day (Marie Bastille); **U4, U5:** Joanna Kerr; **U6:** Kay Coenen (Advocate Art); **F7, U7, CLIL8:** O. Flores.

Video Stills

The following stills are sourced from Getty Images.

U1: Kelvin Murray/Image Bank Film: Signature; Carol Yepes/Moment; NiseriN/iStock/Getty Images Plus; Carol Yepes/Moment; NiseriN/iStock/Getty Images Plus; **U2:** BlackLight Films – Louie Schwartzberg/Image Bank Film: Signature; Carlos Alkmin/Moment; Kostyantyn_Skuridin/Creatas Video+/Getty Images Plus; Carlos Alkmin/Moment; Kostyantyn_Skuridin/Creatas Video+/Getty Images Plus; **U3:** alatriste1/Creatas Video; MADDRAT/Creatas Video+/Getty Images Plus; **U4:** TheStacks/Creatas Video+; BURGER/PHANIE; TheStacks/Creatas Video+; **U5:** Scubazoo Images/Photolibrary Video; GeorgiaCourt/Creatas Video; GeorgiaCourt/Creatas Video; U6: RichVintage/Creatas Video; U7: phaitoons/Vetta; lavoview/Creatas Video+; **U8:** GeorgiaCourt/Vetta; Dalila Jocabed/EyeEm; Ascent Xmedia/The Image Bank; Yagi Studio/DigitalVision; **U9:** fStop/DigitalVision; stock-eye/Creatas Video; stock-eye/Creatas Video.

The following stills are sourced from other libraries:

SU–U9: Lucentum Digital

Typesetting: Aphik, S.A. de C.V.

Cover Illustration: Collaborate Agency

Audio Recordings: Eastern Sky Studios

Video Production: Lucentum Digital

The authors and editors would like to thank all the teachers and consultants who have contributed to the development of the course, in particular:

Mexico: Ana Belem Duran; Nelly Marina Elizalde; Julio Andrés Franco Del Campo; Nimbe García Haro; Raoul Josset Paquette; Adriana Maldonado Torres; Ana Edith Ramos Ramírez

Brazil: Beatriz Affonso; Alessandra Bautista; Ana Carolina De Luca; Esdras Fattobene; Maria Claudia Ferreira; Itana Lins; Maria Helena Meyer; ; Valéria Moraes Novoa; Odinéia Morandi; Regina Pedroso De Araujo; Andrea Perina; Simone Rodrigues; Jacqueline Saback; Clice Sales; Silvia Teles

Turkey: Belgün Akçelik; Peggy Alptekin; Hayri Arslan; Ayşe Aylin Kündüroğlu; Nihan Çalışkan; Selin Dinçkal Erkenci; Bengü Özbek; Saliha Şimşek

Contributing Authors: Liz Walter and Kate Woodford

Versioner: Suzanne Harris

American English Consultant: Multimodal Media

Freelance Editors: Mandie Drucker, Penny Nicholson, Cara Norris-Ramirez, and Rebecca Raynes

SHAPE IT! 3 COMBO

WORKBOOK

Annie Cornford and Andrew Reid

CAMBRIDGE UNIVERSITY PRESS

CONTENTS

STARTER

WELCOME!

VOCABULARY AND READING

Technology

1 **Complete the sentences with the words in the box.**

apps ~~devices~~ emoji
screen social media video chat

1 My grandparents don't have many electronic *devices*.
2 Do your eyes get tired when you look at the computer ________ for a long time?
3 We learn a lot about famous people by following them on ________.
4 Bella likes to use ________ so she can see the person she's talking to.
5 My favorite ________ are Snapchat and BuzzFeed.
6 It's impossible to express some emotions with a(n) ________.

Feelings

2 **Circle the correct words.**

1 Mason gets *embarrassed* / *excited* when his mom puts his baby photos on Facebook.
2 I'm getting *angry* / *excited* about tonight's party!
3 You always do well on exams, so don't be *nervous* / *bored*.
4 Carlos was *angry* / *bored* at Jill because she forgot his birthday.
5 Mandy's crying – what's she *upset* / *excited* about?
6 We're always so busy that we don't have time to get *angry* / *bored*.

3 **Write example sentences for the words.**

1 embarrassed ________
2 app ________
3 screen ________

A Message on an App

4 **Read the conversation. How are Juan and Louise spending the summer?**

____

JUAN Hey! How's the filmmaking course? Are you enjoying it?
LOUISE It's great, thanks. And you? I hope you're not getting bored.
JUAN I hardly ever get bored – I love getting new ideas and dancing in front of the group.
LOUISE Don't you sometimes feel embarrassed?
JUAN Not at all! But I'm new to street dance, so I often get upset if I forget the steps. What kind of movies are you making?
LOUISE We're not making a whole movie until the end of the course. I'm so excited about that!
JUAN So, what do they teach you?
LOUISE We're learning to use different devices like video cameras and music apps.
JUAN Cool!
LOUISE After lunch, we usually write movie scripts or practice doing makeup or costumes.
JUAN They're making a short video of our final show – I'm kind of nervous about that!
LOUISE Why? You're a great dancer! Hey, maybe I can make a movie about you one day!

5 **Answer the questions.**

1 How does Juan show that he is confident?
____
2 When does Juan sometimes feel unhappy?
____
3 What is Louise excited about?
____
4 What idea does Louise have for a movie?
____

GRAMMAR IN ACTION AND VOCABULARY

Simple Present and Present Continuous with Adverbs of Frequency

1 ☆ **Put the words in the correct order to make sentences.**

1 ever / upset / gets / He / hardly

He hardly ever gets upset.

2 steps / remember / I / the / don't / always

______

3 embarrassed / dance / often / Do / when / get / you / you / ?

______

4 music / the / movies / We / for / write / the / sometimes

______

5 him / His / never / teachers / angry / get / with

______

2 ☆☆ **(Circle) the correct words.**

1 She (*'s playing*) / *plays* a computer game now.
2 I *often feel* / *'m often feeling* bored at home.
3 *Does Mario sometimes send* / *Is Mario sometimes sending* you photos?
4 The course is good. I*'m having* / *have* a great time.
5 I *usually text* / *'m usually texting* my friend when I can't do my homework.

Simple Present and Present Continuous for Future

3 ☆☆ **Complete the questions with the correct form of the verbs in parentheses. Then write the answers.**

1 What time does the class *start* (start)? (nine)

It starts at nine.

2 When is Tom ______ (travel) to Japan? (today)

______

3 When do we ______ (get) the exam scores? (on Friday)

______

4 When are you ______ (go) to the concert? (Saturday night)

______

Music

4 ☆ **(Circle) nine more music words in the sound wave.**

(heavymetal)countrydrumsreggaejazzfansbassguitarDJrapkeyboard

5 ☆☆ **Match the definitions with words in Exercise 4.**

1 a loud, round instrument you play with your hands or sticks *drums*
2 a person who plays music and talks on the radio or at a club ______
3 music popular in Jamaica with a strong rhythm ______
4 an electric instrument similar to a guitar with low notes ______
5 popular style of music from the southern and western U.S.A. ______
6 the artist usually speaks the words in this type of music ______

6 ☆☆ **Complete the advertisement with the words in the box.**

DJ drums ~~fan~~ heavy metal jazz rap

Are you a big [1] *fan* of music? Do you sing like a bird or is [2] ______ more your thing (fan of Drake, maybe?). Do you play a musical instrument like the guitar or [3] ______? Or perhaps you want to be a [4] ______ because you prefer to choose the songs for the party? From relaxing, [5] ______ to fast, loud [6] ______, you can learn and practice it all at MLA Music Summer Camp. Click on the link below for more information!

MORE INFO

LISTENING AND GRAMMAR IN ACTION

A Conversation

1 ☆ **Look at the photo. Where are the people?**

____

2 ☆ **Listen to the conversation. Why does Maria go to the event in Exercise 1 every year?** S.01

____

3 ☆☆ **Listen again. Are the sentences *T* (true) or *F* (false)?** S.01

1 The organizers of MusicFest sell the tickets in a lottery. _T_
2 Maria doesn't pay for her ticket. ___
3 She works every evening. ___
4 Maria hears and sees all the bands. ___
5 She loves the music but doesn't like the hot weather. ___

4 ☆☆☆ **Listen again. Why do Maria and Nick mention these words?** S.01

1 excited _Nick says Maria looks excited._
2 upset ____
3 fans ____
4 reggae singers ____

Simple Past

5 ☆ **Complete the sentences with the simple past form of the verbs in parentheses.**

1 Ela _wrote_ (write) a great song and ________ (sing) it for us last night.
2 We ________ (take) the dogs and ________ (go) for a long walk on the beach.
3 I ________ (know) you were here because I ________ (see) your coat.
4 ________ she ________ (make) a playlist for Luca's birthday party?
5 Marcus ________ (not tell) us that he ________ (have) concert tickets for all of us.

6 ☆☆ **Complete the sentences with the correct simple past form of the verbs in the box.**

be (x2)	fall	learn	not enjoy	~~play~~	work

1 The heavy metal band _played_ really loud music.
2 We ________ the words to all the new songs.
3 They ________ very hard on their projects.
4 Joe ________ embarrassed when he ________ on the ice.
5 I ________ the concert. It ________ boring.

7 ☆☆☆ **Write questions about Maria and MusicFest. Then write the correct answers from the audio in Exercise 2.**

1 the organizers of MusicFest / send Maria a letter / ?
Did the organizers of MusicFest send Maria a letter?
No, they didn't. They sent her an email.
2 Maria / ask the organizers for a free ticket / ?
____
3 Maria / get a ticket in the lottery / ?
____
4 Maria / work in the evening last year / ?
____
5 it / rain all weekend at MusicFest last year / ?
____

WRITING

A Review of an App

1 ☆ **Look at the advertisement. What do you think the app does?** ________________

2 ☆☆ **Read Enzo's review and check your answer to Exercise 1.**

1 WordFind is a great app for English language learners, especially when you are studying alone. Our teacher told us about it in class. He said he uses it all the time, so I decided to try it. Last week, I downloaded it on my phone, and I love it!

2 It's good because the definitions are very easy to understand. It tells you what each word means in simple English and how and when you can use it. You can also search for a word by saying it. I can't always find words when I don't know how to spell them, so this is very useful.

3 In my opinion, there are a couple of problems with it. It tells you where each word comes from and when people first used it, but I'm not interested in the history of words. Also, it's expensive – there are a lot of free dictionary apps, though maybe they're not as good.

4 Overall, I think WordFind is a great app because you can use it anywhere and it's easy to use. I would definitely recommend it.

3 ☆☆ **Which paragraph (1–4) …**

a explains the bad things about the app? 3

b gives Enzo's general opinion? ___

c introduces the app? ___

d explains the good things about the app? ___

4 ☆☆ **Complete the *Useful Language* phrases with the words in the box.**

great ~~language~~ opinion Overall problems recommend

1 WordFind is a language-learning app.

2 It's ________ because you can use it anywhere.

3 I would definitely ________ it to all English language learners.

4 ________, I think it's a great app.

5 In my ________, there are a couple of ________ with it.

PLAN

5 ☆☆ **Write your own review. Choose a language-learning app you use and take notes.**

What is it? ________________

____

What's good about it? ________________

____

What isn't good about it? ________________

____

What's your general opinion? ________________

____

____

6 **Decide what information to include in each paragraph. Use the information in Exercise 3 to help you.**

WRITE

7 ☆☆☆ **Write your review. Remember to include four paragraphs, the simple present and present continuous, adverbs of frequency, and phrases from the *Useful Language* box (see Student's Book, p9).**

CHECK

8 **Do you …**

- introduce the app in the first paragraph?
- write about good and bad things?
- give your general opinion?

1 What inspires you?

VOCABULARY
Describing People

1 ☆ **Find 11 more personality adjectives in the word search.**

A	M	C	O	N	F	I	D	E	N	T	R
M	S	A	F	D	A	S	E	G	R	E	G
B	S	L	F	E	Y	C	U	Z	J	X	I
I	E	M	I	D	T	N	V	K	C	S	N
T	P	R	O	F	E	N	T	U	H	O	S
I	A	O	B	A	E	D	C	N	E	C	P
O	T	R	S	C	S	S	E	D	E	I	I
U	I	A	C	T	O	N	F	F	R	A	R
S	E	N	S	I	T	I	V	E	F	B	I
G	N	B	E	V	R	Y	W	B	U	L	N
F	T	R	S	E	N	S	I	B	L	E	G
N	G	H	E	L	P	F	U	L	J	W	B
T	A	L	E	N	T	E	D	B	N	Y	S

2 ☆☆ **Complete the sentences with words in Exercise 1.**

1 People think I'm *confident*, but I'm usually shy.
2 Paul isn't very ________. He likes being alone.
3 He's usually very ________. He's always smiling.
4 Kim and her brother are very different. He's silly and immature, but she's ________.
5 It's better to be ________ and not panic in dangerous situations.
6 I'm very ________ – I get upset easily.

3 ☆☆ **Complete the chart with the opposites of some of the words in Exercise 1.**

in-	1 *sensitive*	im-	7 ________
un-	2 ________ 3 ________ 4 ________ 5 ________ 6 ________		

4 ☆☆ **Complete the sentences with the opposites in the box.**

~~anxious~~ grumpy lazy shy silly

1 Martin isn't calm today. He's *anxious* because of his exam tomorrow.
2 I don't think I'm confident. I'm usually really ________.
3 My mother is always ________. She's not cheerful at all.
4 You're so ________ sometimes. Why can't you be more sensible?
5 When she was young, my cat was always active. Now she's just ________.

5 ☆☆ **Circle the correct adjectives.**

HOME ABOUT ME ARCHIVE FOLLOW

My sister, Alicia, is a very [1]*confident* / *talented* person because she's always sure of herself and knows what she's good at. In fact, she's pretty [2]*active* / *ambitious* – she has a lot of goals and things she wants to achieve. She's also smart and really [3]*patient* / *talented* – she can play the piano and is very good at sports. The only "problem" is that she's not very [4]*cheerful* / *sociable* – she doesn't like going to parties and she doesn't have many friends. But if I have a problem, she's always [5]*helpful* / *calm* and tries to solve it. Alicia is [6]*sensitive* / *patient*, too – she doesn't get angry, even when other people make really big mistakes. My sister is my hero!

Explore It!

Guess the correct answer.

Scientists believe that people who are … live longer than average.

a cheerful b confident c grumpy

Find another interesting idea about how to live longer. Write a question and send it to a classmate in an email, or ask them in the next class.

READING

An Article

1 ☆ **Read the article quickly and answer the questions.**

1 What is the name of the young man in photo A?

______

2 What is the name of the wave in photo B?

______

2 ☆☆ **Match the words in bold in the article with the definitions.**

1 very surprised *amazed*

2 a physical or mental power to do something ______

3 a person who teaches other people ______

4 water that moves over the top of the ocean ______

5 very difficult ______

6 wanting to do something very much ______

3 ☆☆ **Are the sentences *T* (true) or *F* (false)? Correct the false sentences.**

1 Derek's favorite surfer was also named Derek. *F*
Derek's father's favorite surfer was also named Derek.

2 Derek didn't surf until he was a teenager. ___

______

3 Derek's father taught Derek to surf. ___

______

4 Derek can hear which direction he needs to surf in. ___

______

5 People who saw Derek in Hawaii were very surprised. ___

______

6 Derek went to Hawaii to make a movie with a producer. ___

______

4 ☆☆☆ **Answer the questions in your own words.**

1 Why do you think Derek was determined to try surfing?

______

2 What do you think inspired the movie producer to make a movie about Derek?

______

Home Posts Archives

SURFING WITHOUT LIMITS

Derek Rabelo was born in Brazil in 1992. His father named him Derek after a famous surfing champion, Derek Ho – his father's favorite surfer. Derek's father wanted Derek to become a surfer, too, but this was going to be difficult because Derek was born blind. His father's dream to see his son surf seemed impossible!

When Derek was 17, his father told him about his dream. From that moment, Derek was **determined** to become a surfer. He went to the beach with his father every day and started taking surfing lessons with an **instructor**. Derek kept trying, and finally, he learned to surf!

Derek explains that although he can't see, he understands the noises that the **waves** make and he can hear them when they are coming. He says every part of a wave makes a different noise, so he knows which direction to surf in.

In 2012, he flew to Hawaii to surf the famous Banzai Pipeline – one of the most **challenging** and dangerous waves in the world. Local surfers were **amazed** to see the confident young blind man surf the huge wave with no problem at all.

While Derek was surfing in Hawaii, he met a movie producer who believed that Derek had an amazing **ability**. The producer decided to make a movie about him. *Beyond Sight* tells Derek's inspirational story and teaches us that nothing is impossible if you believe in yourself!

GRAMMAR IN ACTION

Simple Past and Past Continuous with *When* and *While*

1 ☆ **Complete the sentences with the past continuous form of the verbs in the box.**

do	look	not watch
rain	~~sleep~~	work

1 I *was sleeping* at eleven o'clock last night. That's why I didn't check my emails.
2 It ______ yesterday, so I didn't go out.
3 My mom ______ late at the office and missed dinner.
4 I ______ for clothes online, but I didn't see anything I liked.
5 What ______ you ______ in the kitchen? I heard a strange noise.
6 She ______ videos on the computer – she was studying!

2 ☆☆ **Complete the conversation with the simple past form of the verbs in parentheses.**

EMMA Hey, Ben! [1] *Did you have* (you / have) a nice vacation?
BEN Hmm, not bad. I [2] ______ (help) my uncle in his store.
EMMA Why [3] ______ (you / do) that?
BEN Because my aunt [4] ______ (be) sick, and my uncle [5] ______ (not have) time to go to the store every day.
EMMA Wow! That's really kind of you. [6] ______ (it / be) difficult?
BEN Yeah. But my uncle [7] ______ (give) me some money for it, so I [8] ______ (buy) some new clothes.
EMMA Cool!

3 ☆☆ **Write sentences with the simple past and past continuous and the words in parentheses.**

1 I / sleep / you / call / me last night (when)
I was sleeping when you called me last night.
2 he / finish / his book / he / wait / for the bus (while)
______
3 we / live / in New York, / we / go / to a lot of museums (while)
______
4 she / not see / the puddle / she / cross / the street (when)
______
5 I / not cry / I / watch / that inspirational movie (while)
______
6 they / say / goodbye / they / leave / the party (when)
______

4 ☆☆ **(Circle) the correct options.**

One day, my wife was sick, so I [1] (*drove*) / *was driving* to the drugstore to get some medicine. While I [2] *walked / was walking* back to the car, I noticed that I [3] *didn't have / wasn't having* my keys. They were still in the car with my phone! I [4] *kicked / was kicking* the wheels of my car when a teenager [5] *was arriving / arrived* on his bike and [6] *asked / was asking* what was wrong. I told him the story and [7] *explained / was explaining* that we had another car key at home, but it was five kilometers away. The boy said, "I'll get the keys" and then [8] *gave / was giving* me his phone to call my wife to explain what was happening. After 30 minutes, he [9] *came / was coming* back with the keys. While I [10] *opened / was opening* my car, he rode away – before I could thank him!

5 ☆☆☆ **Write a short paragraph in your notebook about a time when someone helped you or you helped someone. Use the simple past and past continuous.**

VOCABULARY AND LISTENING

Phrasal Verbs

1 ☆ **Circle the correct options.**

1 If you have a good relationship with someone, you *get along with* / *hang out with* them.

2 When you supervise or care for someone who is old, sick, or very young, you *cheer up* / *take care of* them.

3 When you spend time with friends, you *hang out* / *deal* with them.

4 When you try to solve a problem, you *deal with* / *depend on* it.

5 If you respect and admire someone, you *look up to* / *give up* them.

6 When you make someone feel happier, you *cheer them up* / *hang them out*.

7 When you stop trying to do something because it is too difficult, you *cheer up* / *give up*.

8 When you need someone's help and support, you *look up to* / *depend on* them.

2 ☆☆ **Complete the sentences with the phrasal verbs in Exercise 1.**

1 I can't go out tonight. I have a lot of problems that I need to ___deal with___.

2 I sometimes ________________ my little brother when my parents are not at home.

3 I can't do this homework – it's too difficult. I ________________!

4 I really ________________ my mother. I think she's an amazing woman, and I'd like to be just like her when I'm older.

5 I ________________ my sister for help and advice. I often don't know what to do without her.

6 My grandfather is feeling sad these days, so I'm trying to ____________ him ____________.

7 I usually ________________ with friends at the park or in a café.

8 Paula doesn't ________________ Susana very well. They're very different people.

A Conversation

1.01 **3** ☆ **Listen to the conversation. Why is Gabriel going to a concert?**

a It's a family member's birthday.

b He wants to help people.

c It's his weekend job.

1.01 **4** ☆☆ **Listen again. Complete the notes with key words and information.**

Concert

- Takes place at [1] ___the park___
- Brandon's [2] ________________ was sick in the past
- Concert to make money for people with same illness
- Brandon wants to make a minimum of [3]$ ________________ for charity.

Charity Work

- Brandon made more than [4]$ ________________ last month for charity.
- Jobs he did: washed [5] ________________, cut grass in yards, took trash away
- Worked some afternoons and every [6] ________________

5 ☆☆☆ **Gabriel mentions running a race, giving up chocolate, and cutting off his hair for charity. Think of three other ways to raise money.**

1 ________________________________

2 ________________________________

3 ________________________________

GRAMMAR IN ACTION

Used To

1 ☆ Match sentences 1–6 with a–f.

1 I used to live in the country. [c]
2 I didn't use to like coffee. [ ]
3 I used to be really shy. [ ]
4 I used to like going to the gym. [ ]
5 I used to eat a lot of fast food. [ ]
6 I didn't use to have many friends. [ ]

a Now I don't have time.
b Now I think it's unhealthy.
c I live in a city now.
d Now I have a lot of them.
e I'm much more confident these days.
f Now I have a cup every morning.

2 ☆ Complete the text with *used to* or *didn't use to*.

When I was very young, I [1] used to want to be a swimming teacher because I loved swimming and I [2] ________ like our gym teacher. Sometimes, I [3] ________ want to be an astronaut, as well, because I really liked space. When I got older, I started to get interested in computers. We [4] ________ have a good computer at home, just a very old one, but then my dad decided to buy a really good one. My parents [5] ________ let me spend much time on the computer – just a few hours a week. When I was 13, I started learning how to write my own games. I [6] ________ know how to do that before, but I had a great teacher at school who showed me how. In the future, I'd like to be a game developer!

1 
2 
3 
4 
5 

3 ☆☆ Look at the photos. Complete the sentences with the correct form of *used to*.

1 I didn't use to like ice cream, but now I love it!
2 I ________, but I play tennis now.
3 I ________, but now I want to be a teacher.
4 I ________, but I have one now.
5 I ________. Now I have a new one.

4 ☆☆ Put the words in the correct order to make questions with *used to*.

1 you / use / to / Did / cell phones / have / ?
Did you use to have cell phones?
2 did / How / communicate / with / people / use / to / you / ?
____
3 free / in / your / What / you / did / use / do / to / time / ?
____
4 old / use / people / What / you / think / did / of / to / ?
____

5 ☆☆ Complete the answers to the questions in Exercise 4. Use the correct form of *used to* and the verbs in the box.

be do ~~have~~ read send think (x2) use

1 Twenty years ago, I didn't use to have a cell phone. We ________ the home phone to make calls.
2 We ________ letters and meet up a lot. Life ________ calmer then.
3 I watched TV. I ________ a lot of books, too. A lot of people now go shopping. We ________ that because we didn't have the money.
4 Good question! I ________ about them at all! I ________ I couldn't get old. I still don't think I'm old!

WRITING

A Letter to a Magazine

1 ☆ **Read the competition details. What will the writer win for the best entry?** ______________

____

Competition! Write and tell us about a helpful person in your life who you think deserves an award. As always, the winning letter appears online in next month's edition and the writer receives $100! The person you write about will also win a special award. Answer the following questions.

- Who is the most helpful person you know?
- What do/did they do to help you?
- Why do you think they deserve to win an award?

2 ☆ **Read the letter to a magazine. Does the writer answer the questions in Exercise 1 in the same order?** ______________

The most helpful person I know is my English teacher, Mrs. Davies. In my [1] opinion , she should definitely win an award. Here's why.

A few years ago, I used to go to a different school, and I liked it very much. Then my parents got new jobs in a different city, and I changed schools. In the new school, I was shy and not at all confident. I didn't make any new friends. The only person who really noticed this was Mrs. Davies. She helped me by talking to me in class and putting me in groups with other friendly students. She also often asked questions that she knew I could answer in front of the class. [2] ________ me, that was a very kind thing to do. [3] ________, I think I became more confident and sociable because of Mrs. Davies!

In my [4] ________, Mrs. Davies deserves an award because she's the calmest and most patient teacher at our school. She's also sensitive to people's feelings and always wants to help her students. She helped me through a difficult situation, and she also inspired me to like English!

3 ☆☆ **Complete the *Useful Language* phrases in the letter with the words in the box.**

~~opinion~~ personally to view

4 ☆☆ **Read the letter again. Are the sentences *T* (true) or *F* (false)?**

1. The writer wasn't very happy at her old school. F
2. She went to a new school because her parents wanted to live in the country. ____
3. Her teacher asked her easy questions in class to help her. ____
4. The writer thinks Mrs. Davies should win the award because she helped build her confidence. ____

PLAN

5 ☆☆ **Write your own letter to a magazine. Think of a helpful person you know. What do/did they do to help you? Why should they win an award?**

WRITE

6 ☆☆☆ **Write your letter. Remember to include three paragraphs, past tenses, *used to*, and phrases from the *Useful Language* box (see Student's Book, p17).**

CHECK

7 **Do you ...**

- introduce the person in the first paragraph?
- say why the person should win an award?
- use language for giving opinions?

1 REVIEW

VOCABULARY

1 Match the people with the adjectives in the box.

active	ambitious	calm	cheerful
confident	helpful	inspiring	patient
sensible	sensitive	sociable	talented

1 She runs every morning and goes to the gym on the weekend, too! ________
2 Mark always wants to do things for other people. ________
3 He never gets nervous. He always looks relaxed. ________
4 Sara can play the piano very well. She's also an amazing singer. ________
5 Paula loves talking to people and making new friends. ________
6 John is 100 percent sure about everything he does – he believes he can do anything. ________
7 I was 45 minutes late, but Alex didn't get angry at all! ________
8 We all look up to George. He's an amazing person. ________
9 Kerry is always playing tennis. She wants to be a professional player one day. ________
10 Linda is always smiling, even when everyone else is sad or tired. ________
11 Be careful what you say to Hannah. She gets upset very easily. ________
12 Johann is a serious person. He always says and does the right thing. ________

2 Circle the correct prepositions.

1 I always looked up *with* / *to* my older brother when I was young.
2 Don't look so sad. Cheer *to* / *up*!
3 I might go out today. It depends *on* / *of* the weather.
4 I tried running five kilometers yesterday, but I was tired and gave *up* / *out* after four kilometers.
5 You need to be very patient to deal *with* / *on* little children.
6 Everyone gets *in* / *along* with Eduardo because he's really cheerful and sociable.
7 I was hanging *out* / *on* with my friends last night.
8 I used to take care *with* / *of* my little sister when she was a baby.

GRAMMAR IN ACTION

3 Complete the sentences with the simple past and past continuous form of the verbs in parentheses.

1 I ________ (walk) to the store when it ________ (start) to rain.
2 My friend ________ (call) me while I ________ (write) him a text.
3 What ________ Harry and Abby ________ (do) when they ________ (hear) the news?
4 He ________ (find) an expensive ring when he ________ (clean) their house.
5 We ________ (leave) Tom's house when Lisa ________ (arrive).
6 While I ________ (cross) the street, my phone ________ (fall) out of my pocket.

4 Complete the conversation with the correct form of *used to* and the verbs in parentheses.

A How old is your brother now?

B He's nine.

A Wow! I remember when he was a little baby. He [1] ________________ (be) so sweet!

B Yes. And I [2] ________________ (take) care of him, too! I [3] ________________ (read) him bedtime stories!

A [4] ________________ (you / give) him food and put him to bed?

B No, I [5] ________________ (not do) that. My parents [6] ________________ (do) it. He's changed a lot. He really [7] ________________ (look up) to me, but now he doesn't!

CUMULATIVE GRAMMAR

5 Complete the text with the missing words. Circle the correct options.

When my mother was younger, she [1] _____ a singer. I [2] _____ this until recently! She [3] _____ short, blond hair, and she [4] _____ really strange clothes. In her first year at college, she [5] _____ some other people who wanted to form a band. The other people quickly [6] _____ out that she was a really talented singer, so they asked her to join in. She [7] _____ famous or anything like that, but she had a lot of fun. Unfortunately, I [8] _____ any recordings of her singing. They [9] _____ smartphones or video cameras then, so I can't see what she looked like. It's difficult to believe that my mom used to be a singer because she [10] _____ very serious and sensible these days! She has long, dark hair and she [11] _____ in a bank! Where did that young pop singer [12] _____?

	a	b	c
1	a is	b was being	c was
2	a not know	b didn't knew	c didn't know
3	a was having	b did have	c used to have
4	a wore	b was wearing	c wear
5	a was meeting	b met	c meets
6	a found	b find	c were finding
7	a weren't	b wasn't being	c didn't use to be
8	a don't have	b have not	c doesn't have
9	a weren't having	b didn't used to have	c didn't use to have
10	a always	b is always	c always is
11	a works	b usually works	c work
12	a goes	b went	c go

2 What is art?

VOCABULARY
Visual and Performing Arts

1 ☆ **Complete the visual and performing arts words. Then match the words with photos a–h.**

1 filmmaking [d]
2 s__ee__ a__t [ ]
3 __o__e__o__a__y __a__e [ ]
4 __a__io__ __e__i__n [ ]
5 s__u__p__u__e [ ]
6 p__o__o__a__h__ [ ]
7 a__c__i__e__u__e [ ]
8 il__u__t__a__io__ [ ]

a

b

c

d

e

f

g

h
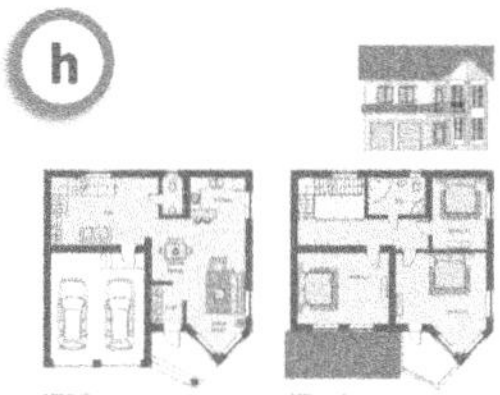

2 ☆☆ **Correct the sentences by changing the underlined words.**

1 You see paintings and other art forms in <u>a performance</u>. ____________

2 <u>Musical theater</u> is an inside or outside event where you can see paintings and other art forms. ____________

3 <u>An exhibition</u> is the action of entertaining people by dancing, singing, acting, or playing music. ____________

4 <u>A gallery</u> is a play in which singing and dancing tell part of the story. ____________

3 ☆☆ **Match the beginnings of the words with the ends to make the names of the people who do an activity.**

danc illustrat art sculpt filmmak fashion design

-or -er -ist

4 ☆☆ **Match the people or things (1–6) with the definitions (a–f).**

1 contemporary dance [e]
2 fashion design [ ]
3 street art [ ]
4 filmmaker [ ]
5 sculpture [ ]
6 illustrator [ ]

a making objects that represent things, people, or ideas
b someone who draws pictures for books
c someone who creates movies for TV or theaters
d working with clothes, shoes, and sometimes hairstyles
e moving to music in a modern style
f paintings, graffiti, etc., outside in urban areas

Explore It!

Guess the correct answer.

Every … minutes, people around the world take more photos than the whole of humanity took in the 1800s.

a 2 b 10 c 45

Find another interesting fact about an art form. Write a question and send it to a classmate in an email, or ask them in the next class.

READING

A Magazine Article

1 ☆ **Look at the photo. What art form can you see and where do you think it is?**

____

2 ☆ **Read the article from an art magazine and check your answer to Exercise 1.**

3 ☆☆ **Match the words in bold in the article with the definitions.**

1 going underwater ___sinking___
2 people who work to protect the environment ______________
3 an orange-brown metal ______________
4 put something into position ______________
5 an ability to achieve something ______________
6 keep or maintain something in its position ______________

4 ☆☆ **Read the article again. Answer the questions.**

1 Where did Lorenzo Quinn study art?
He studied art in the U.S.A.
2 What are Quinn's sculptures normally made from?
____
3 Which important problem does *Support* deal with?
____
4 How are the giant hands "helping" the Ca' Sagredo Hotel?
____
5 How did Quinn's family help with *Support*?
____
6 Who can do something about climate change, according to Quinn?
____

5 ☆☆☆ **Answer the questions in your own words.**

1 What's your favorite form of art? Why do you like it?
____
____
2 What other important issues does art often deal with? Think of two examples.
____
____

Support: An Art Installation

Sculptor Lorenzo Quinn is the first artist to **install** a work of art directly into the Grand Canal in Venice. But who is he, and what does his work of art mean?

Quinn was born in Rome, but he has lived in Spain and in the U.S.A., where he studied art. He hasn't always been a sculptor. He has also been a singer, and he has acted in movies – once as the painter Salvador Dalí!

His sculptures have appeared at exhibitions internationally. He usually works with metals such as **bronze**, steel, and aluminum. But what inspired him to make visual art with two enormous hands?

Together with many scientists and **conservationists**, Quinn believes that the Mediterranean Sea has risen and is still rising because of climate change. Because of higher water levels in the Grand Canal, the historic city of Venice is slowly **sinking**.

The art installation, called *Support*, which Quinn created for the Venice Art Biennale exhibition, warns us about the danger of rising water levels in this amazing city. The two giant hands **"hold up"** the famous Ca' Sagredo Hotel on Venice's Grand Canal.

Quinn used his son's hands as models for the huge sculptures to show the **potential** of the next generation. The message is that the future is in their hands.

GRAMMAR IN ACTION

Present Perfect with Regular and Irregular Verbs

1 ☆ **Circle the correct options.**

1 He has *use* / *used* bronze to make the sculpture.
2 *Have* / *Has* you watched that video about Dalí?
3 They haven't *visit* / *visited* many exhibitions.
4 I have never *meet* / *met* a street artist.
5 *Has* / *Have* your art teacher taught you how to use spray paint?
6 A Have they visited the new gallery?
B Yes, they *have* / *haven't*.

2 ☆ **Complete the sentences with the present perfect form of the verbs in parentheses.**

1 We *have been* (be) to a very interesting exhibition.
2 She ________ (not do) any contemporary dance.
3 The children ________ (make) some plastic models.
4 I ________ (see) some beautiful artwork today.
5 ________ you ________ (take) photography classes?
6 Sofia's mom ________ (write) to her art teacher.

3 ☆☆ **Complete the sentences with the present perfect form of the verbs in the box.**

be	draw	~~have~~	make	not see	not write

1 The art installation *has had* an enormous number of visitors.
2 We ________ the new exhibition yet.
3 ________ Lorenzo Quinn ________ any new sculptures this year?
4 My favorite singer ________ many good songs this year.
5 ________ you ever ________ a picture of a rabbit? It isn't easy!
6 I ________ never ________ on a gondola on the Grand Canal. Have you?

4 ☆☆ **Complete the sentences with *been* or *gone*.**

1 I've *been* to the art store. Look what I bought.
2 Helena's ________ into town, but she's normally back home by five o'clock.
3 My parents have ________ to Venice many times.
4 We've ________ to see the exhibition and we loved it.
5 He's ________ to the gallery. He's meeting the artist.

5 ☆☆ **Complete the text with the present perfect form of the verbs in the box.**

change	ever take	~~join~~	make	train

JOIN OUR SALSA DANCE CLASSES!

Read what some of our students wrote about it:

"My friends and I [1] *have joined* many different classes, but the salsa class is the best – it's awesome!"

"This is the best class I [2] ________. Everyone is so welcoming. I [3] ________ some great new friends."

"Salsa dancing [4] ________ my life! My teacher [5] ________ in Colombia and the Caribbean, and her classes are fun and very exciting!"

6 ☆☆☆ **Write questions and answers.**

1 your brother / ever read / *Death in Venice* / ?
No / see / the movie
Has your brother ever read Death in Venice?
No, he hasn't, but he has seen the movie.

2 they / ever visit / Rio / ?
No / be / to São Paulo
____
____

3 she / ever win / first prize in a competition / ?
No / come in second
____
____

4 you / ever make / a video / ?
No / take / some great photos on my phone
____
____

VOCABULARY AND LISTENING

Music and Theater

1 ☆ **Match the beginnings of the sentences (1–6) with the ends (a–f).**

1 The words of a song [f]
2 A recording studio is where [ ]
3 The words an actor says [ ]
4 The audience is the people [ ]
5 You have an audition when [ ]
6 During a rehearsal [ ]

a are called the lines.
b you practice a play, concert, or show.
c who are listening to the orchestra.
d singers and musicians record their music.
e you want a part or role in a play or show.
f are called the lyrics.

2 ☆ **(Circle) the correct options.**

1 When the (*orchestra*) / *audience* stopped playing their instruments, we stood up and clapped.
2 In the final *show* / *scene*, the friends say goodbye and the movie ends.
3 I really want the *line* / *part* of Romeo in the school production of Shakespeare's *Romeo and Juliet*.
4 What's your favorite type of *part* / *show*: dance, music, or theater?

3 ☆☆☆ **Answer the questions.**

1 Have you ever written lyrics for a song? What was the song about?

______

______

2 Have you ever performed in a play or a show? What part did you have?

______

______

3 Have you ever played in or been to see an orchestra? Which one?

______

______

A Conversation

4 2.01 ☆☆ **Listen to Melanie and David talking about Alma Deutscher, a young musician. Answer the questions.**

1 How does Melanie feel about Alma at the beginning of the conversation?

______

2 Does she feel differently at the end?

______

5 2.01 ☆☆ **Listen again and answer the questions.**

1 How does David know so much about Alma Deutscher?
He watched a show about her on YouTube.
2 What art form is Alma's *Cinderella*?

______

3 What musical instruments does Alma play?

______

4 Where was the performance of *Cinderella*?

______

5 How does Alma get some of her ideas and melodies?

______

6 What activity is a waste of time, according to Alma?

______

6 ☆☆☆ **Find out about another talented young person like Alma Deutscher. Write a short paragraph about their life and achievements in your notebook.**

GRAMMAR IN ACTION

Present Perfect with *Already*, *Just*, *Still*, and *Yet*

1 ☆ **Match sentences 1–6 with a–f.**

1 My mom's just found her glasses. [c]
2 I haven't seen that movie yet. [ ]
3 The show has already started. [ ]
4 She still hasn't heard from Joel. [ ]
5 I've just had a second audition. [ ]
6 The children haven't gone to bed yet. [ ]

a She hopes he calls soon.
b I hope I get the part.
c Now she can see the stage.
d They'll be tired in the morning.
e We've missed the beginning.
f We have tickets to see it tomorrow.

2 ☆☆ **Look at the photos. Write sentences about what has just happened.**

1 she / cut his hair
She has just cut his hair.
2 The children / finish school for the day
____
3 they / go swimming
____
4 he / make a cake
____
5 the girls / see a funny movie
____
6 the girl / give her some flowers
____

3 ☆☆ **(Circle) the letter of the correct sentence.**

1 (a) I've already seen the art exhibition.
  b Already I've seen the art exhibition.
2 a Dylan just has left for school.
  b Dylan has just left for school.
3 a She hasn't cleaned up her room still!
  b She still hasn't cleaned up her room!
4 a Have you bought the orchestra tickets yet?
  b Have you bought yet the orchestra tickets?
5 a Liz and Eva have come back from the movies just.
  b Liz and Eva have just come back from the movies.

4 ☆☆ **Rewrite the sentences putting the words in parentheses in the correct position.**

1 The gallery has announced an exciting event. (just)
The gallery has just announced an exciting event.
2 Have you heard about the Picasso exhibition? (yet)
____
3 Someone has discovered an unknown painting. (just)
____
4 The gallery has bought it from a collector in Paris. (just) __________
5 It seems they have agreed on a fair price. (already)
____
6 They haven't told anyone how much they paid, though. (still) __________

5 ☆☆☆ **Put the words in the correct order.**

1 you / yet / seen / new / the / Shrek movie / Have / ?
Have you seen the new Shrek movie yet?
2 art gallery / already / to / Enzo / the / has / gone / .
____
3 still / art project / finished / Susie / her / hasn't / .
____
4 audition / you / your / had / yet / Have / ?
____
5 have / They / in town / just / held / an exhibition / .
____
6 three times / been / have / We / to / already / the theater / this month / !
____

WRITING

A Review

1 ☆ **Look at the photo. Circle the correct answer.**

The New Dance School is …

a a classical orchestra.

b a music group.

c a group of dancers.

2 ☆ **Read the review. Why does the reviewer recommend The New Dance School?**

____

____

1 Have you seen The New Dance School yet? I've never heard anything like it before. The band is perfect for lovers of international music – it's the best performance I've ever been to!

2 The New Dance School's music isn't exactly rock. It's a bit like world music, but you can really dance to it! The musicians are all really talented. They create powerful rhythms with a number of different instruments, like sitars, bongos, and steel drums – it's amazing.

3 What I liked about it was that the performers were so happy and there was a lot of movement in their music. They make you feel cheerful. I was sitting in the audience, but I really wanted to get up and dance!

4 I saw them at my local community center. It was so cool! These musicians haven't been together very long, but they have a big future! The New Dance School is playing at the Newport Music Festival, so don't miss it. I recommend it because the music has great energy and it makes you want to dance.

3 ☆ **Which paragraph (1–4) …**

a gives a description of the band and its music? 2

b explains what the reviewer liked / didn't like about it? ____

c gives details of where you can see the band? ____

d explains who the band's audience is? ____

4 ☆ **Circle the correct words in the *Useful Language* phrases. Then check in the review.**

1 I've *never* / *ever* heard anything like it before.

2 It's *play* / *playing* at …

3 I *recommend* / *recommending* it because …

4 It's the best performance I've *ever* / *never* been to.

5 *How* / *What* I liked / didn't like about it was …

5 ☆☆ **Read the review again. Answer the questions.**

1 Who is the concert for, in the reviewer's opinion?

____

2 What instruments do the musicians play?

____

PLAN

6 ☆☆ **Write your own review. First, take notes in your notebook about a music concert you have been to or seen on TV.**

Who was the concert for?

What was it like?

What did you like / not like about it?

Where did you see it?

7 **Decide what information to include in each paragraph. Use the information in Exercise 3 to help you.**

WRITE

8 ☆☆☆ **Write your review. Remember to include four paragraphs, the present perfect, and phrases from the *Useful Language* box (see Student's Book, p29).**

CHECK

9 **Do you …**

- say who it is for?
- describe the event?
- say what you liked / didn't like about it?

2 REVIEW

VOCABULARY

1 Complete the sentences with the words in the box.

architecture contemporary dance exhibition filmmaking gallery illustrations performance photography sculptures street art

1 Eduardo goes to the movies a lot because he's interested in ________________.
2 Lorenzo Quinn makes ________________ of people and things with different metals.
3 I love ________________, but you need a lot of energy and rhythm to move your body to the music.
4 The Louvre in Paris is the most famous art ________________ in the world – the *Mona Lisa* is there.
5 They saw a wonderful ________________ of paintings and sculptures by a local artist.
6 The ________________ in this book are in black and white, not color.
7 We saw a ________________ of *High School Musical* at our local theater – it was really good.
8 I bought a new camera for my ________________ class. I've taken some great pictures.
9 ________________ is an art because you need creativity to design, plan, and make buildings.
10 Some ________________ is OK, but I really don't like graffiti. It looks messy.

2 Read the definitions and complete the nouns.

1 o________________: a big group of musicians who play different instruments together

2 p________________: one of the people in a movie, play, or dance show

3 s________________: a part of a play or movie in which the action happens in one place

4 a________________: the group of people together in one place to watch or listen to a play, movie, etc.

5 a________________: a short performance that an actor, dancer, etc., gives to show they can play a particular part

6 l________________: the words of a song

7 r________________: the time when all the people in a play, dance, etc., practice to prepare for a performance

8 l________________: the words that an actor speaks when performing in a movie, play, etc.

9 s________________: a theater performance or a TV or radio program

10 r____________ s____________: a place where a musician makes and records their songs

GRAMMAR IN ACTION

3 Write questions and short answers (affirmative or negative) in the present perfect.

1 you / see the new Almodóvar movie? (✓)
____
2 he / take photos of his sculpture? (✓)
____
3 the visitors / come from all over the world? (✗)
____
4 she / ever sing in front of a big audience? (✗)
____
5 they / hear your new song? (✓)
____
6 you / have many exhibitions? (✗)
____
7 she / be to that gallery before? (✓)
____
8 the show / win many awards? (✗)
____

4 Make the sentences negative using the words in parentheses.

1 I've just done my homework. (not yet)

____

2 He's read that book already. (still not)

____

3 We've been to Venice. (still not)

____

4 The performance has just begun. (not yet)

____

5 The sculptor has explained his work. (still not)

____

6 We've just bought your new song. (not yet)

____

7 She's just met the photographer. (still not)

____

8 I've been into Paul's recording studio. (not yet)

____

CUMULATIVE GRAMMAR

5 Complete the conversation with the missing words. Circle the correct options.

INTERVIEWER Hello and welcome. We have some great music for you today, but I [1] _____ that one of our most talented young singers, Lexi West, is in the recording studio. Welcome to Miami, Lexi!

LEXI Thanks! It's great to be here. Actually, I [2] _____ an apartment in the city. It's all very new and exciting for me!

INTERVIEWER Yeah? Where [3] _____ live? You were born in Mexico, right? But of course you [4] _____ all over the world.

LEXI That's right. I [5] _____ back from New York, but while I [6] _____ and working abroad, I didn't have my own place. I [7] _____ with my parents.

INTERVIEWER Was there a lot of music in your home when you [8] _____, Lexi? I believe your father [9] _____ songs for you.

LEXI Yes, that's right. My dad was definitely my inspiration, but he was also very sensible. I [10] _____ on TV as a teenager, but he never let me miss school! I still [11] _____ his advice: it's OK to be ambitious, but don't get impatient!

INTERVIEWER Well, Lexi, you [12] _____ three number one hits, so you didn't have to wait very long to be famous!

	a	b	c
1	've still heard	haven't heard	've just heard
2	didn't buy	've just bought	was just buying
3	did you use to	were you used to	use you to
4	haven't traveled	've traveled	weren't traveling
5	was coming	have already come	've just come
6	was singing	wasn't singing	used to sing
7	didn't use to	was living	haven't lived
8	have grown up	grew up	were growing up
9	has just written	didn't use to write	used to write
10	performing	was performing	have just performed
11	used to forget	was forgetting	haven't forgotten
12	've already had	haven't had	were having

3 How do we communicate?

VOCABULARY

Communicating

1 ☆ **Put the letters in order to make words about communicating.**

1 tereg — g*reet*
2 retgesu — g______
3 besiredc — d________
4 ptreertin — i__________
5 stpo — p___
6 eksha nsdah — s____ h____
7 leims — s____
8 vewa — w___
9 latsenrta — t__________
10 wrheips — w______
11 tsuho — s____

2 ☆☆ **Complete the sentences with words in Exercise 1.**

1 A thumbs-up sign is a *gesture* that means "good."
2 I don't know what Jackie looks like. Can you ________ her to me?
3 Don't speak loudly. You'll wake up the baby. Please ________.
4 These instructions are in French. I need someone to ________ them for me.
5 There's Lucy across the street. Let's ________ at her. Maybe she will see us.
6 I only ________ when I'm very angry.
7 Everyone understands when you ________ at them. It means you're happy.
8 It's good to ________ comments online and then wait for people to reply to them.

3 ☆☆ **Complete the spidergrams with the words in Exercise 1.**

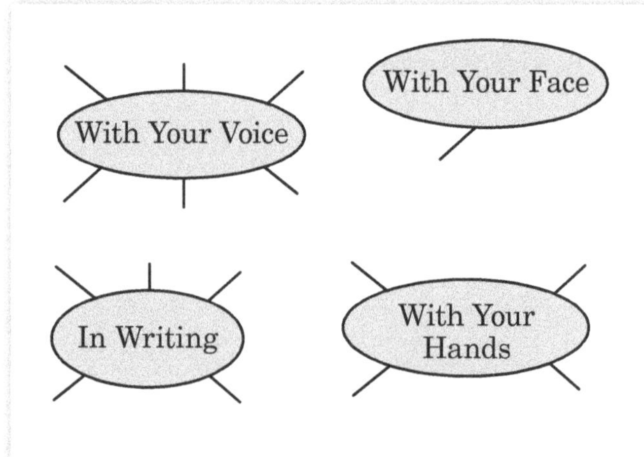

4 ☆☆ **Complete the story with the correct form of words in Exercise 1.**

I met my friend Kazue yesterday for the first time! Actually, I first met her online about six months ago. She's from Japan, and now she's visiting my country with her family. I [1] *greeted* her at the airport when she arrived. In her emails, she [2] ________ herself as pretty short, but in fact she's as tall as me. I also met her brother and her parents. I wanted to [3] ________ hands with them, but Kazue quietly [4] ________ in my ear that Japanese people don't usually do that when they meet. I already knew what her brother looked like because Kazue sometimes [5] ________ photos of him online. He was very friendly and he [6] ________ a lot. Kazue's parents don't speak English, but Kazue [7] ________ everything I said into Japanese. Kazue and her family were tired and wanted to go to their hotel. I arranged to meet Kazue the next day, and we [8] ________ goodbye as they drove away in a taxi.

Explore It!

Guess the correct answer.

People originally shook hands because …

a they wanted to find out how strong the other person was.
b they wanted to show that they didn't want to start a fight.
c they wanted to check that the other person had clean hands.

Find another interesting fact about greetings. Write a question and send it to a classmate in an email, or ask them in the next class.

READING

An Article

1 Look at the photo. What emotions/actions do the emojis show? ______

2 Read the article and complete the paragraphs (1–4) with the missing headings.

From Japan to the World — Japan's Alphabets — The Most Popular Symbol — A World Language

3 Find adverbs in the article with the meanings below.

1 in a good way (paragraph 1) ___well___
2 with no problems (paragraph 2) ______
3 very much (paragraph 3) ______
4 not how you expect (paragraph 4) ______

4 Read the article again. Are the sentences *T* (true) or *F* (false)? Correct the false sentences.

1 For verb endings like *-ing*, Japanese people use the *hiragana* alphabet.
T______

2 *Katakana* has the most symbols.
______

3 You can't use more than one alphabet in one text.
______

4 The first emojis didn't express many different feelings.
______

5 In paragraph C, "ones" refers to "people."
______

6 The writer hopes emojis will become an international language in the future.
______

5 Answer the questions in your own words.

1 Which emojis do you use most often? Why?
______

2 Apart from using emojis, how else can we show emotions in text messages?
______

3 Is the alphabet in your language different from English? If so, how?
______

Emojis

The World's Most Popular Alphabet?

1 ______

Did you know that the Japanese language has three alphabets? One alphabet, *katakana*, is mostly for foreign words, like "pizza" (ピザ). This alphabet has 48 characters, or letters and symbols. Another alphabet, *hiragana*, is usually for grammar words, like the word ending "した," which changes a verb into the past tense – similar to *-ed* in English. *Hiragana* has 46 characters. A third alphabet, *kanji*, has about 50,000 different symbols. It is usually for verbs, adjectives, and nouns. For example, "山" is the Japanese symbol for "mountain." Often a piece of writing contains all three alphabets at the same time! Learning written Japanese well can be difficult!

2 ______

But there is another kind of "alphabet" from Japan, which everyone can easily recognize. You probably use it a lot when you communicate with friends. It doesn't use letters; it uses emojis, which translates as "picture characters" in English. We can all recognize emojis when we see them. They show a huge range of feelings or actions, from love and sadness to dancing and waving.

3 ______

The Japanese have used emojis since 1999. Of course, these early emojis were very simple, and people could only use them to show basic emotions. Since then, they have become more and more popular around the world, and the number of emoji symbols has greatly increased – now there are nearly 3,000 official ones. Everyone can understand emojis – it doesn't matter which country they are from.

4 ______

And what is the most common emoji symbol that people use? Surprisingly, it is not a smiley face or a heart. It is the "tears of joy" emoji, showing a face laughing and crying happily. Perhaps in the future, there will be an emoji for every possible emotion, and we will be able to communicate with anyone in the world only by using emoji symbols!

GRAMMAR IN ACTION

Can, Could, Will Be Able To

1 ☆ **Are these sentences about the *past*, *present*, or *future*?**

1 Most people couldn't send each other quick messages 30 years ago. *past*

2 It's possible that we will be able to interpret any language on a smartphone app. ______

3 Animals can't communicate in the same way that humans can. ______

4 I couldn't speak until I was three years old. ______

5 I won't be able to use my phone in the mountains. ______

2 ☆☆ **Complete the conversation with the correct form of *can*, *could*, or *will be able to* and the verbs in parentheses.**

KIM [1] *Can you tell* (you / tell) me why you didn't reply to my email?

DAN Sorry! I was at my grandparents' house out in the country. I [2] ______ (not use) my phone.

KIM Really? But you [3] ______ (post) messages online. I saw them.

DAN Uh, yes, but I [4] ______ (not check) my email.

KIM OK, anyway, [5] ______ (you / help) me practice my presentation tomorrow for next week's test?

DAN Sorry, I [6] ______ (not do) it then. I'm really busy. I [7] ______ (help) you now, though.

KIM Oh, I [8] ______ (not practice) now. I haven't written anything yet.

DAN Well, we [9] ______ (write) it together now, if you want. What's the topic of the presentation?

KIM How to communicate successfully!

3 ☆☆ **Complete the blogs with the correct words.**

HOME ABOUT ME ARCHIVE FOLLOW

Julia

I [1] *couldn't* play the piano very well when I was younger. I didn't like practicing because the piano was in our living room downstairs. That meant everyone had to listen to me when I played, and no one [2] ______ watch TV or read. Now I have an electric piano and I [3] ______ use headphones. It's great because my family [4] ______ hear anything I'm playing! So now I'm practicing a lot, and I [5] ______ play very well.

Liam

I [6] ______ swim at all, but I'd like to. Last summer, I went with my friends to the beach, and I [7] ______ join in the fun in the water. That made me feel sad, so I hope I [8] ______ be able to start taking lessons in the next few months. I know that I [9] ______ be able to swim like a fish after just a few lessons, but I just want to be confident in the water so that I [10] ______ be able to swim with my friends next summer!

4 ☆☆☆ **Look at the information about Vero. Write sentences with the correct form of *can*, *could*, and *will be able to*.**

	**1** play the piano	**2** type quickly	**3** sleep ten hours a night	**4** ask her parents for money
when she was younger	✗		✓	
now	✓	✗	✗	✓
in the future		✓		✗

1 *Vero couldn't play the piano when she was younger, but she can now.*

2 ______

3 ______

4 ______

VOCABULARY AND LISTENING

A Radio Interview

1 ☆☆ **Listen to a radio interview about dolphins. Mark (✓) the topics that the people talk about.** (3.01)

1 ☐ dolphin communication and language
2 ☐ dolphin greetings
3 ☐ the language of human babies
4 ☐ dolphin body language
5 ☐ how quickly dolphins can swim
6 ☐ new technology

2 ☆☆ **Listen again. Are the sentences** *T* **(true) or** *F* **(false)?** (3.01)

1 Sara thinks that all dolphins speak the same language. F
2 Scientists believe dolphins have names. ___
3 Dolphins talk to each other at the same time without stopping. ___
4 In one experiment, two dolphins spoke on a phone. ___
5 Dolphins can communicate over long distances. ___
6 Scientists have the technology to translate what dolphins are saying. ___

Collocations with *To Say* and *To Tell*

3 ☆ **Complete the flashcards with** *to say* **or** *to tell.*

1 to say hello
2 ______ sorry
3 ______ the truth
4 ______ a story
5 ______ a lie
6 ______ (someone) a secret
7 ______ yes / no
8 ______ (something) in Italian
9 ______ a joke

4 ☆☆ **Complete the sentences with the correct form of the collocations in Exercise 3.**

1 Can I tell you a secret? But promise you won't tell anyone else.
2 How do you ______ "thank you" ______?
3 Let me ______ you a ______ about how I met my best friend.
4 The interviewer asked me if I wanted the job. I ______, of course!
5 Maria says she doesn't have any money, but I don't think she's ______. She always wears expensive clothes.
6 I ______ to your brother in the street, but he didn't hear me and he continued walking!
7 I like ______, but I can never make them sound funny.
8 I want to ______ for shouting at you last week.
9 Ed just ______ me a big ______. I'll never believe him again!

5 ☆☆☆ **Answer the questions.**

1 Have you ever told a "good" lie to help someone? What lie did you tell?

______

2 When you have a secret, who do you tell?

______

3 How many languages can you say something in? Which languages?

______

GRAMMAR IN ACTION

Present Perfect with *How long* ... ? and *For/Since*

1 ☆ **Circle the best ending for each sentence.**

1 I've lived here for …
 (a) two years. b I was 14 years old.

2 I've had this phone for …
 a a long time. b 2015.

3 I haven't eaten anything since …
 a about three hours. b this morning.

4 I've been able to speak French since …
 a ten years. b I was a child.

5 My best friend and I have known each other for …
 a six years. b we started school together.

6 Max has been on the computer since …
 a all day. b he woke up.

2 ☆☆ **Complete the questions with *How long* and the present perfect form of the verbs in the box.**

be	have	know	like	~~live~~

A [1] *How long have you lived* here?

B For about six months. I really like it here. It's a nice city.

A So, Emma and Kirsty are friends?
[2] ________________ each other?

B Since they were about three years old. They've been best friends for ages!

A I didn't know Olivia liked watching tennis.
[3] ________________ it?

B For a long time. She's played on the school team since she was really young.

A I see that Will has a new bike.
[4] ________________ it?

B For about a week. He needed a new one. The old one was too small for him.

A I'm sorry I'm late, everyone.
[5] ________________ here?

B Not long. Don't worry. We only got here ten minutes ago.

Present Perfect and Simple Past

3 ☆☆ **Complete the joke with the simple past or present perfect form of the verbs in parentheses.**

My friend [1] *told* (tell) me a funny joke this morning. I [2] ________________ (hear) a lot of jokes in my life, but this one [3] ________________ (make) me laugh when I [4] ________________ (hear) it.

A girl and her father [5] ________________ (be) at the dinner table having some soup. The girl [6] ________________ (ask) her dad, "Dad, are spiders good to eat?" "What a horrible question," [7] ________________ (say) her dad. "Can't you think of anything nice to say at dinnertime? Please let me eat. I [8] ________________ (not eat) anything since this morning!" The girl [9] ________________ (decide) to be quiet. They both [10] ________________ (eat) their dinner in silence. Later, the girl's father [11] ________________ (ask), "Why did you want to know about spiders earlier?" She replied, "Oh, there was a spider in your soup. But it [12] ________________ (go) now."

4 ☆☆ **Write questions with the present perfect or the simple past.**

1 a you / ever / tell / a lie? *Have you ever told a lie?*
 b Who / you / tell / the lie to?
 ____
 c Why / you / tell / it?
 ____

2 a anyone / ever / tell / you a secret?
 ____
 b it / a very big secret?
 ____
 c you / ever / tell / another person the secret?
 ____

5 ☆☆☆ **Choose question 1 or 2 from Exercise 4. Write your answers.**

____

____

WRITING

A Listicle

1 ☆ **Read the listicle and circle the best title.**

1 How to Communicate with People from Other Countries
2 How to Be a Good Language Learner
3 How to Be a Better Communicator
4 How to Tell Jokes

Over the last few years, I've learned a few things, and now I can communicate much better than before. Here are my top five tips.

- **Use Body Language**

Use your hands and gesture to make a point, and always make eye contact. Since I started doing this, people have paid a lot more attention to me!

- **Use Intonation**

Your tone of voice, that is, how it sounds, shows your feelings. If your voice sounds flat and bored, your listener will be bored, too! Before, I didn't use to think about intonation, but now I understand that how you say something is very important.

- **Be a Good Listener**

Good communicators listen. Of course, say what you want to say, but later on, ask questions to find out what the other person is thinking.

- **Be Yourself!**

Most people can tell when someone is telling a lie. All my life, I've never been very confident or sociable. Be honest and don't try to appear more confident than you really are. Always be yourself.

- **Tell Jokes**

Smile and try to find the funny side whenever you can – this will make your listener more relaxed. This is especially important these days, when the world can be such a serious place.

Try to use some of these helpful tips and you'll soon be able to see the difference it makes!

2 ☆☆ **Read the listicle again and complete the sentences.**

1 People pay more attention to you when you *use your hands and gesture, and make eye contact.*
2 ________________ lets the listener know how you are feeling.
3 Good communicators listen and ________________.
4 It's a bad idea to not tell the truth when you meet people because ________________ ________________.
5 Telling jokes helps the listener be ________________.

3 ☆☆ **Circle the correct meanings for the *Useful Language* words and phrases.**

1 **over the last few years** *recently / since I was a baby*
2 **since** *at the moment / from a specific time in the past*
3 **before** *earlier / after some time has passed*
4 **later on** *after some time has passed / recently*
5 **all my life** *at the moment / since I was born*
6 **these days** *at the moment / earlier*
7 **soon** *earlier / in the very near future*

PLAN

4 ☆☆ **Write your own listicle. Choose one of the other titles from Exercise 1 and take notes in your notebook. Use these headings.**

Title:
Introduction:
A List of Five Tips
A Short Ending

WRITE

5 ☆☆☆ **Write your listicle. Remember to include an introduction, five tips and a short ending, *can*, *could*, *will be able to*, the correct past tenses, and words and phrases from the *Useful Language* box (see Student's Book, p41).**

CHECK

6 **Do you …**

- have an introduction that will interest the reader?
- have an ending to make the reader think?

3 REVIEW

VOCABULARY

1 Circle the correct words.

People [1]*greet / gesture* each other in many ways when they meet. All around the world, it's very common to [2]*whisper / wave* when you want to attract someone's attention and then simply [3]*smile / shout* to show that you are happy. If we don't do this, then the other person might [4]*interpret / translate* your serious face as meaning that you don't want to meet them. Perhaps the most common way to say hello in Europe and North America is to [5]*wave / shake hands*. In other places, like Japan, people bow (move their head and body forward). In the Philippines, some people perform a [6]*gesture / shake* called *mano* (this Spanish word [7]*posts / translates* to "hand" in English), putting the other person's hand on their head. In some cultures, people put their noses together when they meet. In Costa Rica, however, people [8]*shout / whisper* "Ooooooooopppe!" in a very loud voice when they meet!

2 Complete the sentences with the correct form of *to say* or *to tell*.

1 Can I ______________ you a secret?
2 I'd like to know how to ______________ "I love you" in Italian.
3 When you don't want to do something, you can always ______________ no.
4 I know I said I was 16, but I wasn't ______________ the truth.
5 Paula didn't ______________ hello to me at the party.
6 George ______________ me the story of how his parents met. It was really funny.
7 I'm not very good at ______________ lies – my face always turns red!
8 Fernando ______________ a really terrible joke and no one laughed.

GRAMMAR IN ACTION

3 Mark (✓) the correct sentences and correct five incorrect sentences

1 I can swim when I was only two years old. ☐
____
2 I think I can be able to get a good job in the future. ☐
____
3 I couldn't come to the party last night because I was sick. ☐
____
4 Will you be able to call me when you get home? ☐
____
5 I can't speak English until I went to school. ☐
____
6 Can you watch TV late at night on the weekend? ☐
____
7 The school will be able let me know about my test score next week. ☐
____
8 Now I could speak Italian well, but in the past I couldn't. ☐
____

4 Complete the sentences with the simple past or present perfect form of the verbs in parentheses.

1 I ____________ (live) in London for about ten years – I love it here.
2 Before you came to London, how long ____________ (you / live) in New York?
3 It ____________ (be) 50 years since the first man stepped on the moon.
4 They ____________ (not learn) much Russian in Moscow – they were only there for two months.
5 My sister ____________ (not finish) reading that book, but she will soon.
6 I ____________ (not do) any exercise last week, so I want to do a lot this week.
7 You and Frank get along really well. How long ____________ (you / know) him?
8 I can't play soccer this afternoon because I ____________ (fall) off my bike yesterday.

CUMULATIVE GRAMMAR

5 Complete the text with the missing words. Circle the correct options.

[1] ____ heard the story *The Boy Who Cried Wolf*? The parents of a young boy asked him to take care of their sheep on a lonely mountain. The boy [2] ____ yes, but he soon found that it was a very boring job. After about four hours, he decided to do something interesting. He started shouting, "Help! Wolf!" There [3] ____ no wolf, of course, but his parents came running.

"Where's the wolf?" they asked.

"Sorry!" said the boy, "I [4] ____."

The parents [5] ____ very angry and went back to the village. A few hours [6] ____ and then suddenly the boy saw a real wolf! "Help! Wolf!" he shouted. But this time, no one came. They thought it was a joke again! This [7] ____ an old story, but the message is still relevant. For example, once I [8] ____ to go to school, so I told my parents I was sick. I don't [9] ____ tell lies, so they believed me, and I didn't go to school that day. But unfortunately, the next week, I really was sick. My parents didn't believe me this time, and I [10] ____ stay at home – I felt terrible! I [11] ____ lied since then! So remember: don't cry wolf because you [12] ____ get help when you really need to!

	a	b	c
1	Have you ever	Have ever you	Haven't you never
2	is saying	said	told
3	is	were	was
4	was joking	joke	have joked
5	was	were	have been
6	are passing	have passed	passed
7	has been	is being	is
8	didn't want	didn't wanted	couldn't want
9	usually	never	sometimes
10	won't be able	couldn't	can't
11	don't	didn't	haven't
12	can't	couldn't	won't be able to

4 How can I stay healthy?

VOCABULARY

Health and Fitness

1 ☆ **Complete the words and phrases with the vowels (a, e, i, o, u).**

1 sw*e* *a*t
2 c__ __gh
3 r_l_x
4 tr__ __n
5 sn__ __z__
6 g_t b_tt_r
7 g_ j_gg_ng
8 h_v__ __ f_v_r
9 g_t s_ck
10 g_t str__ss_d
11 w_rm __p
12 w_rk __ __t
13 g_t __n__ __gh sl__ __p

2 ☆ **Mark the words and phrases that are in the correct column (✓) and those that are in the incorrect column (✗). Then write one extra word for each column.**

HEALTH		FITNESS	
1 *cough*	✓	7 *go jogging*	☐
2 *get better*	☐	8 *have a fever*	☐
3 *work out*	☐	9 *train*	☐
4 *relax*	☐	10 *sneeze*	☐
5 *warm up*	☐	11 *get enough sleep*	☐
6 ________		12 ________	

3 ☆☆ **Complete the sentences with the correct form of the words in Exercise 1.**

1 Is it true that you can't *sneeze* with your eyes open?
2 Sam is ________ for a half marathon at the moment.
3 A Isabel can't come today. She's not feeling very well.
B Oh, no! I hope she ________ soon!
4 He ________ a lot when he exercises. His clothes get very wet!
5 Remember to ________ before you run or do exercise, especially in cold weather.
6 Don't ________ about your exams – relax, you'll be OK!

4 ☆☆ **Circle the correct options.**

CARO Hey, Leo! Do you want to go [1]*jogging* / *sweating* in the park? Meet me there?

LEO Sorry, I can't. I'm getting [2]*better* / *stressed* about my exams.

CARO Oh, come on! Working [3]*out* / *in* will be good for you!

LEO I have a [4]*sneeze* / *fever*, too. I'm really hot and I feel terrible.

CARO Oh, no! But it isn't a good idea to do schoolwork if you want to get [5]*better* / *stressed*.

LEO I know … anyway, you're [6]*training* / *relaxing* for the marathon – it's very difficult to run with you! ☹

CARO OK. Get enough [7]*exercise* / *sleep*. Don't study all night!

LEO OK, and don't forget to [8]*work out* / *warm up* before running. You hurt your leg last time!

Explore It!

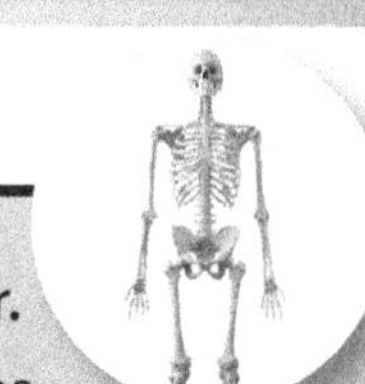

Guess the correct answer.

Almost half of all the bones in the human body are in the …

a hands and feet.
b legs and arms.
c head and back.

Find another interesting fact about exercise and the human body. Write a question and send it to a classmate in an email, or ask them in the next class.

READING

Online FAQs

1 ☆ **Match the photos (a–d) with the FAQs and answers (1–4).**

a 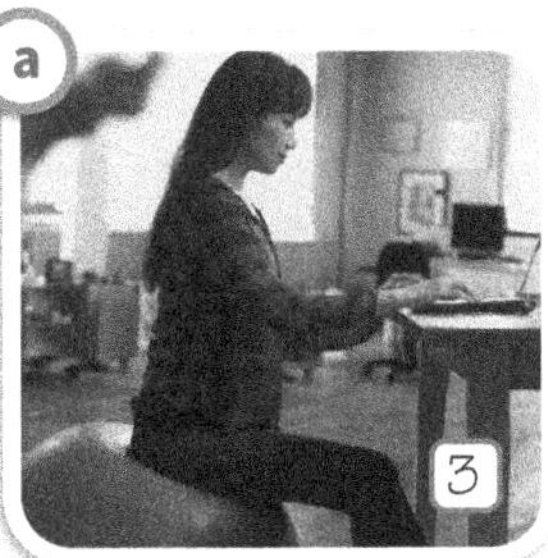

b 

c 

d 

Home News FAQs

Read some of our FAQs about staying fit and healthy during the school week and study sessions.

1 **Q** What can I do to get active during a school day and when can I do it?

A Getting exercise on a school day can be easy. Not enough people cycle or walk to and from school. And if that takes too much of your time, then use your lunch break to exercise or join a sports team after school.

2 **Q** I spend too much time sitting at a desk and not enough time on my feet. What can I do?

A We spend too many hours sitting at a desk or in front of a **screen**. Standing up exercises many different **muscles**. These muscles can become **weak** when we don't use them enough. You can now buy **adjustable** desks, which you can make higher so you can stand up while working. It's a good idea to stand and walk around every half an hour during long study sessions.

3 **Q** What are fitness balls and how can they help me?

A Some people say they feel too silly sitting on a big plastic ball. But fitness balls are a great way to work out, as they help build the muscles in your **back** and **stomach** … all while you're sitting down! A fitness ball for home study is perfect for long hours sitting at a desk.

4 **Q** There is too much noise and stress in my life. How can I get a little quiet time?

A One word: yoga. The practice of yoga is thousands of years old, and when you find a little time between studying and exams to relax in this way, you can concentrate better. It's free and it's easy to do alone!

GET MORE INFORMATION HERE

2 ☆☆ **Match the words in bold in the online FAQs with the meanings.**

1 you need these to carry heavy objects *muscles*
2 the opposite of strong ______
3 where food goes in the body ______
4 the part of a computer where you see words or pictures ______
5 if something is this, you can change it to make it better ______
6 the part of the body that is opposite to the front ______

3 ☆☆ **Read the online FAQs again and answer the questions.**

1 What times of the day can students do exercise, according to the FAQs?
before and after school and at lunchtime
2 What can happen to the body when we don't stand up regularly?
______
3 How often do you need to move around when studying?
______
4 Why is the fitness ball unpopular with some people?
______
5 How can a fitness ball help your body?
______
6 Which activity can students do to relax, according to the FAQs?
______

4 ☆☆☆ **Answer the questions.**

1 Which of the things in the FAQs have you tried?
______
2 Think of one more FAQ about young people's health and fitness.
______

GRAMMAR IN ACTION

Quantifiers

1 ☆ **Complete the sentences with *much* or *many*.**

1 Kylie did too _much_ exercise yesterday and now she's very tired.
2 Is it possible to have too ________ fun on the weekend?
3 There were too ________ people in the pool, so we didn't swim.
4 Everyone I know has too ________ work to take a vacation.
5 Skiing costs too ________ money for most students.
6 Too ________ students get stressed at exam time.

2 ☆ **Match the beginnings of the sentences (1–6) with the ends (a–f).**

1 Swimming is great, but only a few [c]
2 Please give me a little more [ ]
3 Relaxing is hard: I need a little [ ]
4 The nearest gym is a few [ ]
5 It's very hot, so take a little [ ]
6 Stand up for just a few [ ]

a minutes every half an hour.
b kilometers away.
c schools have swimming pools.
d water with you.
e help from my yoga teacher.
f time to finish my homework.

3 ☆☆ **Put the words in the correct order to make sentences.**

1 long / school / aren't / enough / days / Normal
Normal school days aren't long enough.
2 noisy / My / too / friend's / are / dogs
____
3 enough / I'm / drive / can't / not / because / I / old
____
4 her / Gisela / desk / too / says / low / is
____
5 everyone / aren't / chairs / for / There / enough
____

4 ☆☆ **Match the meanings (a–e) with the sentences (1–5) in Exercise 3.**

a He/She's too young. [3]
b They're not quiet enough. [ ]
c There are too many people. [ ]
d They are too short. [ ]
e It's not high enough. [ ]

5 ☆☆☆ **Complete the online post and its response with the phrases in the box.**

a few problems	enough strength	
not enough answers	not enough options	
~~too many questions~~	too old	too young (x2)

Young Teen Health **FORUM**

Posts:

I'd like to see more advice about health and fitness for boys on this website. There are [1] _too many questions_ from teenage girls and [2] ________________ for boys. What advice can you give young male teens for a regular workout?
Andrés

Thanks for your comment, Andrés! Teenage boys can also have [3] ________________ with their body image as they are growing up and changing. Fitness for boys is easy when you're young, but the early teenage years can be complicated. You feel you're [4] ________________ to play silly games with friends but [5] ________________ to work out at the gym with older guys. Perhaps you don't have [6] ________________ yet to join an adult sports team. But you're never [7] ________________ to exercise regularly. If there are [8] ________________ where you live, think about running or parkour, or working out at home. Hope this helps!

VOCABULARY AND LISTENING Healthy Eating

1 Complete the puzzle. Use the clues.

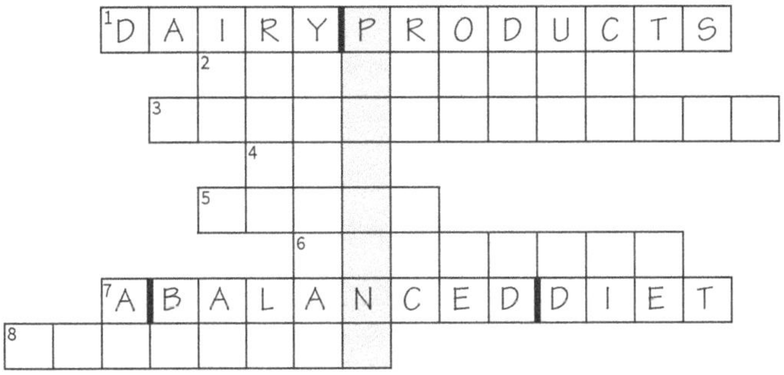

1 These foods usually come from milk.
2 You can study this to learn about food and a healthy diet.
3 We get most of our energy from these. You find them in bread and pasta.
4 There is a lot of this in cheese and chocolate.
5 This helps food pass through the body.
6 We get these natural substances from fruit (C) and sunlight (D).
7 This is a good mixture of many food types.
8 We count these to find out how much energy there is in our food.

2 Circle the correct definition for the secret word (in gray) in Exercise 1.

a They help your bones grow longer.
b They help your body grow stronger.
c They help your heart work.

3 (4.01) Underline the words that are the same or similar in your language – notice any differences in spelling. Then listen to the English pronunciation.

1 A balance between mental and physical health is important.
2 We know that calcium is good for our bones.
3 Do you know why grains are good for you?
4 Basketball practice always ends with a fun activity.

An Interview

4 (4.02) Listen to an interview about "Blue Zones." Number the topics the speakers mention in the order you hear them (1–4).

a [ ] regular exercise
b [ ] the Mediterranean diet
c [1] centenarians
d [ ] eating food from the ocean

5 (4.02) Listen again and circle the correct answers.

1 A Blue Zone is a place where people often … .
a become large.
(b) live to an old age.
c eat seafood.

2 Philippa was surprised because many Blue Zones are … .
a very big. b in Asia. c islands.

3 The food tofu is very high in … .
a carbohydrates. b calories. c protein.

4 Philippa says people in the Mediterranean often eat … .
a too much meat.
b very little fat.
c a lot of sweet things.

5 Philippa thinks that … also important for a long life.
a family and friends are
b working outside is
c getting up early is

GRAMMAR IN ACTION

Should, Shouldn't, and Ought To

1 ☆ **Look at the photos. Complete the sentences with *should* or *shouldn't* and the correct verb.**

1

2

3

4

5

6

1 You ___should eat___ enough fruit.
2 You ________ too much coffee.
3 You ________ too much chocolate.
4 You ________ enough fish.
5 You ________ too many sweet drinks.
6 You ________ enough vegetables.

2 ☆☆ **Complete the sentences with *should*, *shouldn't*, or *ought*.**

1 If you're always late for class, you ___should___ get up earlier.
2 People who can't get up ________ go to bed so late.
3 Ilona can't relax: I think she ________ to do yoga.
4 Our teacher said we ________ to eat our lunch outside because it's hot today.
5 You ________ give chocolate to dogs – it's bad for them.
6 We ________ eat more tofu because it's full of protein.

3 ☆☆ **Underline and correct one mistake in each sentence.**

1 You don't look well; perhaps you shouldn't see a doctor. ___should___
2 Our fridge is empty, so we ought go to the store. ________
3 You should worry so much about your exams. ________
4 What should I to do to get healthier? ________
5 He oughts to eat more protein. ________
6 You shouldn't to eat unhealthy food if you want to live to be 100. ________

4 ☆☆☆ **Complete the article with the phrases in the box.**

ought to check ~~ought to know~~ ought to start should be should drink should take shouldn't carry shouldn't spend

Top Tips for a Road Trip – By Bike!

Planning a road trip by bike? Here's what you [1] ___ought to know___ to stay fit and healthy!

Your bike [2] ________ light enough because if it's too heavy, cycling becomes difficult in hot weather. But you [3] ________ that it's big enough for you – a bike that's too small soon gets uncomfortable.

You [4] ________ too many things with you. Too many bags slow you down, so you [5] ________ two small bags, maximum. You [6] ________ a lot of water, so take a one-liter water bottle.

You [7] ________ too much money on maps: paper maps are heavy. Download maps onto your smartphone before you leave home. And finally, you [8] ________ early in the day – before it gets too hot!

5 ☆☆☆ **Choose one of the topics in the box and write three pieces of advice in your notebook. Use *should*, *ought to*, and *shouldn't*.**

eating more healthily preparing for an exam writing an essay

WRITING

A Post on a Forum

1 ☆ **Read the post on a forum and the response. Who does Carlos want to help? What does Tom suggest?**

Forum:
We ♥ Animals
Posts:

Carlos: My grandma lives alone now. She sits and thinks about the past and gets stressed about her health. I think she ought to get a cat or a dog, but she thinks she's too old. What do you think?

Tom@the Den: Hey, great that you've written to me – thanks! We all have stress in our lives and especially old people living alone. Pets make people feel happier and more relaxed. In fact, did you know that they can also help with stress? Have you ever tried sitting with a cat or walking a dog when you're stressed? It really helps! Why? Stress often causes high blood pressure, and just being near an animal can help lower it. I think your grandma should definitely try having a pet. If she likes dogs, for example, but doesn't want to keep a dog as a pet, I can recommend trying a therapy dog. There are specially trained dogs that can visit old people with their owners or volunteers. Your grandma can enjoy the dog without worrying about it! Why don't you look online for a therapy pet center near you? Or you could always ask at your local vet – they ought to be able to help. That way, your grandma can relax and beat stress.

2 ☆☆ **Read the post and response again. Answer the questions.**

1 Why doesn't Carlos's grandma want a pet?
She thinks she's too old.
2 How can pets help with stress?
3 Why is a therapy pet a better option for Carlos's grandma?
4 Where should Carlos find out about a therapy pet?

3 ☆☆ **(Circle) the correct options in the *Useful Language* phrases. Then check in the forum response.**

1 You *would* / (*could*) always ask …
2 Have you ever tried *sitting* / *sit* … ?
3 *This* / *That* way, your grandma can relax …
4 Why *don't* / *not* you look … ?
5 I can recommend *to try* / *trying* …

PLAN

4 ☆☆ **Write your own response to a post on a forum. Use the problem below or your own ideas. Take notes.**

> Please help! I drink two liters of soda a day! I know it's bad for me, but I think I'm addicted to the sugar and caffeine! What can I do?

Advice:

Reasons:

WRITE

5 ☆☆☆ **Write your response. Remember to include a greeting and thanks, *should, shouldn't, ought to*, quantifiers, and phrases from the *Useful Language* box (see Student's Book, p53).**

CHECK

6 **Do you …**
- give advice with reasons?
- use an informal style?

4 REVIEW

VOCABULARY

1 Look at the photos and circle the correct options.

2 Match the beginnings of the sentences (1–8) with the ends (a–h).

1 Nutrition is the food we eat ☐
2 Hamburgers, ice cream, and chocolate ☐
3 The number of calories in food ☐
4 Carbohydrates give us ☐
5 Protein helps our bodies ☐
6 Fruit and vegetables contain ☐
7 A balanced diet ☐
8 A lot of fiber is good for the stomach ☐

a tells us how much energy it has.
b grow and be healthy and strong.
c a lot of vitamins A and C.
d and how our body uses it.
e the energy we need to move.
f have a lot of fat in them.
g and travels through the body quickly.
h is eating a good variety of healthy food.

GRAMMAR IN ACTION

3 Circle the correct options.

1 Is there *little / enough* food for everyone, or should I cook more?
2 We don't use too *many / much* milk products in our restaurant.
3 Owen's just gone out to buy *a few / a little* eggs.
4 We all need to relax and have *much / a little* fun.
5 My baby sister isn't *old enough / enough old* to make her own breakfast.
6 This article gives you *a little / few* ideas on healthy diets.

1 *sneeze / cough*

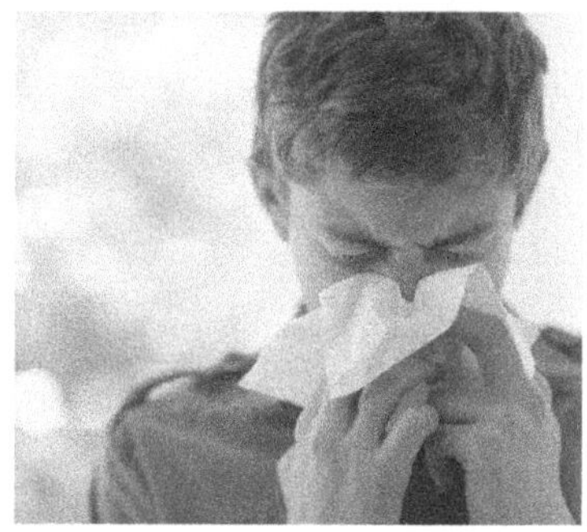

2 *sneeze / cough*

3 *go jogging / warm up*

4 *relax / get sick*

5 *warm up / sweat*

6 *have a fever / get enough sleep*

7 *sweat / warm up*

8 *get stressed / get enough sleep*

4 Complete the sentences with *should*, *shouldn't*, or *ought*.

1 What ________ we eat to grow stronger?
2 The children ________ to eat fewer chips and candy.
3 A balanced diet ________ to have a little of everything.
4 You ________ drink coffee at night – it stops you from sleeping.
5 How much exercise ________ we do?
6 You ________ eat more than you need.

CUMULATIVE GRAMMAR

5 Complete the conversation with the missing words. Circle the correct options.

INTERVIEWER You've just completed a marathon; well done! I'm sure you're tired, but [1] ______ to answer a few questions?

BERNADETTE Sure, I just need [2] ______ water. OK, so yeah, it was a great run.

INTERVIEWER It was! You [3] ______ a runner, did you? Tell us how it started.

BERNADETTE I often got sick when I was younger, and I wasn't [4] ______ to play sports.

INTERVIEWER That's hard to believe! You've [5] ______ a marathon in record time!

BERNADETTE As a child, I spent [6] ______ time in bed, and I really wasn't fit at all.

INTERVIEWER Not enough young people exercise as much as they [7] ______ to. What changed for you?

BERNADETTE One day, my mother [8] ______ a TV show about foods that some people [9] ______ eat because it makes them sick. We later discovered that I [10] ______ eat bread or anything with gluten in it.

INTERVIEWER And what [11] ______ then?

BERNADETTE I changed my diet right, and I [12] ______ gluten since then. I felt better, started playing sports, and the rest is history!

	a	b	c
1	can you	will you be able	should you
2	too much	a few	a little
3	didn't use to be	used not be	didn't use be
4	enough strong	too strong	strong enough
5	just completed	still completed	yet completed
6	enough	too little	too much
7	should	ought	shouldn't
8	is seeing	has seen	saw
9	can't	can't to	can
10	shouldn't to	shouldn't	ought to
11	happens	happen	happened
12	didn't eat	haven't eaten	still didn't eat

5 How can we save our planet?

VOCABULARY

Planet Earth

1 ★ Complete the crossword. Use the clues.

DOWN ↓

1 We usually separate our paper, plastic, and food … into different trash cans.
2 I try to save … at home – I always turn off the lights when I'm not using them.
3 Cycling or walking is better for the … than traveling by car.
5 Governments want to reduce the carbon … (or CO_2) that their countries produce.
8 We all live on … Earth.

ACROSS →

4 Tigers are an … species. It's possible they will all die in a few years.
6 There used to be a lot of … near here, like birds and butterflies, but not now.
7 Trees produce … for us to breathe.
8 Traffic causes a lot of air … in cities.
9 … change causes hotter weather around the world.
10 … power from the sun produces a lot of electricity.
11 Plastic in the ocean is bad for all … life, from large whales to small fish.

Explore It!

Guess the correct answer.

How much of the plastic that we use every year ends up in the seas and oceans?

a 1 percent b 5 percent c 10 percent

Find another interesting fact about pollution in the ocean. Write a question and send it to a classmate in an email, or ask them in the next class.

2 ★★ Complete the notes with words from Exercise 1.

Things We Should Reduce

- *the amount of carbon* [1] *dioxide* *that we produce*
- [2] ______ *(e.g., air, water, and noise)*
- [3] ______ *(e.g., plastic and food)*
- *the effects of* [4] ______ *change (e.g., rising temperatures and sea levels)*
- *the amount of* [5] ______ *that we use (e.g., electricity and gas)*

Things We Need to Protect or Save

- *the* [6] ______ *(the air, our water, etc.)*
- [7] ______ *life (e.g., fish)*
- [8] ______ *Earth (our home – we only have one!)*
- *all animals, but especially* [9] ______ *species (e.g., tigers and gorillas)*

3 ★★★ Circle the correct words.

We face many environmental problems, such as rising levels of [1]*carbon* / *oxygen* dioxide in the air, which cause [2]*climate* / *planet* change. Plastic is also a big cause of [3]*pollution* / *energy*. Every year, we put a lot of plastic [4]*energy* / *waste* into our oceans. This is a huge problem for [5]*endangered* / *marine* life. It ends up in the stomachs of fish, which bigger animals then eat, including us. Many animals are therefore becoming [6]*endangered* / *marine*. But plastic is all over the [7]*planet* / *environment*. Even high mountains now have millions of tiny pieces of plastic on them, carried there by the wind.

READING

A News Story

1 ☆ Look at the photos and read the news story quickly. Circle the best title.

a Why We Should Use Drinking Straws

b The History of Drinking Straws

c The End of Drinking Straws?

News | Search

Home | News | Articles | Sign In | Register

Most of us have used straws. They are useful and [1] c. When we get a soda or juice from a café or restaurant, for example, it often comes with a straw, [2] ______. We usually use them once and then **dispose of** them immediately. In fact, people in the U.S.A. use 500 million every day. That's enough straws to go around the planet 2.5 times!

The big problem with straws is that many of them [3] ______. Europeans **recycle** only about 30 percent of their plastic, and straws are in the top ten **items** of **litter** found on beaches every year.

The good news is that [4] ______. More and more big companies are deciding not to use straws, or to provide them only when customers have asked for them. The city of Seattle, in the U.S.A., has already put a **ban** on straws, and the European Union wants to do the same by 2030. England plans to do this in 2020. Even the British Queen [5] ______.

So, it is possible that plastic drinking straws will soon be a thing of the past. Many people believe that we can continue to protect our environment by also reducing all the other plastic objects that we only use once, [6] ______.

2 ☆☆ Complete the article with the missing sentence parts (a–f).

a end up in the ocean, as waste

b such as bags, cups, and bottles

~~c they can be fun to drink with~~

d people are starting to do something about the problem

e including when we haven't asked for one

f has decided not to have plastic straws in any of her houses

3 ☆☆ Match the words in bold in the news story with the definitions.

1 things on a list items

2 put something in the trash can after we have used it ______

3 an official law that stops something from happening ______

4 use something again, or change it into something different ______

5 small pieces of trash in public places ______

4 ☆☆ What do these numbers in the news story describe?

1 30 percent is the amount of plastic that Europeans recycle

2 500 million ______

3 2.5 ______

4 2020 ______

5 10 ______

5 ☆☆☆ Apart from a ban, how can we reduce the number of plastic straws people use? Write three ideas.

______

______

______

GRAMMAR IN ACTION

The First Conditional

1 ☆ **Circle the correct options.**

1 If I (see) / *don't* see any litter on the beach, I'll pick it up.

2 I won't use my bike tomorrow *unless* / *if* it's raining. I don't want to get wet.

3 Unless we *use* / *don't use* alternative forms of energy, we will create more air pollution.

4 If you *will leave* / *leave* your computer on all night, it will waste energy.

5 Some cities *may* / *may be* underwater if sea levels rise.

6 I'll travel by train if I *go* / *might go* on vacation this year.

2 ☆☆ **Complete the sentences with the phrases in the box.**

climate change will get worse if we stop using so much plastic ~~it will help the planet~~ many types of plants may be in danger there might be more plastic than fish by 2050 unless we protect them

1 If we reduce our energy use,
it will help the planet .

2 Many animals could become endangered
__________________ .

3 If we lose a lot of insect species,
__________________ .

4 If we don't reduce the amount of carbon dioxide,
__________________ .

5 Unless we stop polluting our oceans,
__________________ .

6 It will help the planet
__________________ .

3 ☆☆ **Complete the text with the verbs in the box.**

act continue is might be ~~might not see~~ will need

If you drive somewhere on a summer night and check the front window of your car after, you [1] *might not see* many dead insects on it. This doesn't sound like a problem. In fact, if your car [2] __________ clean, you will probably be pleased. However, this is a worrying sign. Over the last 30 years, the number of insects has fallen by 75 percent. But if there are fewer flies and mosquitoes in the future, the world [3] __________ a better place, right? Wrong! The problem is that if insects [4] __________ to disappear, we will all be in trouble. Many plants depend on them. As insects move from one plant to another, they carry pollen, which helps plants grow again. And if the number of people on the planet keeps on rising, we [5] __________ more and more food. Unless we [6] __________ quickly, insect numbers could fall even more. This could be very bad news for both humans and the planet.

4 ☆☆☆ **Complete the second sentence so that it has a similar meaning to the first. Use the word in parentheses.**

1 If we don't do something soon, it's possible that endangered species will disappear.
Endangered species could disappear if we don't do something soon. (could)

2 There will be huge problems if we don't protect our environment.
__________________ our environment, there will be huge problems. (unless)

3 If we don't stop using chemicals on farms, it's possible that insect numbers will fall.
__________________ if we don't stop using chemicals on farms. (might)

4 If we do something now, we might stop climate change.
Unless we do something now, we __________________ climate change. (might)

5 ☆☆☆ **Complete the sentences with your own ideas.**

1 Unless we do something about climate change,
__________________ .

2 We might be able to help the planet if
__________________ .

VOCABULARY AND LISTENING

Natural Environments

1 Look at the photos and complete the natural environment words.

1 bay

2 v______

3 c______

4 c______

5 c______

6 i______

7 r______

8 s______

9 v______

10 w______

2 Choose the three most difficult words to remember in Exercise 1. Then draw a picture of each one in your notebook (see the *Learn to Learn* tip in the Student's Book, p62).

3 Circle the correct options.

1 A (stream) / *bay* is a small river, usually in the country.
2 You only find *icebergs* / *cliffs* in very cold places like the Arctic.
3 A *valley* / *cave* is a big hole in a mountain or under the ground.
4 A *cliff* / *valley* is a high area of vertical rock, often near the ocean.
5 A *stream* / *waterfall* is where a river falls from a high point to a lower point.
6 A *volcano* / *bay* is a mountain with a hole at the top. Sometimes gases and hot liquids come out.
7 A *rainforest* / *waterfall* is a hot place with trees and a lot of animals.
8 A *bay* / *valley* is an area between hills or mountains. There is often a river at the bottom.

A Class Discussion

5.01 **4 Listen to the class discussion. Which four natural environments in Exercise 1 do the students mention?**

1 ______ 2 ______
3 ______ 4 ______

5.01 **5 Listen again and complete the notes.**

Harry talks about caves in [1] New Zealand. Inside the caves there is a small [2] ______. To travel through the caves, you need to take a [3] ______. If you look up at the top of the cave, you can see thousands of [4] ______ – they look like stars.

Abbie talks about [5] ______ in Papua New Guinea – these are very difficult to get to. There are also rainforests where scientists have found a lot of [6] ______. They have discovered a colorful fish, a river [7] ______, and a tree kangaroo. There are only [8] ______ tenkile tree kangaroos alive today.

6 Think of three examples of natural environments in Exercise 1 that are in your country. What are their names?

______
______
______

GRAMMAR IN ACTION

The Second Conditional

1 ☆ **Circle the correct options.**

1 If I could travel anywhere in the world, …
   a I'll visit a jungle.
   (b) I'd visit a jungle.
   c I visited a jungle.

2 I don't know what would happen …
   a if all the insects will disappear.
   b if all the insects would disappear.
   c if all the insects disappeared.

3 What would happen if …
   a we cut down all the rainforests?
   b we'd cut down all the rainforests?
   c would we cut down all the rainforests?

4 If I were you, …
   a I'd find out more information.
   b I found out more information.
   c I'm finding out more information.

5 People wouldn't buy plastic products …
   a if they have a better alternative.
   b if they had a better alternative.
   c if they'd have a better alternative.

2 ☆☆ **Complete the second conditional sentences using the verbs in parentheses.**

1 If I _had_ a bike, I _would use_ it to go to school. (have / use)

2 I __________ out today if it __________ cold. (go / not be)

3 If they __________ near the ocean, they __________ to the beach a lot. (live / go)

4 The waterfall __________ more interesting to look at if it __________ raining. (be / be)

5 If we __________ so much meat, we __________ so many rainforests. (not eat / not cut down)

3 ☆☆ **Complete the blog post with the correct form of the verbs in the box to make second conditional sentences.**

be (x3)	~~can~~	check	find	not continue	not use	~~try~~

HOME ABOUT ME ARCHIVE FOLLOW

If I [1] _could_ do anything to help the planet, I [2] _would try_ to stop people from buying so many things with palm oil in them. If you [3] __________ the ingredients in the things you buy, you [4] __________ palm oil in many of them – from cookies to toothpaste. It's a cheap type of oil, and our products [5] __________ more expensive if companies [6] __________ it.

The oil comes from trees that only grow in hot countries. This means that we need to cut down rainforests to grow them. This is a problem for the animals that live in rainforests, including the orangutan. If we [7] __________ to destroy their natural habitat, orangutans wouldn't be endangered. So, if there [8] __________ one useful thing everyone could do to protect the environment, it [9] __________ to buy things that don't contain palm oil.

4 ☆☆ **Write second conditional questions and then write short answers (affirmative or negative).**

1 be so much waste / people not use so much plastic / ? (✗)
   Would _there be so much waste if people didn't use so much plastic?_
   No, there wouldn't.

2 we recycle more waste / help the environment / ? (✓)
   If __________

3 they use solar power / they have enough sunlight / ? (✓)
   Could __________

4 companies use palm oil / it not be cheap / ? (✗)
   Would __________

a

b

c

WRITING

An Opinion Essay

1 **Read the essay. Which environmental problem in the photos (a–c) does the writer think is the most serious?** ______

2 **Complete the essay with the words in the box. Sometimes more than one answer is possible.**

addition	~~believe~~	Furthermore	
However	opinion	summary	view

Our Most Serious Environmental Problem

There are many environmental problems nowadays, and it is difficult to know which one is the most important. Some people [1] *believe* that we should protect the rainforests. Other people might think that we need to stop using plastic. Which is the most important?

It would be good if we could solve both of these problems. [2] ______, in my [3] ______, the most serious problem is air pollution. This is something that is getting worse in cities around the world. [4] ______, it has an effect on everyone as it is a major cause of health problems, especially in children.

In my [5] ______, the first step would be to reduce the number of cars in cities. This is one of the biggest causes of pollution. In [6] ______, we need to make more people use public transportation or cleaner forms of personal transportation like bicycles. We also need cleaner factories that don't produce dangerous gases that are bad for our health.

In [7] ______, if we have cleaner cities with cleaner air, we will all become healthier. We will also spend more time outdoors, exercising and enjoying our natural environment.

3 **Circle the correct options.**

1 The first paragraph includes an introduction and *a question / the writer's main opinion*.

2 The second paragraph gives *the writer's main / other people's* opinion.

3 The third paragraph offers *reasons for / possible solutions to* the problem.

4 The last paragraph *introduces / summarizes* the writer's opinion.

PLAN

4 **Write your own opinion essay. Decide what you think is the biggest environmental problem and think of two possible solutions to the problem. Take notes.**

Problem: ______

Solution 1: ______

Solution 2: ______

5 **Decide what information to include in each paragraph. Use the information in Exercise 3 to help you.**

WRITE

6 **Write your opinion essay. Remember to include four paragraphs, the first and second conditional, and words and phrases from the *Useful Language* box (see Student's Book, p65).**

CHECK

7 **Do you …**

- have an introduction with a question for the reader to think about?
- have solutions and examples to support your opinion?
- have a conclusion?

5 REVIEW

VOCABULARY

1 Match the beginnings of the sentences (1–10) with the ends (a–j).

1 Too much carbon ☐
2 It's important to save ☐
3 The biggest environmental problem is climate ☐
4 We all need to recycle and reduce waste to help protect the ☐
5 Plastic is a big problem for marine ☐
6 Plants produce ☐
7 The white rhino is ☐
8 We all live on the same ☐
9 Cars are the main cause of air ☐
10 Sunny countries produce a lot of energy from ☐

a change.
b an endangered species.
c oxygen, which all animals need to survive.
d planet, so we should take care of it.
e life, like fish, whales, and sea birds.
f dioxide causes global warming.
g pollution in cities.
h energy and not waste it.
i solar power.
j environment.

2 Match the sentences with the words in the box.

cave cliff coast icebergs rainforest stream volcano waterfall

1 We walk here by the water as it flows through the forest. ______
2 My grandparents have a house there. It's nice because you can just walk out onto the beach and you can hear the ocean at night. ______
3 You can walk into it and it's really interesting. It's dark, but you can hear the sound of water deep below you. ______
4 Don't stand too close to the edge. I know it's nice to look down at the ocean, but it can be dangerous. ______
5 They cut down a large area. It will take hundreds of years for the trees and plants to grow again. ______
6 They're very dangerous to boats and ships. Remember that you can only see 10 percent of them. The rest is below the ocean. ______
7 Every second, almost 3 million liters of water drops to the river below at Niagara! ______
8 It's still active and you can often smell the gases – the heat and noise is incredible sometimes! ______

GRAMMAR IN ACTION

3 Mark (✓) the correct sentences and correct five incorrect sentences.

1 If I pass my exam tomorrow, I am really happy. ☐
______
2 I might go for a drive along the coast tomorrow if the weather will be nice. ☐
______
3 Will you call me if you're late? ☐
______
4 Unless I don't do my homework now, I won't have time to go out later. ☐
______
5 If I will have money, I will go to the movies on Friday. ☐
______
6 I won't buy a new phone unless this one breaks completely. ☐
______
7 If you look in the stream, you will may see some fish. ☐
______
8 You could take a break if you feel tired. ☐
______

4 Complete the sentences with the words in the box.

didn't have	had	knew	took	was	were	would be
would have	would need	would stop	would take	wouldn't be		

1 If I ________ time, I ________ a trip to the bay.
2 The town ________ in trouble if that volcano ________ active.
3 If you ________ more sociable, you ________ more friends.
4 You ________ sick if you ________ better care of yourself.
5 If I ________ a bike, I ________ to use the bus.
6 More people ________ eating meat if they ________ about the effects on the environment.

CUMULATIVE GRAMMAR

5 Complete the text with the missing words. Circle the correct options.

I [1] ____ a TV documentary last month about marine life and plastic. Every day, we [2] ____ a lot of plastic waste into the oceans, and even a little drinking straw can have a terrible effect on an animal. For example, if a fish [3] ____ one, it could easily die. And if a sea bird ate the fish, it [4] ____ the plastic, too. Plastic in the oceans is a big problem because it [5] ____ away. It just breaks down into smaller and smaller pieces! [6] ____ we do something about this problem, it will get worse. So, I [7] ____ to make some changes to my life. They're small, but if everyone [8] ____ something small, it would add up to something big. In the past, I [9] ____ a lot of plastic straws and bags. I [10] ____ straws without thinking about it in cafés. Now, I just say I don't need one when they offer. They haven't stopped using straws in cafés in my city [11] ____, but I hope they do soon. Anyway, we all need to do something. If we don't, then soon we [12] ____ to enjoy the natural beauty of the ocean and its marine life.

	a	b	c
1	have watched	watched	watch
2	have put	used to put	put
3	eats	would eat	will eat
4	ate	would eat	will eat
5	doesn't go	wouldn't go	isn't going
6	If	Furthermore	Unless
7	have decided	am deciding	will decide
8	did	does	would do
9	use to use	used to use	did use
10	will use	am using	have used
11	yet	already	since
12	couldn't	can't	won't be able

6 How can inventions change our lives?

VOCABULARY

Making Things

1 ☆ **Circle 12 more verbs in the word snake.**

increasestirboiladdremovedipplacepullcoverfreezepourreducepress

2 ☆☆ **Complete the sentences with the correct form of the verbs in Exercise 1.**

1. *Increase* the oven temperature from 150°C to 200°C.
2. I want to ________ the time I spend watching TV from four hours to one hour a day.
3. Water ________ at 100°C.
4. She ________ her feet in the ocean for a few seconds – it was really cold!
5. ________ the hot water into the cup and ________ sugar and milk.
6. ________ the cake from the oven and ________ it on a plate to cool.
7. You should ________ the soup with a spoon so it doesn't burn and stick to the pot.
8. I ________ my eyes so I couldn't see the frightening scenes in the movie.
9. Lara collects flowers – she ________ them flat and puts them in a scrapbook.
10. We use our car to ________ our camper when we go on vacation.
11. You should ________ fresh fish at –20°C for at least seven days before eating it.

3 ☆ **Choose one of the words in Exercise 1 and think of an image to go with it. Draw your image in your notebook (see the *Learn to Learn* tip in the Student's Book, p71).**

4 ☆☆ **Circle the correct words.**

1. When the milk boils, *pour* / *pull* it into your coffee cup.
2. *Reduce* / *Increase* the temperature so that it's really cold.
3. Take a spoon and *remove* / *stir* the butter, sugar, and milk together for a few minutes.
4. *Add* / *Cover* the glass with paper and put it in the fridge overnight.
5. I'll *freeze* / *press* any food that we don't eat, and we can have it next month.
6. Don't *dip* / *freeze* your finger into the hot liquid!

Explore It!

Guess the correct answer.

A chef in the U.S.A. invented chips when he …

a accidentally cooked some potatoes for too long.
b cut potatoes very thinly for an angry customer.
c poured hot fat over some frozen vegetables.

Find another interesting fact about an invention or discovery. Write a question and send it to a classmate in a text, or ask them in the next class.

READING

A News Story

1 Read the news story. Complete the paragraphs (1–4) with the headings.

What Was the Problem? What Do People Use It for Now?
What Was the Solution? Who Was Vesta Stoudt?

The Story of Duct Tape

1 ____________

In the early 1940s, the U.S. army was fighting in Europe in World War II. Vesta Stoudt was a woman from Illinois who had two sons in the military. As part of the war effort, she was working in a factory in the U.S.A. Her job was to **inspect** and pack equipment for the soldiers in Europe.

2 ____________

At the factory, they closed and **secured** the boxes of equipment using a thin paper **tape**. However, the boxes were difficult to open quickly, especially when they were wet. Vesta was worried that soldiers' lives might be in danger because they might not be able to get their equipment out fast enough.

3 ____________

Vesta suggested that they close the boxes with a stronger, **waterproof** tape. She designed a basic **prototype** of how she thought the tape should be. The boxes were easier to open quickly with this new tape. Vesta's managers in the factory didn't listen to her, but she didn't give up. She decided to write to Franklin Roosevelt, the president of the United States.

4 ____________

The letter worked and Vesta received a letter of thanks from Roosevelt. The government then asked a company to make the tape based on Vesta's idea. The tape was a great success and probably helped save lives! Nowadays, duct tape, as it is known, is used for many different things and in many different industries. It is used by NASA on its spaceships, and clothes are even made from it. And it's all thanks to the **patience** of one inspiring woman.

2 Match the words in bold in the news story with the meanings.

1 made safe from damage *secured*
2 stopping liquid from entering somewhere ____________
3 the ability to stay calm and continue doing something difficult ____________
4 view closely to check condition ____________
5 a long, narrow piece of material we use to close things ____________
6 the first example of something ____________

3 Read the news story again and answer the questions.

1 Where did Vesta Stoudt work?
She worked in a factory in the U.S.A.
2 What did Vesta do at the factory?
____
3 What problem did Vesta want to solve?
____
4 Why was Vesta's prototype better than the paper tape?
____
5 How did Vesta show patience?
____
6 What examples does the writer give of how people use duct tape now?
____

4 Can you think of any other ways people use duct tape? Write two ideas.

____

GRAMMAR IN ACTION

Simple Present Passive

1 ☆ **Complete the chart with the past participle form of the verbs. Mark if the verb is *R* (regular) or *I* (irregular).**

Verb	Past Participle	R	I
add	*added*	✓	
break			
catch			
collect			
connect			
design			
develop			
eat			
manufacture			
throw			

2 ☆☆ **Complete the sentences with the simple present passive form of the verbs in parentheses.**

1 How many smartphones *are made* every year in Asia? (make)
2 Something new and exciting ______ every day. (invent)
3 The potatoes ______ in very hot oil to make chips. (place)
4 These new inventions ______ enough, in my opinion. (not test)
5 ______ these materials ______ online or should we go to a store? (sell)

3 ☆☆ **Complete the sentences with the simple present passive form of verbs in Exercise 1.**

1 Food waste *is collected* for recycling.
2 Sugar ______ to chocolate to make it sweet.
3 How many plastic bottles ______ in the trash every day?
4 New ideas ______ here by brilliant young inventors.
5 ______ your computer ______ to the Internet by a cable or Wi-Fi?
6 This system ______ to help blind people use a computer.

4 ☆☆ **Write questions in the simple present passive. Then write the correct answers using the places in parentheses.**

1 coffee beans / grow / Iceland? (South America)
Are coffee beans grown in Iceland?
No, they aren't. Coffee beans are grown in South America.
2 most chocolate / produce / in Switzerland? (the U.S.A.)
______
3 these cars / manufacture / in Malta? (China)
______
4 insects / eat / in the UK? (Thailand)
______
5 bananas / grow / in Denmark? (Ecuador)
______

5 ☆☆☆ **Complete the text with the simple present passive form of the verbs in parentheses.**

It's difficult to believe, but glass [1] *is made* (make) of liquid sand. That's right, the same sand that [2] ______ (find) on the beach or in the desert. When sand [3] ______ (heat) to about 1,700°C, it changes into a liquid. Other minerals [4] ______ (add), and when it cools to a much lower temperature, it changes into glass. To make glass containers, like jars and bottles, liquid glass [5] ______ (pour) into containers in a particular shape, called molds. Of course, glass [6] ______ also ______ (use) for windows, and we [7] ______ (protect) by glass, for example, in cars, but glass breaks easily, too. Glass [8] ______ easily ______ (recycle), so manufacturers can often use the same glass again and again in their products.

VOCABULARY AND LISTENING

Materials and Containers

1 ☆ **Match the materials with the containers in the box to make six objects. Then write the words in the correct column. Use each word only once.**

~~bag~~ box can cardboard case glass jar leather rubber ~~silk~~ tin tube

Material	Container
1 silk	bag
2	
3	
4	
5	
6	

2 ☆☆ **Complete the sentences with the objects in Exercise 1.**

1 Julia's dress doesn't have pockets. She needs a little silk bag to put her phone and wallet in.

2 A garden hose is a ________. It's long and thin. You use it to water your flowers.

3 When Dad goes to work every morning, he carries his laptop and all his important papers in a ________.

4 Our new computer came in a big ________. We used it to put old books and clothes in.

5 Tuna, peas, and beans – what other things come in a ________?

6 My grandma used to have a ________ full of candy and chocolate for visiting children.

A Conversation

3 ☆ **Look at the questions and think about possible answers.**

1 What are jeans made of?

2 Who wears jeans?

3 How much do jeans cost?

4 What are the best styles?

5 What effect do jeans have on the environment?

6.01 **4** ☆ **Listen to two friends shopping for jeans. Which three questions in Exercise 3 do the girls discuss?**

____

6.01 **5** ☆☆ **Listen again. Are the sentences *T* (true) or *F* (false)? Correct the false sentences.**

1 Nicole prefers white jeans to blue jeans. F
Nicole prefers blue jeans.

2 The word "denim" comes from the name of a French town. ___

3 Camila says good jeans can cost about $100. ___

4 Nicole says that some jeans factories use too much energy. ___

5 Nicole says Camila should find out information before she buys jeans. ___

6 Camila doesn't want to go to the store that Nicole suggests. ___

GRAMMAR IN ACTION

Simple Past Passive

1 ★ **Complete the sentences with the simple past passive form of the verbs in parentheses.**

1 Tolstoy's novel *War and Peace* was published (publish) in 1867.

2 The world's most expensive violins ______ (make) by Antonio Stradivari.

3 Facebook ______ (start) by Harvard University students in 2004.

4 Is it true that some of Shakespeare's plays ______ (not write) by him?

5 A lot of my photos ______ (lose) when my phone broke.

6 Paper ______ (not invent) in Europe but in China.

2 ★★ **Write questions in the simple past passive.**

1 when / first antibiotic / discover?
When was the first antibiotic discovered?

2 where / the world's first subway / open?
______

3 where / the first modern Olympics / hold?
______

4 what / the first Pixar movie / call?
______

5 where / the largest Egyptian pyramids / build?
______

6 when / the first email / write?
______

7 where / the first CD / make?
______

8 when / Google / start?
______

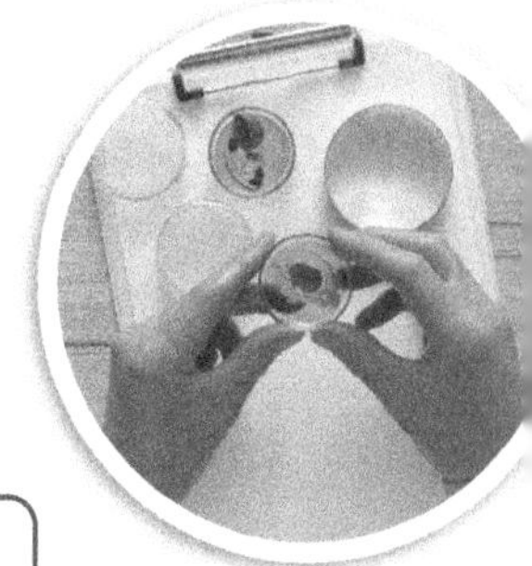

3 ★★ **Match the answers in the box with the questions in Exercise 2. Check your answers on the Internet if necessary. Then write sentences in the simple past passive.**

~~1928~~ 1971 1998 Athens Germany Giza London *Toy Story*

1 The first antibiotic was discovered in 1928.
2 ______
3 ______
4 ______
5 ______
6 ______
7 ______
8 ______

4 ★★★ **Read the text about Stonehenge. Rewrite the underlined phrases using the simple past passive.**

Who built Stonehenge and why [1]someone built it continues to be a great mystery. It is one of the most famous prehistoric monuments in the UK. [2]Someone started the building of Stonehenge about 5,000 years ago. Some people believe that [3]someone used Stonehenge in a celebration of the sun. [4]Someone designed it in exact mathematical detail, as the stone circle perfectly matches the direction of the midsummer sunrise and the midwinter sunset. There are two types of stone at Stonehenge. The larger stones are called "sarsens." The tallest sarsen stands nine meters high and weighs 25 tons – [5]someone carried the stones 32 kilometers to Stonehenge! The smaller "bluestones" weigh much less, but [6]someone brought these stones from Wales, a distance of 225 kilometers. Nobody knows how [7]someone transported such heavy stones so far in those days.

1 it was built
2 ______
3 ______
4 ______
5 ______
6 ______
7 ______

WRITING

A Review

1 ☆ **Look at the photo and read the review. Is everything about the smartwatch positive?**

____

1 If you're serious about your fitness training, you'll find this smartwatch very helpful. It counts the calories used in every activity you do. It also gives information on goals, such as distance and speed, and tells you your heart rate. You can connect it to your favorite fitness apps so that your performance can help improve your training.

2 This smartwatch is light and comfortable. The strap looks like silk, though it's actually made from soft rubber. It looks cool and modern, and it feels like silk on your skin, too, so you won't know you're wearing it! It's also waterproof, so you can walk straight into the shower after your workout. The battery life is very good: it lasts up to 20 hours and it recharges very quickly.

3 What I like about this smartwatch is that it's sporty and strong, but it's also really comfortable, so you can wear it all day. However, I should point out that it's not cheap. Overall, I think it's a really cool invention and I'm really happy I bought this model!

2 ☆☆ **Read the review again. In which paragraph (1–3) can you find …**

a a description of what the invention does? [1]
b what the reviewer likes the most? [ ]
c a physical description? [ ]
d the reviewer's general opinion? [ ]
e a disadvantage? [ ]
f who the invention is for? [ ]

3 ☆☆ **Put the words in the correct order to make the *Useful Language* phrases.**

1 made from / soft rubber / is / The strap
The strap is made from soft rubber.
2 it's a / really cool invention / Overall, / I think
____
3 it's sporty and strong / about this smartwatch / is that / What I like
____
4 it's not cheap / point out that / I should / However,
____
5 The strap / looks / silk / like
____

PLAN

4 ☆☆ **Write your own review. Choose an amazing digital device or gadget and take notes.**

Who the device or gadget is for: ______________________

What it does: ______________________

What it looks like: ______________________

The advantages: ______________________

One disadvantage: ______________________

Your opinion: ______________________

WRITE

5 ☆☆☆ **Write your review. Remember to include the parts of the review from Exercise 2, the passive, and phrases from the *Useful Language* box (see Student's Book, p77).**

CHECK

6 Do you …

- describe what the device/gadget does and who it's for?
- give a physical description?
- say what the advantages/disadvantages are?
- give your general opinion?

6 REVIEW

VOCABULARY

1 Match the beginnings of the sentences (1–8) with the ends (a–h).

1 If the fruit has pits in it, ☐
2 You should reduce the ☐
3 Don't dip your fingers into ☐
4 Palm oil boils ☐
5 Add the sugar to the water ☐
6 We waited for the liquid to freeze ☐
7 Carefully pour the liquid ☐
8 Pull the paper off the ☐

a temperature when the sauce gets too hot.
b at about 300°C.
c solid before we ate the ice pops.
d and stir both of them together.
e into the molds.
f remove them before you cook it.
g ice pops before the children eat them.
h very hot water – it's dangerous!

2 <u>Underline</u> and correct one mistake with materials and containers in each sentence.

1 The clothes and shoes were packed in cardboard jars. ________
2 It's better to use glass boxes for jam so you can recycle them. ________
3 We gave our mom a pretty silk tube for her birthday. ________
4 We don't know what is in this tin bag because there's no label. ________
5 Our teacher always carries our homework and exam papers in a leather can. ________
6 Hospitals have a lot of rubber cases for medical use. ________

GRAMMAR IN ACTION

3 Complete the conversation with the simple present passive form of the verbs in parentheses.

RYAN Do you know how much coffee [1] ________ (make) every year?
HARI I'm sure it's a lot. I know that loads of coffee [2] ________ (use) in my house!
RYAN Well, they estimate that over two billion cups of coffee [3] ________ (drink) worldwide every day.
HARI Wow! That is amazing! And where [4] ________ all that coffee ________ (grow)? South America?
RYAN Yes, well, most of the coffee that [5] ________ (buy) in the U.S.A. [6] ________ (produce) in Brazil.
HARI I guess the climate is just right there.
RYAN Yes, it's perfect because coffee [7] ________ (plant) in the wet season, but sunshine [8] ________ (need) later in the process. The coffee beans [9] ________ (dry) in the sun and [10] ________ (test) by experts.
HARI Hmm, how about a cup right now?
RYAN Good idea!

4 **Put the words in the correct order to make simple past passive questions. Then write answers using the words in parentheses.**

1 was / When / the / build / Taj Mahal / ? (around 1640)

____

____

2 open / was / this / When / middle school / ? (in 2010)

____

____

3 were / Where / these / make / computers / ? (in Japan)

____

____

4 cave paintings / were / those / Where / old / find / ? (in France)

____

____

5 was / Where / tea / grow / first / ? (in China)

____

____

6 write / was / When / *Macbeth* / ? (in 1606)

____

____

CUMULATIVE GRAMMAR

5 **Complete the text with the missing words. Circle the correct options.**

I [1]_____ an interesting article about important inventions the other day. [2]_____ that plastic shopping bags [3]_____ in the 1960s by a Swedish engineer? Before plastic was invented, shoppers [4]_____ paper bags. These were much better for the environment. Nowadays, governments [5]_____ to find ways to reduce the use of plastic bags. Ideas include "Bags for Life." These bags [6]_____ of cotton and are very strong, so shoppers can use them again and again. Supermarkets have also [7]_____ charging customers for their plastic bags. The article also said that scientists believe they [8]_____ a special bacteria that [9]_____ eat plastic. The bacteria was discovered in a Japanese recycling center in 2016. While the scientists [10]_____ the bacteria, they accidentally made it even better at eating plastic! At the moment, the bacteria can only eat the plastic in drink bottles, but in the future, it [11]_____ be able to eat all types of plastic! If scientists [12]_____ a super bacteria to eat all plastic, plastic bags would become a thing of the past!

1 a read b have read c did read
2 a Were you knowing b Did you knew c Did you know
3 a was invented b were invented c invented
4 a used to use b use to use c use to using
5 a try b tried c are trying
6 a are made b is made c made
7 a begin b begun c began
8 a invented b are invented c have invented
9 a can b can to c can will
10 a investigated b have investigated c were investigating
11 a might b can c may not
12 a would create b could create c might create

7 What do you celebrate?

1 a *fair* / *parade*

2 *an atmosphere* / *a stall*

VOCABULARY
Festivals

3 *a costume* / *decoration*

4 *a parade* / *float*

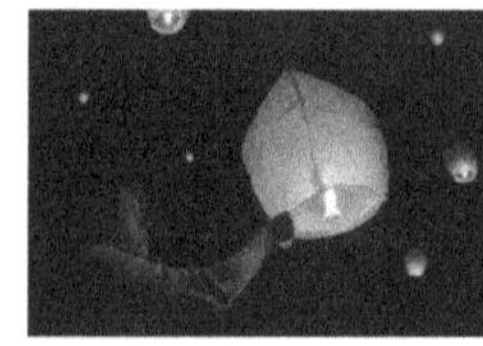
5 *a lantern* / *fireworks*

1 ☆ **Look at the photos and circle the correct options.**

2 ☆☆ **Complete the article with the correct form of words in Exercise 1.**

6 *decorations* / *a float*

7 *a program* / *fair*

8 *a parade* / *program*

9 *fireworks* / *a lantern*

Celebrations Around the World

One of the biggest festivals in Japan is the Gion Festival in Narita, a small town near Tokyo. It's a celebration of the summer. There are colorful [1] *decorations* all over the town, and people dress up in traditional Japanese [2] ________. Visitors can enjoy food and drinks at the many [3] ________ in Narita's narrow streets. The best part of the festival is when decorated [4] ________ with people on them are pulled through the streets to Narita's main temple. The streets of Narita are beautiful at night when they are lit up by [5] ________ on the sides of the buildings.

New Year's Eve is always special in Sydney, Australia. You can see a beautiful display of [6] ________ in the night sky, with thousands exploding over the Sydney Opera House. There are a lot of things to do during the day, too. Children can enjoy fantastic rides at the [7] ________, like a 40-meter Ferris wheel or a super-fast train. In the evening, people love the [8] ________ of boats traveling up and down the harbor with special lights on them!

3 ☆☆ **Circle the correct options.**

1 There was already *a crowd* / *an atmosphere* of 50,000 people at ten o'clock!
2 The band marched in the *ceremony* / *parade* down Main Street.
3 Great music and a lot of people usually make a good *program* / *atmosphere*.
4 A *fair* / *ceremony* is usually a formal event with a long history.

4 ☆☆ **Underline the stressed syllable in each word.**

Two Syllables	Three Syllables	Four Syllables
costume	atmosphere	ceremony
fireworks		decoration
lantern		
parade		

Explore It!

Guess the correct answer.

The famous Japanese ... ceremony began around 700 years ago.

a tea b coffee c milk

Find another interesting fact about an ancient ceremony. Write a question and send it to a classmate in an email, or ask them in the next class.

READING

A Folktale

1 **Look at the pictures. What do you think the folktale is about? Read the story and circle the correct answer.**

a a prince who lost his son
b a very brave dog
c a brave prince who killed a wolf

2 **Match the words in bold in the folktale with the meanings.**

1 very shocked horrified
2 a long piece of metal used for fighting ______
3 chasing and trying to catch and kill an animal ______
4 a place in the ground where a dead body is put ______
5 strong and not changing in your friendship with someone ______
6 put something into a hole in the ground and covered it ______

3 **Read the folktale again. Circle the correct answers.**

1 Why did the prince have dogs?
   a because he was lonely
   b to take care of his castle
   (c) to look for other animals
2 What did the prince think when he saw blood on his dog?
   a His son was hurt.
   b Something was missing.
   c The dog was hurt.
3 What did the dog do?
   a He killed the prince's son.
   b He killed a dangerous animal.
   c He hid behind a bed.
4 What happened at the end?
   a Everyone forgot about the dog.
   b The village was given the dog's name.
   c The prince found another dog.

The Wolf and a Baby Boy

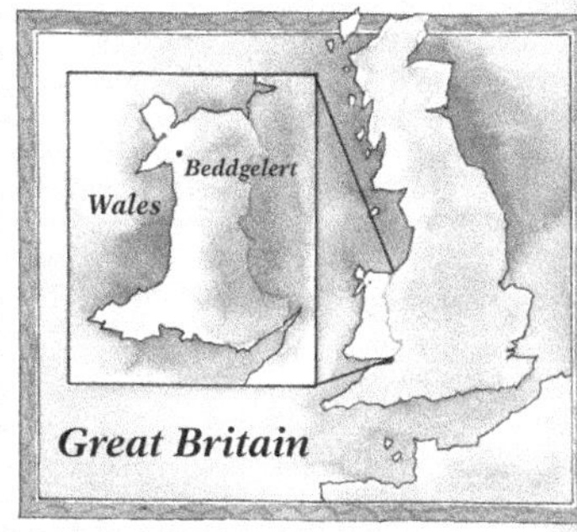

In the north of Wales, there is a small village named Beddgelert. According to an old story, many hundreds of years ago, a prince lived in the area. It was a place of forests and dangerous wild animals. The prince loved **hunting**, so he had many dogs. They spent a lot of time chasing animals through the forests for sport. His favorite dog was named Gelert – a **faithful** dog who the prince loved.

One day, the prince decided to go hunting and called for Gelert. To the prince's surprise, the dog came with blood around its mouth. The prince was **horrified**. Where had the blood come from? He had a terrible thought. He ran to his son's bedroom and saw an awful sight. His baby was missing and the floor was covered in blood. The prince realized what the dog had done. With anger, he took a **sword** and killed Gelert. Seconds later, the prince heard a cry from behind the bed. There was his son, completely safe. And next to his son was a wolf – killed by Gelert, just a few minutes earlier. The prince felt very sad. He carried his favorite dog outside and **buried** it under some stones.

Beddgelert means "Gelert's grave" in the Welsh language, and you can see stones marking the **grave** in the village. However, the story might not be true. Some people say that a hotel owner placed the stones there 200 years ago and, perhaps, invented the story to bring in more tourists. And it worked! Now there are many events in the town, from music festivals to fireworks displays on New Year's Eve. In the summer, people in the town grow lots of flowers as decorations, and Beddgelert has won competitions for being the most beautiful town in the country!

4 **Think of a folktale from your country. Write a paragraph about it in your notebook.**

GRAMMAR IN ACTION

Past Perfect

1 ★ **Match sentences 1–6 with a–f.**

1 I felt very tired. [f]
2 I couldn't go to the concert. [ ]
3 I already knew the story of the movie. [ ]
4 I said I was sorry for being late. [ ]
5 I got lost when I went to Quito. [ ]
6 I didn't know what time the concert started. [ ]

a I hadn't looked at the program.
b I hadn't bought any tickets.
c I had read the book.
d I hadn't finished my work on time.
e I hadn't been there before.
f I hadn't slept enough.

2 ★★ **Read the sentences. Circle the action that happened first, *A* or *B*.**

1 She went to see the fireworks because her friends had invited her.
   A She went to see the fireworks.
   (B) Her friends invited her.
2 When I saw the program, I knew I'd seen the show before.
   A I saw the program.
   B I saw the show.
3 They'd arranged to meet at the food stall, but Tom couldn't find Katy.
   A They arranged to meet.
   B Tom couldn't find Katy.
4 After he'd called his mom, he ordered a pizza.
   A He ordered a pizza.
   B He called his mom.
5 Megan felt a little upset after she'd said goodbye to them.
   A Megan said goodbye to them.
   B She felt a little upset.

3 ★★ **Complete the sentences with the past perfect form of the verbs in parentheses.**

1 I _hadn't bought_ (not buy) a costume, so I didn't have anything special to wear to the parade.
2 Talia __________ (not hear) of the festival before she went there.
3 He got to the concert 20 minutes after it __________ (start).
4 They went to Miami last year, and they were also there 30 years ago. It __________ (change) a lot.
5 We didn't want to see the new *Bond* movie because we __________ (not see) the previous one yet.
6 When I got home, I realized that I __________ (leave) my phone at school.

4 ★★ **Circle the correct options.**

PAULA [1](*Did you go*) / *Had you been* anywhere interesting for your vacation?

MARCO Well, I [2]*visited* / *had visited* my grandparents in northern Italy in September. They took me to a town named Marostica. I [3]*didn't go* / *hadn't been* there before.

PAULA Was it nice?

MARCO Yes, they have a chess festival there.

PAULA Chess festival? That doesn't sound very interesting!

MARCO But it was! My grandparents [4]*told* / *had told* me a lot about it before I [5]*went* / *had been*, and I'd thought the same as you. But there was a giant chess set in the middle of the town! And people were dressed in costumes as chess pieces, and they [6]*moved* / *had moved* around the board.

PAULA Oh, do they do that every year?

MARCO Every two years. It's to celebrate a famous chess match that two princes [7]*played* / *had played* about 600 years ago. They [8]*fell* / *had fallen* in love with the same woman, but instead of fighting, they decided to play chess!

VOCABULARY AND LISTENING

Music Festivals and Live Music

1 ☆ **Complete the lists with the words in the box. One word can go in more than one list.**

~~band member~~ campsite encore gig headliner stage supporting act tent track venue

1 where you can see a band: ______ ______ ______

2 where you can stay the night: ______ ______

3 singers or musicians: band member ______ ______ ______

4 ways to hear a song ______ ______ ______

2 ☆☆ **Complete the text with the correct form of words in Exercise 1.**

The [1] venue for the Coachella Festival is a polo club in California. Thousands of music fans go there to see their favorite bands. [2] ______ at Coachella have included some of the biggest names in music, like Radiohead and Beyoncé. There are also lots of interesting, less famous [3] ______ to see. These bands play on smaller [4] ______ in front of smaller crowds. Visitors to the festival can stay at a big [5] ______ with a lot of [6] ______. There's always a great atmosphere at Coachella, and the bands always leave the fans shouting for an [7] ______.

A Conversation

3 7.01 ☆ **Listen to the conversation. What is unusual about the Secret Solstice Festival?**

______

4 7.01 ☆☆ **Listen again. Are the sentences *T* (true) or *F* (false)?**

1 Antonio hasn't been to the Secret Solstice Festival. T

2 The weather isn't very cold at the festival. ______

3 Famous bands don't play at the festival. ______

4 One of the venues is in a dangerous place. ______

5 Antonio's brother didn't have a ticket for the volcano gig. ______

5 ☆☆ **Look at Exercise 6. What type of information (object, number, or place) is missing in 1–7? (See the *Learn to Learn* tip in the Student's Book, page 86).**

______

6 7.01 ☆☆☆ **Complete the summary about the Secret Solstice festival. Then listen again and check.**

The Secret Solstice is a festival. It takes place each year in [1] Iceland during the summer solstice. Antonio says the festival feels like a [2] ______ - hour day. When Antonio's brother went, there were about [3] ______ bands. One venue at the festival was inside a volcano. You needed to fly in a [4] ______ to get there and then go down [5] ______ meters to reach the venue. Only [6] ______ people could see the gig, and the tickets cost about [7] ______ dollars each.

GRAMMAR IN ACTION

Reported Statements

1 How do the tenses and verbs change in reported speech? Complete the table.

Direct Speech	Reported Speech
Simple Present	1 Simple Past
Simple Past	2
Present Perfect	3
Present Continuous	4
Will	5
Can	6

2 Complete the sentences with *said* or *told*.

1 My sister ___said___ she went to a really interesting music festival last year.

2 George ______ me that he had some new tracks for me to listen to.

3 I ______ everyone that I had a spare ticket for the concert.

4 Sally ______ that she couldn't go to the campsite because she didn't have a tent.

5 Laura ______ us to meet her in front of the stage.

6 I ______ I didn't know who the supporting act was.

3 Rewrite the reported speech as direct speech.

1 Ashraf said that he was in a café.
"I'm in a café. ______"

2 He told me that he was having lunch.
"______"

3 He said he wanted to meet me.
"______"

4 He said that he had been in the café for an hour.
"______"

5 He told me he would leave in about 30 minutes.
"______"

6 He told me to come quickly.
"______"

4 Read the conversation. Then complete the reported speech below.

ME Hi, Dan!

DAN Hi! I'm really happy to see you! I have some exciting news. I'm thinking of going to a festival in the summer. I want you to come with me.

ME Hmm, I'm not sure. Where is it? How much is it?

DAN It's not far away. It's in the country. The tickets are about $30. I've been there before. I had a great time.

ME OK, but where would we stay?

DAN Well, there's a campsite. We can stay in a tent. It won't be expensive.

ME OK, I'll think about it.

DAN Great!

I went to the café to meet Dan.
He said that he 1 ___was___ happy to see me and that he 2 ______ some exciting news. He told me that he 3 ______ of going to a festival in the summer, and then he told me that he 4 ______ me to go with him. I said that I 5 ______ sure, and I asked where the festival was and how much it was. Ashraf said that it 6 ______ far away, in the country, and the tickets 7 ______ about $30. He said that he 8 ______ there before and that he 9 ______ a great time. He also said that we 10 ______ in a tent, so it 11 ______ very expensive. I said that I 12 ______ about it.

5 Think of a conversation you had with someone recently. What did you talk about? Write at least five sentences using reported speech.

I was talking to Mom yesterday. She told me ...

WRITING

An Email to a Friend

1 ★ Read the email quickly. Circle the photo that matches it.

a 

b 

c 

Home Inbox Sent New

From: Karen | To: Matt

Hello Matt,

[1] I just got your message, thanks. [2] It was nice of you to write!

You said you wanted to know all about the festival. I'd never been to anything like it before, but it was great! I only spent a day there, but I saw so many amazing things. There were a lot of people dressed as characters from movies and TV. I'm attaching a photo of some people I met. They live near you! They told me to say hello to you! I think I was the only one not wearing a costume! I felt strange walking around in normal clothes!

In the afternoon, there was an event with some really famous actors from *Star Wars*. There were probably around 500 people in the audience, asking questions. Unfortunately, I didn't get the chance to ask anything. But one of the guests said that she had just filmed something really exciting for the next movie. Then she told us! I can't say anything – it's a spoiler!

OK, [3] I have to go now. [4] I hope to hear from you soon.

[5] I'll be in touch later,

Karen

2 ★★ Put a–e in the order they appear in the email (1–5).

- a ☐ request for a reply
- b ☐ goodbye
- c ☐ description of the festival
- d [1] greeting
- e ☐ thanks for writing

3 ★★ Match the underlined phrases in the email (1–5) with the *Useful Language* phrases (a–e).

- a Write back soon. [4]
- b Anyway, that's all from me. ☐
- c Bye for now. ☐
- d It was great to hear from you. ☐
- e Thanks for your email. ☐

PLAN

4 ★★ Write your own email about a festival you have been to. Take notes.

What kind of festival was it? ____________

What did people wear? ____________

What did people do? ____________

What did you see and do? ____________

How did you feel? ____________

5 Decide what information to include. Use the structure in Exercise 2 to help you.

WRITE

6 ★★★ Write your email. Remember to include the past perfect, reported speech, and phrases from the *Useful Language* box (see Student's Book, p89).

CHECK

7 Do you …

- have a greeting and a goodbye?
- describe the festival?
- request a reply?

7 REVIEW

VOCABULARY

1 Match the definitions with the words in the box.

costume decoration fair fireworks float lantern parade program stall

1 something you use to make things look more interesting or beautiful ______

2 a plan of all the activities and events at a festival ______

3 a big table on the street where people can buy things ______

4 a big decorated truck that moves through the streets at festivals ______

5 a light that people can hold or hang up in public places ______

6 the clothes you wear for a special activity ______

7 something that makes beautiful lights and noises in the night sky ______

8 a large number of people walking together, usually to celebrate something ______

9 a place with games and machines you can ride on ______

2 Complete the sentences with words for live music and festivals.

1 There were three b______ m______ in Clean Bandit: Grace Chatto, and Jack and Luke Patterson.

2 At the end of the concert, the audience shouted for more, and the band came back for an e______.

3 It was a terrible v______ for a concert. I couldn't see the stage because it was really far away.

4 I don't think this year's festival will be very good. The h______ is a band from the 1990s that no one has heard of.

5 We went to a small g______ last night – it was one of the best live events I've been to.

6 Did you know that there is a bonus t______ at the end of the album? Most people don't know about it.

7 Sometimes, the s______ a______ is better than the main performer.

8 The festival has a big c______ with space for nearly 500 tents.

GRAMMAR IN ACTION

3 Complete the sentences with the past perfect form of the verbs in the box.

be buy decorate hear not see sell

1 I didn't go to the festival because I ______ that it was going to rain.

2 I'm glad that we ______ the tickets early because they became really expensive later.

3 By the time the headliners appeared, the supporting acts ______ on stage for an hour.

4 My sister loved the concert. She ______ anything like it before.

5 When you checked the tickets online, ______ they ______ them all?

6 People ______ the street with lanterns and it looked beautiful.

4 What did Mike say? Change the direct speech into reported speech.

1 "I want to go home."
Mike said that ______________________.

2 "I don't feel well."
Mike said that ______________________.

3 "I've taken some medicine."
Mike said that ______________________.

4 "I'll take a taxi home."
Mike said that ______________________.

5 "I can't find a taxi number!"
Mike said that ______________________.

6 "I'll ask my mom to come get me."
Mike said that ______________________.

CUMULATIVE GRAMMAR

5 Complete the text with the missing words. Circle the correct options.

I live in a small town. It's nice, but nothing interesting ever [1]_____. So I was really surprised when my dad [2]_____ me that there would be a big celebration. He said that the bridge in the town [3]_____ 200 years old this summer, and there would be a huge party. At first, I said that I wasn't interested. I [4]_____ over that bridge thousands of times going to school and I [5]_____ see it during my summer vacation. But then my dad said, "If you [6]_____ to the festival, you'll have a great time." So I went. And it really was great! Everyone was dressed up in costumes, and they had a parade through the center of town. The whole town [7]_____ like a big history lesson! And in the evening, there [8]_____ a big fireworks display. Earlier that day, I [9]_____ that the bridge was really important in history. It [10]_____ by a famous architect. I [11]_____ it was just a boring bridge! It was a great day, but I still don't think there are [12]_____ in my town!

	a	b	c
1	happens	had happened	is happening
2	said	asked	told
3	is being	would be	should be
4	have been	had	was
5	not want	didn't want to	didn't wanted
6	come	will come	came
7	looks	looking	looked
8	was	were	had been
9	was learning	had learned	have learned
10	is built	built	was built
11	was thinking	used to think	don't think
12	festivals enough	too festivals	enough festivals

8 What is education?

VOCABULARY

School

1 ☆ **Circle the correct verbs to complete the phrases about school.**

1 *cheat* / *pay* on a test
2 *tell* / *fail* an exam
3 *get* / *pay* detention
4 *study* / *get* good grades
5 *pay* / *give* (somebody) a talk
6 *hand* / *pass* in homework
7 *cheat* / *pass* an exam
8 *pay* / *get* attention to the teacher
9 *study* / *take* for a test
10 *take* / *pay* an exam
11 *write* / *study* an essay

2 ☆ **Look at phrases 1–8 in Exercise 1. Write them in the correct column.**

Positive Things	Negative Things
______	cheat on a test
______	______
______	______
______	______

3 ☆☆ **Complete the sentences with the correct form of phrases in Exercise 1.**

1 I took an exam last week, but I'm not sure how well I did.
2 If you ______ for bad behavior, you won't be able to go to basketball practice after school!
3 He doesn't always ______ on his schoolwork – last week he got a D on an essay.
4 Tania was very pleased when she ______ all her ______ – she got As in history and science!
5 I can't go out tonight. I need to ______ on capital cities, and I haven't learned them all yet.
6 I ______ on ancient history – I got an F! I need to take it again.
7 Why did the teacher ______ you ______? What did you do to make him angry?
8 Please try to ______ on time, Sam! That's the second time you've given it to me late this week!
9 Someone ______ in Ms. Clarke's class. They used their phone to look up the answers!
10 Unless you ______ and listen to everything he says, you won't know how to do the project.

4 ☆☆☆ **Complete the sentences so they are true for you.**

1 If I saw someone cheating on a test, I would ______.
2 It's important for me to get good grades because ______.
3 The last time I failed an exam was ______.
4 One important exam I will take this year is ______.
5 I usually study for tests ______.

Explore It!

Guess the correct answer.

The highest school in the world is called Phumachangtang in the Himalayas.
The school is more than … meters above sea level.

a 4,000 b 5,000 c 6,000

Find an interesting fact about education in your country. Write a question and send it to a classmate in an email, or ask them in the next class.

Home News Articles Sign In Register

READING

A Report

1 ☆ What do you think is happening in the photo? Read the report and check your ideas.

SCHOOL'S OUT

More than a million people are homeschooled in the U.S.A. **Reasons** for homeschooling can include a child's special needs, **bullying**, or **a lack of** good school options in the area. We spoke to one "homeschooler," Andrew James, from Atlanta, Georgia, about his experiences of homeschooling.

"I started homeschooling three years ago – I'm 14 now. When I left elementary school, I went straight to homeschooling, so I've never been to middle school. My mom was also homeschooled, so she was **into** us having a similar education to hers. My parents believe that education is not just about getting good grades or taking exams – they think a **balanced** education, including practical skills, is also important.

My younger brother and I study at home with our parents for seven hours a day. Both our parents used to be teachers – so that helps! But having school at home doesn't mean there aren't any rules. We're not allowed to stay in bed all day, obviously, but we can also choose what we learn. Of course, we study normal subjects, but we also frequently go to libraries, museums, exhibitions, concerts, and sporting events as part of our education.

We can also do other things that maybe you can't do at an ordinary school. For example, each year my brother and I are allowed to plan a big trip to a place connected to something we are studying. My brother studies geology, so we went to Mount Vesuvius in Italy to learn about volcanoes. Next year, I want to go to Amsterdam to visit the house of Anne Frank because I'm learning about her famous **diary** in my history lessons.

It's not all vacations and day trips – we work really hard and study a lot! But I really love my home education. I wouldn't change it for anything!"

2 ☆☆ Match the words in bold in the report with the meanings.

1 having equal amounts of something *balanced*
2 a book with someone's thoughts and feelings ______
3 the causes of an event or situation ______
4 very interested in ______
5 not enough of something ______
6 when someone hurts or frightens someone else ______

3 ☆☆ Read the report again. Are the sentences *T* (true) or *F* (false)? Correct the false sentences.

1 Andrew has never attended an ordinary school.
F. He went to an ordinary elementary school.
2 Andrew started homeschooling because his mom didn't like his school.
______
3 His parents taught at schools before they homeschooled Andrew.
______
4 Andrew and his brother do some studying outside their home.
______
5 Their trips to other places are part of their education.
______
6 Andrew would like to go back to ordinary school in the future.
______

4 ☆☆☆ Think of two possible disadvantages of homeschooling.

______
______

GRAMMAR IN ACTION

Can/Can't

1 ★ **What do the sentences express? Write *permission*, *prohibition*, or *ability*.**

1 Marcus can't leave yet because he has detention. ____________

2 You got a very good grade on your essay. Can I read it? ____________

3 Sonia can play two instruments, and she's a great singer, too. ____________

2 ★ **(Circle) the correct options.**

1 In my school, we (*can*) / *can't* learn Latin if we want.

2 My sister *can* / *can't* speak Italian, but she speaks German well.

3 Mrs. Evans says I *can* / *can't* leave until I've finished this exercise.

4 *Can* / *Can't* I borrow your dictionary, please?

5 We *can* / *can't* understand you when you speak clearly.

6 You *can* / *can't* stay in bed all day. It's bad for you.

To Be Allowed To

3 ★★ **Put the words in the correct order to make sentences. Then mark (✓) the sentences that are true for your school.**

1 school / at / wear / allowed / Students / aren't / jewelery / to ☐

Students aren't allowed to wear jewelery at school.

2 lunchtime / allowed / phones / We / at / use / to / are / our ☐

____

3 break time / soccer / play / Students / at / are / allowed / to ☐

____

4 shout / allowed / aren't / the / You / teachers / to / at ☐

____

4 ★★ **Write questions and short answers with the correct form of *to be allowed to*.**

1 you / cycle to school? (yes)

Are you allowed to cycle to school? Yes, I am.

2 your teachers / give detention? (yes)

____

3 students / wear any clothes they like? (no)

____

4 students / talk during exams? (no)

____

5 your best friend / sit next to you? (yes)

____

6 your parents / help with homework? (no)

____

5 ★★ **Complete the text with the missing words. (Circle) the correct options.**

I think it's hard to be the youngest in the family. My big sister [1] ______ to go to bed when she wants, but I [2] ______. On Fridays and Saturdays, I [3] ______ stay up later, but not as late as my sister. And my big brothers [4] ______ watch late shows on TV! But they [5] ______ to leave the house without helping our parents. They [6] ______ go to college by car, but I [7] ______ drive yet, so I cycle to school. All the people in my family [8] ______ give me a talk because I'm the youngest – it's so unfair!

	a	b	c
1	(a) is allowed	b are allowed	c can
2	a can	b 'm not	c isn't
3	a can't	b can	c 'm not allowed to
4	a can to	b is allowed to	c are allowed to
5	a aren't allowed	b can't	c not allowed
6	a can	b can't	c aren't allowed to
7	a 'm allowed to	b can	c can't
8	a are allowed to	b is allowed to	c aren't allowed to

VOCABULARY AND LISTENING

A Phone Call

1 ☆ **You will hear an exchange student in the Netherlands talking about what she likes about the country. Write two questions you'd like to ask.**

____

____

8.01 **2** ☆☆ **Listen to the phone call. Does it answer any of your questions in Exercise 1?**

____

8.01 **3** ☆☆ **Listen again and answer the questions.**

1 What is the subject of the phone call?
studying and living in another country

2 How long will Julia be in the Netherlands?
____

3 What's her favorite thing about life in the Netherlands?
____

4 Why are drivers from the Netherlands usually polite, according to Julia?
____

5 How did Julia travel to school this morning?
____

6 Which country does Julia compare with the Netherlands?
____

Attitude and Behavior

4 ☆ **Complete the words with the correct vowels (*a*, *e*, *i*, *o*, *u*).**

1 r*u*d*e*
2 c_r_f_l
3 _mm_t_r_
4 p_l_t_
5 m_t_r_
6 c_r_l_ss
7 _rg_n_z_d
8 d_s_b_d__nt
9 d_s_rg_n_z_d
10 w_ll-b_h_v_d

5 ☆☆ **Complete the sentences with the words in Exercise 4.**

1 Rohan is a very *well-behaved* student: the teachers never need to give him a talk.
2 Patricia is a very ________ child. She never says "please"!
3 Our teacher likes us to be ________ and keep our desks clean and neat.
4 Please be ________ when you cycle in the rain.
5 Don't be ________ – you should check your homework for mistakes before you hand it in.
6 Our parents teach us to be ________ and thank visitors for coming to the house.
7 Bella's pens and pencils are all over the floor. She's so ________ with her things!
8 My little cousin is very ________! My aunt's always giving him a talk, but he never listens.
9 Molly is nearly 16, but sometimes she is very ________ – like a little girl.
10 Paul is younger than his sister Molly, but he's much more ________ and sensible.

6 ☆☆ **Match sentences 1–5 with a–e.**

1 Jorge is so careless. [*c*]
2 He's usually very mature. [ ]
3 Jon's a disobedient boy at home. [ ]
4 Try to be more polite. [ ]
5 Miguel isn't disorganized. [ ]

a He hardly ever does anything that is immature.
b It's so rude not to say "thank you."
c He should try to be more careful.
d His schoolwork is always neat and organized.
e But he's well-behaved at school.

GRAMMAR IN ACTION

To Have To, Must, and To Need To

1 ☆ **Circle the correct options.**

1 You (need to) / *don't have to* / *must not* study for exams.
2 He *must* / *doesn't need to* / *doesn't have to* be better-behaved in class – he's very disobedient!
3 Students *don't have to* / *don't need to* / *must not* wear makeup. It's not allowed.
4 We *don't need to* / *have to* / *must not* ask if we don't understand the questions.
5 You *don't have to* / *must* / *have to* finish the essay right now. It's for next week.

2 ☆☆ **Put the words in the correct order to make the Exam FAQs.**

Home | News | FAQs | Sign In | Register

Exam FAQs

1 need / we / to / an optional question / answer / Do / ?
Do we need to answer an optional question?
2 have / we / Do / to / a pen / use / ?
____
3 do / What / first / need / to / we / do / ?
____
4 if / we / What / have / do / to / do / not sure / we're / ?
____
5 do / need / What / to / we / do / before / finish / we / ?
____
6 have / we / to / Do / the exam room / stay / in / ?
____

4 ☆☆ **Are the sentences about the school notices *T* (true) or *F* (false)? Correct the false sentences with (*don't*) *have to* or *must*(*not*). Sometimes there is more than one possible answer.**

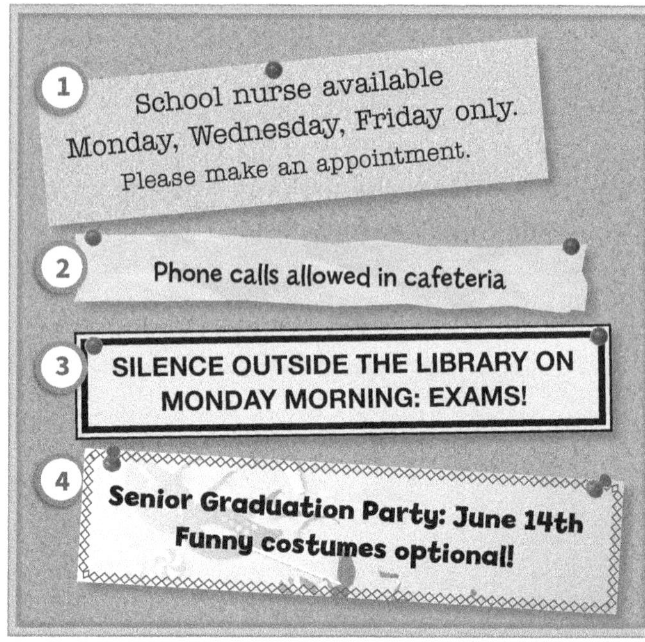

1 You don't have to make an appointment to see the nurse.
F. You have to / must make an appointment to see the nurse.
2 Students don't have to turn off their phones in the cafeteria.
____
3 You must not make noise outside the library on Monday morning.
____
4 Students must wear a funny costume to the graduation party.
____

3 ☆☆ **Complete the sentences with the phrases in the box. Then match the answers (a–f) with the FAQs (1–6) in Exercise 2.**

don't have to stay	don't need to answer	have to use	have to write	~~need to check~~	need to read

a You *need to check* all your answers before you finish. ☐
b You ________ in the room, but please leave quietly. ☐
c You ________ all the questions carefully before you answer. ☐
d If a question is optional, you ________ it. ☐
e Yes, you ________ a black pen. ☐
f You ________ something, so if you're not sure about an answer, don't leave it blank – guess! ☐

WRITING

An Essay

1 ☆ **Make a list of the advantages and disadvantages of digital technology in school education. Then read the essay. Does it have your ideas?**

____

____

Should We Reduce Digital Technology in the Classroom?

1 Most of us find it difficult to imagine schools without laptops or tablets, but some people believe that using electronic devices in class too much can be a bad thing. [1]essay, / In / outline / I / this some of the advantages and disadvantages of technology and give my own opinion.

2 [2]hand, / the / On / one using digital technology in the classroom can be more exciting than learning from books. Technology can also encourage more students to take part in group work through online activities. It is also believed that using technology can help students remember what they learn.

3 [3]other / On / the / hand, technology may cause students to stop paying attention in class. [4]that / Some / say technology is also bad for social skills, as students might speak to each other less during class. [5]argue / that / Others technology can make cheating easier for students – both in classwork and homework.

4 In my opinion, there are more important advantages than disadvantages, but there should be a balance between technology and traditional classroom work. Computers can never take the place of the teacher!

2 ☆ **Match the parts of the essay (a–d) with the correct paragraphs (1–4).**

a a conclusion with the writer's opinion 4

b bad things about digital technology ___

c an introduction to the topic ___

d good things about digital technology ___

3 ☆☆ **Put the underlined words in the essay in the correct order to make the *Useful Language* phrases.**

1 In this essay, I outline

2 _______________

3 _______________

4 _______________

5 _______________

PLAN

4 ☆☆ **Write your own essay. Look at the title and think of two good things and two bad things about weekend homework. Take notes.**

Is weekend homework a good or bad thing?

Good Things: _______________

Bad Things: _______________

5 **Decide what to include in each paragraph. Use the information in Exercise 2 to help you.**

WRITE

6 ☆☆☆ **Write your essay. Remember to include four paragraphs, *can/can't*, *to be allowed to*, *to have to*, *must*, *to need to*, and the phrases from the *Useful Language* box (see Student's Book, p101).**

CHECK

7 **Do you …**

- have an introduction and conclusion?
- write about good things and bad things?

8 REVIEW

VOCABULARY

1 Match the beginnings of the sentences (1–6) with the ends (a–f).

1 The teacher will give you a talk if ☐
2 If you study hard for a test, ☐
3 It's always wrong ☐
4 If students don't pay attention, ☐
5 We usually have to write an essay ☐
6 If you study hard, you won't fail ☐

a when we take an English exam.
b the exam – you'll pass it.
c they won't know what to do.
d you'll get a good grade.
e to cheat on a test.
f you don't hand in homework on time.

2 Circle the correct words.

1 Jonty is very *well-behaved* / *disobedient*: he never gets detention.
2 It's *polite* / *rude* to talk when your teacher's talking.
3 I'm so *organized* / *disorganized* that I can never find anything.
4 She's only ten, but she's really *mature* / *immature* for her age.
5 *Careful* / *Careless* work doesn't usually get good grades.
6 You're so *well-behaved* / *disobedient*. You never do anything I tell you!
7 *Immature* / *Mature* people behave like someone a lot younger.
8 Be *careless* / *careful* with Ahmet – he's very sensitive!
9 He's very *rude* / *polite*: he always says "please" and "thank you."
10 Very *organized* / *disorganized* people plan everything they do.

GRAMMAR IN ACTION

3 Complete the sentences with *can*, *can't*, or the correct form of *to be allowed*.

1 In some countries, girls ______________ go to school because their parents need their help.
2 Boys in that school ______________ to wear long pants. They all wear shorts.
3 We ______________ to have smartphones in the exam room. That's cheating.
4 You ______________ use the library after lunch but not in the morning.
5 If you're late for an exam, you ______________ to take it – you have to do it another day.
6 Your parents ______________ help you because they don't know Latin.

4 Complete the sentences with the words in the box.

have to wear	have to worry	must run	must not run	need to come	need to meet

1 You really __________. The test starts soon.

2 We don't __________ school uniforms on the weekend.

3 Sally doesn't __________. She's studied hard for the test.

4 My parents __________ my teacher after school.

5 We __________ in the hallways. It's dangerous.

6 Do I __________ with you, or can you go alone?

CUMULATIVE GRAMMAR

5 Complete the text with the missing words. Circle the correct options.

HOME ABOUT ME ARCHIVE FOLLOW

Hello! In this week's blog I [1]_____ at exam preparation. Now, if you usually [2]_____ my blog, you'll know that I hate exams. I just [3]_____ do them! If I [4]_____ make exams disappear, I would do it! Anyway, I [5]_____ this subject a lot since my last post, and I think one important thing is planning: you [6]_____ start studying hard before your exams. You [7]_____ start months before, but at least a [8]_____ weeks. You [9]_____ also study at school as well as at home. Find a quiet place, like the library, so you [10]_____ concentrate. Little and often is the best way to study; an hour a day is great. Also, do exercise between study sessions – this helps you relax. I [11]_____ for a run in my local park. Finally, get a good night's sleep before the exam! For my last exam, I [12]_____ well the night before and I got a really bad grade. OK, that's all for now. More tips next week!

1 a look b 'm looking c had looked
2 a read b will read c have read
3 a can b can't to c can't
4 a could b can c would
5 a 'm studying b 've studied c 'd studied
6 a must b don't have to c must to
7 a have to b haven't to c don't have to
8 a few b little c enough
9 a shouldn't b should c should to
10 a need to b have to c 'll be able to
11 a 'm going often b go often c often go
12 a hadn't slept b haven't slept c wasn't sleeping

9 Where would you go?

VOCABULARY

Travel

1 ☆☆ **Complete the puzzle. Use the clues.**

1 the place someone is traveling to
2 in or to a different country from yours
3 a family place with hotels, pools, and restaurants
4 when you travel somewhere and go back home in a short time
5 a large boat that you can go on vacation on (two words)
6 when you visit a place and look around it, often with a group of people
7 when you travel from one place to another, usually a long distance
8 a place to stay on vacation, e.g., a hotel, RV, or youth hostel
9 traveling with a large bag, usually visiting many places
10 visiting famous or interesting places on vacation
11 reserve a hotel room or a seat on a plane.

2 ☆☆ **What are the hidden words in gray in the puzzle in Exercise 1?**

3 ☆☆ **Complete the text with the correct form of words in Exercise 1. Sometimes more than one answer is possible.**

HOME DESTINATIONS FAQS

If you enjoy going [1] *abroad* and visiting exotic places, then Indonesia is one of the world's most interesting [2] ______. You can fly directly to the capital, Jakarta. Flights can be expensive, so it's best to [3] ______ early. You can also arrive by [4] ______, but this is a much longer [5] ______ by sea through Singapore or Australia. Jakarta is a lively city, and it's just a short [6] ______ by plane to the ancient city of Yogyakarta, where you can go [7] ______ and enjoy old buildings, temples, and even an active volcano. Many tourists go to the island of Bali, which offers many types of [8] ______, from expensive hotels to cheap hostels. You can, of course, stay in a large [9] ______, some with their own restaurants and private beaches. Finally, if you have a lot of time, Indonesia is a popular place to go [10] ______: you could spend months traveling around the country, enjoying the local food and culture.

Explore It!

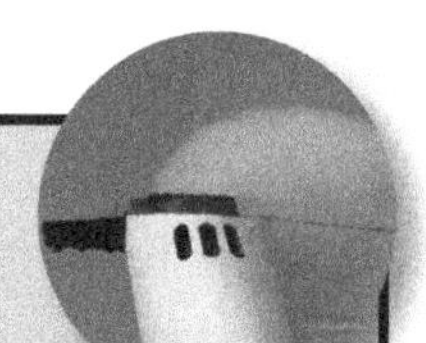

Guess the correct answer.

A cruise ship creates the same amount of pollution in one day as … cars.

a 5,000 b 20,000 c 1 million

Find another interesting fact about tourism and the environment. Write a question and send it to a classmate in an email, or ask them in the next class.

READING

A Magazine Interview

1 Look at the photos of drones. Then read the interview and circle the best title.

a The Dangers of Drones

b Why Drones Will Never Solve Transportation Problems

c How Drones Will Change the Way We Travel

2 Match the words in bold with the definitions.

1 staying away from someone or something avoiding

2 taking things like food or books to someone's house ______

3 working quickly and in an organized way ______

4 arrive on the ground after moving down through the air ______

5 not having a driver ______

6 big vehicles used to transport things ______

3 Read the interview again. Complete it with the missing questions.

Isn't this going to create a lot of problems?

Won't this make people lazy?

What other changes will there be?

~~How will we be traveling in the future?~~

What are the advantages?

4 Read the interview again. Answer the questions.

1 How will companies save money with new technology?

They will use driverless trucks.

2 Where might we see flying taxis soon?

______

3 What might be the biggest danger for flying taxis?

______

4 What three things make flying taxis better than normal taxis?

______

______

5 How will drones help people in danger?

______

Computer scientist Jeremy May answers our questions about the future of transportation.

1 How will we be traveling in the future?

I think **driverless** taxis will become common. Not only that, but companies will soon be using **trucks** that don't have a driver. This will save companies a lot of money. Some companies have developed a kind of flying taxi, too. It works like a helicopter, but it doesn't need a pilot – it's actually a drone. It's possible that some cities, like Dubai, will have a lot of flying taxis in the near future.

2 ______

Well, some people are worried that driverless taxis aren't safe. Flying taxis have to be even safer, of course. The skies are already full, so one challenge will be **avoiding** objects, like other drones, buildings, and birds. But most of us won't need to worry. It's likely that only the very rich will be able to travel by flying taxi – in the beginning anyway.

3 ______

First, these taxis will use electricity, so they will be more environmentally friendly. Second, they will be able to travel up to 180 kilometers per hour. This, plus the fact that they will be able to take off and **land** anywhere, means that they will be much more **efficient** than normal taxis.

4 ______

Companies will soon start **delivering** things by drone. In Dubai, a company tested a service for people who wanted a coffee but didn't want to travel to a café. The people just ordered online and got their coffee in a few minutes!

5 ______

It might! But the technology has a more serious use. We will be using drones to quickly send medicine or food to difficult-to-reach places like mountains and islands. This will be very useful in emergencies.

GRAMMAR IN ACTION

To Be Going To and Present Continuous for Future

1 ☆ **Complete the sentences with the phrases in the box. Then write *A* for the arrangements and *P* for the predictions.**

aren't going to find	is going to make	~~'m going to~~	're traveling	's leaving

1 Next week, I *'m going to* Spain on vacation. *A*
2 He ________ for the airport in an hour by taxi. ___
3 Technology ________ travel more environmentally friendly. ___
4 We ________ to Bali by plane, not cruise ship. ___
5 They ________ a way to travel that is 100 percent safe. ___

2 ☆☆ **Decide if the sentences are *A* (arrangements) or *P* (predictions). Then complete them with the best form of the verb in parentheses.**

1 I *'m meeting* (meet) Ed at four o'clock today. ___
2 She ________ (not enjoy) the cruise – she hates boats. ___
3 We ________ (go) camping in July. ___
4 They ________ (like) Madagascar next summer. The wildlife there is incredible! ___
5 Todd and Laura ________ (have) lunch at the airport tomorrow before their flight. ___

Future Continuous

3 ☆☆ **Put the words in order to make sentences in the future continuous. Then mark (✓) the sentences you agree with.**

1 abroad / in / I / 20 / living / be / years / will
I will be living abroad in 20 years. ☐
2 will / by 2035 / be / traveling / by flying taxi / Everyone
________ ☐
3 doing / all / Robots / jobs / in / will / be / ten years
________ ☐
4 50 years / living / other / won't / We / be / planets / on / in
________ ☐
5 using / won't / be / 15 years / gas / We / in / cars / in
________ ☐

4 ☆☆ **Circle the best options. For one answer, both options are possible.**

I read the other day that we [1]*are living* / *will be living* on Mars in the next 30 years. Well, you and I [2]*aren't going to live* / *aren't living* on Mars – they [3]*are only sending* / *are only going to send* their top astronauts in the near future! Normal people [4]*aren't living* / *won't be living* there for a long time. The famous scientist Professor Stephen Hawking said that we [5]*are going to need* / *are needing* to find a new planet in 100 years because we [6]*are having* / *are going to have* more problems with climate change and other things in the future. I [7]*'m giving* / *'m going to give* a presentation on space travel next week at school, so I've done some research! Hawking had previously said that in 1,000 years, people [8]*aren't living* / *won't be living* on the Earth at all. I'm not sure I agree – a lot of things can happen in 1,000 years!

5 ☆☆☆ **Write three predictions in the future continuous. Use the ideas in the box or your own ideas.**

communication	houses	music	relationships	work

By 2050, people won't be communicating face-to-face anymore.
____
____
____
____

VOCABULARY AND LISTENING

Travel Phrasal Verbs

1 ★ Complete the phrasal verbs in the sentences. Use the words in the box.

around	away (x2)	back	in	off (x2)	out

1 After we've checked __in__ to our hotel, I want to rest and then have some lunch.
2 We didn't go ________ this summer. We stayed at home for our vacation.
3 I always feel nervous when the plane is taking ________.
4 We have to check ________ of the hotel early – at nine o'clock – but we can leave our bags.
5 Out plane is at 2 p.m., so we need to set ________ for the airport at around 11 a.m.
6 I went to Guadalajara for a short business trip, but I didn't have time to look ________ the city.
7 It's nice to get ________ on vacation once a year and see a new place.
8 Our train was delayed, so we didn't get ________ home until late at night.
9 What time is your plane expected to get ________?

2 ★★ Complete the email with the correct form of phrasal verbs in Exercise 1.

Home Inbox Sent **New**

From: Marco To: Carmen

Hello Carmen,

I hope you're well! I'm really looking forward to your visit. What time does your plane [1] __get in__ on Tuesday? Let me know, and I'll [2] ________ early enough for the airport and pick you up. You won't need to take a taxi. I expect you'll be tired when you arrive, so I'll just let you [3] ________ to your hotel, and you can relax. You said you wanted to [4] ________ the city with my parents and me and maybe try some good local restaurants. Unfortunately, my parents are [5] ________ on business tomorrow. They won't be here when you arrive on Tuesday, but they're going to [6] ________ the day after. So why don't we all go to a nice restaurant later in the week?

Talk to you soon,

Marco

Conversations

3 ★ You will hear two people planning a vacation. Look at the map and answer the questions.

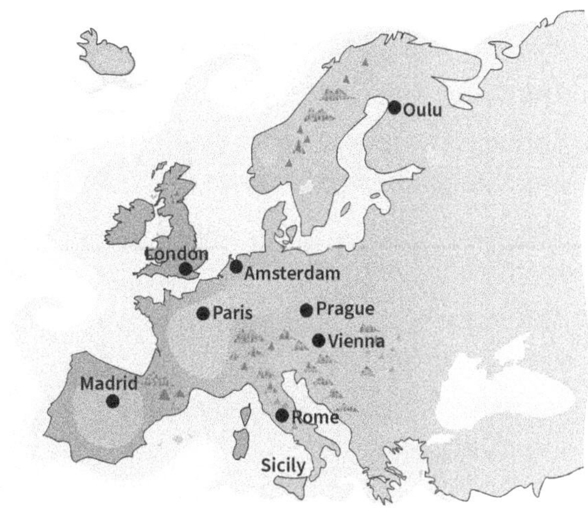

1 Which part of the world are they going to visit?

____

2 What's the best way to travel around and see all these places?

____

3 How much time do you think you would need?

____

9.01 4 ★ Listen to the conversation and check your answers to Exercise 3. Do Emma and Mason have the same ideas as you for questions 2 and 3?

____

9.01 5 ★★ Listen again. Are the sentences *T* (true) or *F* (false)?

1 Emma and Mason can travel anywhere in Europe with their train tickets. __T__
2 Mason wants to go to the beach first. ___
3 Emma would like to visit museums. ___
4 Mason doesn't want to go to Finland because it's cold. ___
5 Mason would like to visit some European capitals. ___
6 Emma doesn't want to go to large cities. ___

GRAMMAR IN ACTION

Relative Pronouns and Relative Clauses

1 ☆ Complete the sentences with relative pronouns.

1 The town _where_ we went on vacation last year was very cheap.

2 The plane _____ I took was two hours late.

3 Spring is the time of year _____ you can see beautiful pink trees in Japan.

4 The reason _____ I want to go to Peru is to try the food.

5 The woman _____ suitcase was damaged was very upset.

6 New York is a good place for people _____ like sightseeing.

2 ☆☆ Correct one mistake in each sentence.

1 I remember the time where we went to London to see the Houses of Parliament.
I remember the time when we went to London to see the Houses of Parliament.

2 This is the resort I will be staying.
_____

3 Is that the girl who bag got lost?
_____

4 I lost the camera I brought it with me.
_____

5 I have an app on my phone what tells me about all the best tourist attractions.
_____

6 Mark is the person who I'm going to visit him in London.
_____

3 ☆☆ Complete the text with the clauses in the box and the correct relative pronouns.

brings you	has traveled to lots of countries	I can see	I got a package in the mail	~~I want to visit Japan~~	opinion I trust

The reason [1] _why I want to visit Japan_ is my brother Jonathan. He's someone [2] _____, including the U.S.A. and Australia, but he always says that Japan is his favorite place. He was working there when I was really young, and he often used to send me presents. I loved the moment [3] _____, and there was something inside, like a cool toy, food, or a *maneki-neko* (this is like a little cat [4] _____ good luck). So, Jonathan is the person [5] _____ the most about traveling to different countries – I always ask him for advice. I hope I can visit Tokyo one day and also other smaller towns [6] _____ traditional Japanese life.

4 ☆☆☆ Join the sentences using a relative pronoun.

1 These are the people. I met them on vacation.
These are the people who I met on vacation.

2 France is the country. It has more tourists than any other country.
_____

3 The departures lounge is a place in an airport. You wait for your plane there.
_____

4 Drones are a new invention. They might replace normal taxis.
_____

5 Norway is the place. I will be traveling there next summer.
_____

6 Check-out is the time. We need to leave the hotel.
_____

7 Linda is the person. Her brother is a pilot.
_____

WRITING

An Email to a Host Family

1 **Read the email quickly. Mark (✓) the information that Bedour wants to find out.**

1 where Boston is ☐
2 what she will study in the course ☐
3 where she can find a place to stay ☐
4 when the course starts ☐
5 when the course finishes ☐
6 how to travel to Boston ☐

2 **Put a–e in the order they appear in Bedour's email (1–5).**

a ☐ goodbye
b ☐ questions about the trip
c [1] greeting
d ☐ reason for writing
e ☐ thanks

3 **Complete the email with the *Useful Language* phrases.**

a Best wishes
b ~~Dear~~
c Do you know
d I'm writing to
e thank you very much for

Home Inbox Sent **New**

From: bedour2004@mymail.com

Subject: Summer Course

[1] *Dear* Mr. Hamilton,

I hope you're well. [2] ________ check some details about my visit to Boston this summer. I'm looking forward to starting the course, and I hope I'm going to really improve my English!

As you may know, this is going to be my first time in the U.S.A. Is it possible to ask some questions? I received your welcome pack that gives information about accommodations. Unfortunately, the places that were listed all look a long way from the center of Boston. [3] ________ if I could find somewhere closer? I'd prefer not to spend too much time traveling each day.

I'd also like to ask about the exact dates of the course. I know the course will be starting on June 25, but do I have to arrive earlier? Could you also tell me when the course ends, exactly? I'm asking because it's important for me to book my flights.

Finally, [4] ________ accepting me into this course. My family is so happy for me!

[5] ________,

Bedour

PLAN

4 **Write your own email to a school abroad. First, decide what you are going to study and where. Write questions to ask your course organizer about these things.**

Your Travel Plans and When You Arrive:

____

____

Your Accommodation:

____

____

Your Course Content and Timetable:

____

____

5 **Decide what information to include. Use the information in Exercise 2 to help you.**

WRITE

6 **Write your email. Remember to include *to be going to*, the present continuous, the future continuous, and phrases from the *Useful Language* box (see Student's Book, p113).**

CHECK

7 **Do you ...**

- use a greeting at the beginning and say goodbye at the end?
- say why you are writing?
- say thank you?

9 REVIEW

VOCABULARY

1 Match the beginnings of the sentences (1–8) with the ends (a–h).

1 We arrived at our final ☐
2 I didn't stay in my own country for my last vacation; I went ☐
3 People like to visit the old market in my city – it's a popular ☐
4 I stayed in a big ☐
5 We went on several day ☐
6 I went online and ☐
7 If I had a lot of time, I'd like to ☐
8 Hotels, hostels, or villas: any ☐

a trips to local towns.
b abroad.
c accommodation is OK for me.
d resort, and my room looked out over the beach.
e destination on time.
f go backpacking across the country.
g tourist attraction.
h booked tickets for my trip next week.

2 Underline and correct six travel phrasal verbs in the sentences. Mark (✓) the correct sentences.

1 You need to check on at the airport two hours before your flight. ______
2 Please check in of the hotel right after breakfast, no later. ______
3 My plane gets in at five o'clock in the morning. I'm going to be so tired! ______
4 We're going out on vacation next week. Can you take care of our cat? ______
5 My dad is on a business trip right now, but he'll get away tonight. ______
6 I looked on the city, but everything was closed. ______
7 After the plane took out, I had an amazing view from the window. ______
8 What time are you setting off for the airport tomorrow morning? ______

GRAMMAR IN ACTION

3 Complete the sentences with the correct form of the verbs in the box. Use the tense in parentheses.

have	live	meet	not learn	study	visit

1 Next week, I ______ lunch with my grandparents. (present continuous)
2 This time next year, I hope I ______ science at college. (future continuous)
3 Some people think that we ______ on other planets in the future. (future continuous)
4 We ______ a lot of interesting places on vacation, I'm sure. (*to be going to*)
5 My host family ______ me at the airport at six o'clock. (present continuous)
6 Emma ______ much Spanish; she's only staying in Madrid for two weeks. (*to be going to*)

4 Write sentences using the correct relative pronoun from the options in parentheses.

1 The person was sitting near me on the plane is a famous actor! (who / whose)

____

2 I stayed at a resort is one of the best in the country. (why / that)

____

3 That's the passenger father is the pilot. (who / whose)

____

4 Cambodia is a country you can visit a lot of interesting old cities. (where / that)

____

5 The main reason I want to visit Italy is all the great food. (which / why)

____

6 June and July is a time there is a lot of rain in Japan. (when / where)

____

CUMULATIVE GRAMMAR

5 Complete the text with the missing words. Circle the correct options.

Usually, it only takes about 12 hours to fly from the UK to Thailand. That's not [1] ______, but so far it's been 32 hours [2] ______ I left home! I had set off for the airport early. I wanted to relax after checking in. After I [3] ______ in, the first thing I saw on the screens was that my flight [4] ______! At first, it was only two hours, then four, then eight! I [5] ______ that there were problems with the airplane. It [6] ______ in London yet. It was still in Moscow – about five hours away! The airline told me I [7] ______ stay in a hotel near the airport and they would pay for it. At 3 a.m., I [8] ______ a phone call saying that my plane had arrived, and that [9] ______ I went immediately to the airport, I would miss the flight! I got on the plane, and many hours later it landed at a new destination – Dhaka, the capital of Bangladesh! My plane needed [10] ______ some other passengers. I'm still in Dhaka now! [11] ______ here for four hours so far! I [12] ______ think that traveling was fun, but now I'm not so sure!

1 a long enough b enough long c too long
2 a since b for c from
3 a have checked b check c had checked
4 a was delayed b delayed c is delayed
5 a was told b was said c told
6 a hasn't arrived b didn't arrive c hadn't arrived
7 a can b could c would
8 a get b got c was getting
9 a if b when c unless
10 a to pick up b picking up c pick up
11 a I was b I've been c I'd been
12 a used to b use to c did use to

EXAM TIPS: Reading Skills

Reading: Multiple Matching

You will read short descriptions of five people and match them with the best options. The options typically give information about places, services, entertainment, restaurants, etc.

There are eight options for five people, so there will be three extra. These extra options usually fit only partially.

Exam Guide: Multiple Matching

- To do this task, you should first read through the short description of each person. You should then decide what the most important information about each one is and underline it.
- Before reading through the options, think about what sort of thing you would recommend for each person. For example, if they like eating fish, you might recommend a restaurant that specializes in fish dishes.
- Then read through each option and underline the important information.
- Always double-check and read the information carefully. Are there any traps? For example, a young man might be looking for a summer job on an organic farm and one of the options offers this. But beware! The young man also says he wants to improve his **French** and the job is in **Spain**, so it is not the perfect match.
- Be careful not to "word spot." If the same word is in the description and in one of the options, it might be a trap and not a match.

REMEMBER!

Make sure the text you choose matches all the requirements in the person's description.

Reading Practice: Multiple Matching

1 Read the text and match the words in bold with the words in the box.

accommodation easygoing famous secretary
said we were sorry said we would star talk show

Tip! The descriptions and the texts often have the same information, but they are written using different words.

I can really recommend the vacation [1]**apartment** in Pocos, where we spent two weeks. The owner is a TV [2]**celebrity** who has a popular late-night [3]**chat show** and is very [4]**well-known** in Brazil. We didn't meet her, but her [5]**assistant** was waiting for us when we arrived. We [6]**apologized** for being so late, but he was very friendly and [7]**not at all difficult**. We [8]**promised to** write a good review when we left!

1 ______ 4 ______ 7 ______
2 ______ 5 ______ 8 ______
3 ______ 6 ______

2 **Look at the word in bold in each sentence and choose the option you think has the closest meaning.**

1 That actor played the **lead** in a movie we went to see last week.

A director B hero C role

2 Parents shouldn't be too **harsh** with teenagers at exam time.

A strict B proud C miserable

3 This restaurant offers a wide **range** of vegetarian and vegan options.

A variety B line C sort

4 He works with a team of exciting and **innovative** young designers.

A athletic B creative C gentle

Tip!

Sometimes you have to guess the meaning of a word you don't know. Look at the context by reading the words and sentences that come before and after the word.

Tip!

Look out for traps! A useful way to check if your answer is correct is to think about why the other options are incorrect.

3 **Read the descriptions of two people. Answer the questions.**

A Gabriela wants to study English at a language school in Cambridge, where she has an aunt she can stay with. She loves soccer and wants to play on a team. Her language level is not very advanced, but she is very excited to learn. She wants small classes of mixed nationalities so that she has to speak English with her classmates.

B Winston is 25. He is very good at soccer and has played professionally. Now he wants to be a gym teacher, so he needs a teaching certificate in different sports. He is looking for a college outside a city with good sporting facilities and cheap college accommodation.

1 Which description mentions accommodation: A, B, or both?

2 Which description mentions student accommodation: A, B, or both?

3 Which person likes sports, especially soccer? Gabriela, Winston, or both?

4 Which person wants to teach sports? Gabriela, Winston, or both?

4 **Read the descriptions of two colleges. Answer the questions.**

Greystones College was built in 2003 in an attractive open area in the country just outside of Oxford. Places are available for our language-learning courses, which are taught in small numbers or intensively, one-on-one. Students stay with local families to give them the greatest opportunities to practice their language skills. There are good sporting and social activities all year round.

Hinton College is located in Cambridge, one of the UK's oldest and most beautiful university cities. The college has a a high level of success in English language learning. Our beginner classes are taught in groups of three or four by qualified native speakers. Social activities are arranged as part of the course, and team sports are encouraged. All of our courses are from one to six months in length.

1 Underline four important facts about each college:

- where they are
- what courses they offer
- how big the classes are
- what other activities they offer

2 What information tells you Greystones College is not suitable for Gabriela?

3 What information tells you Hinton College is suitable for Gabriela?

EXAM TIPS: Writing Skills

Writing: An Email

Writing an Email Response

For this question, you are given a short message from an English-speaking friend. You have to respond to the message in around 100 words. This tests your ability to understand a message and to write a clear response.

Exam Guide: Writing an Email

- Read the instructions carefully so that you understand who you are writing to and why you are writing.
- Your answer should be around 100 words. Don't write much more or much less than that.
- Begin and end your email correctly. Use:
  - your friend's name
  - an opening phrase.
  - one sentence for each point from the original email
  - a phrase to close
  - your name at the end.
- Start your sentences in different ways to make your email interesting.
- Don't copy too much language from the question. Try to think of synonyms where possible.

Writing Practice: Writing an Email

1 **Read the instructions and the statements that follow. Are the statements true or false?**

You are planning to visit your friend Robin in Canada. Read Robin's message. Then write an email to him.

From: Robin
Subject: Your trip!
Hi there!
I'm so happy to hear you are coming to visit me. You are going to love Canada!
On the first weekend you are here would you like to go ice-skating or to see a hockey game?
Let me know what kind of food you like to eat so we can buy it from the store. And don't forget to bring warm clothes. In January it's going to be freezing.
Can't wait to see you.
Bye!
Robin

		True	False
1	Your friend Robin is in Canada.	☐	☐
2	The message is from Robin.	☐	☐
3	Robin is planning to visit you.	☐	☐
4	You might go see a hockey game.	☐	☐
5	Robin has bought some food for you.	☐	☐
6	Your answer should be in email form.	☐	☐

2 **Read the sentences from two emails from the same boy. One is to his teacher, and the other to his friend. In your notebooks, write them in the correct order under the right heading, formal or informal.**

Formal	Informal

Tip! Make sure you use the appropriate style: it should not be formal if you're writing to a friend.

I hope to be back at school on Monday.
I have a very bad cold and a high temperature.
Dear Mr. Jacobs,
Yours truly, Michael Fanshaw
Can you please send me this week's homework?
I apologize for my absence from class yesterday.

Bye, Mike
See you next week with any luck.
I have an awful cold – I'm coughing and sweating.
Hi Ana,
Let me know if there's any homework, OK?
Sorry I wasn't there yesterday.

3 **Change the words in bold to make the sentences more interesting. Use the words in the box or your own ideas.**

Tip! Use a range of vocabulary: make sure you don't use the same word too many times.

amazing awesome boring colorful cool
freezing great hate love pleasant prefer rainy

1 There's a **good** skate park with a **good** café near my home.

2 We had a **nice** camping vacation, but the weather was **not nice**.

3 I **like** swimming, but if you **don't like** it we can do something you'd **like more**.

4 The art galleries in my town are **not very interesting**, but the Museum of Tomorrow is **very interesting.**

5 We could go to the parade. It's very **nice** and the costumes are usually **nice**.

4 **Correct the mistake in each sentence.**

Tip! Check your writing for any mistakes in spelling or grammar.

1 Don't forget turn off the lights when you leave.

2 Are you scared thunder and lightning?

3 The weather forecast says it's going snowing tonight.

4 I can't sing because I have a very hurt throat.

EXAM TIPS: Listening Skills

Listening: Multiple Choice

You will listen to short unrelated extracts and choose from three options. This tests your ability to listen for specific information and answer a question about what you hear.

Exam Guide: Three-Option Multiple Choice

- Use the time before you listen to read the questions. Read them carefully because they tell you what you need to listen for.
- All the possible answers may be in the recording, but only one will answer the question.
- Focus on the general meaning of what you hear. You may have to listen for the person's opinion, which is not necessarily a single word or phrase.
- If you're not sure, mark the answers you think are possible and check on the second listening.
- Always give an answer, even if you're still not sure. A guess might be right.
- Use the second listening to check, even if you're sure you're right. Don't stop listening!

REMEMBER!

You will hear the instructions on the recording. Listen carefully and read the question at the same time because this will help you understand the topic and the context.

Listening Practice: Multiple Choice

1 Underline two key words or phrases in each question.

1 What time does the girl's exam start?
2 What is the man going to buy?
3 Which evening activity is for beginners?
4 Why did Caroline leave her job?
5 Where are the teacher's keys?
6 What did Hari do this morning?

Tip!
Underline the key words in the question. Then listen for the words that mean the same as the key words.

E.01 **2 You will hear a teenage girl speaking to her mother about an exam. Read the question below.**

What time does the girl's exam start?

A It starts at 11:30.
B Four o'clock.
C It begins at nine.

Now listen to the conversation. Why are options A and B not correct?

____

____

Tip!
If the recording is a conversation, listen for the right person: who does the question refer to?

3 **You will hear two people talking about a play they've just seen. What words do you expect to hear in connection with the three options? Choose from the words in the box or use your own ideas.**

bad boring great impressive interesting
old-fashioned too long too short

The Length	The Acting	The Costumes

E.02 **4** **Listen to the conversation and answer the questions.**

1 What did the woman think about the play?

A She thought the play was too long.

B She thought it was very disappointing.

C She liked the actors.

2 What did the man think of the costumes?

A He thought they were old-fashioned.

B He likes fifties fashion.

C He thought the clothes were terrible.

3 When is the play supposed to be set?

A the 1950s

B It's not mentioned.

C in the present

Adverbs of Frequency

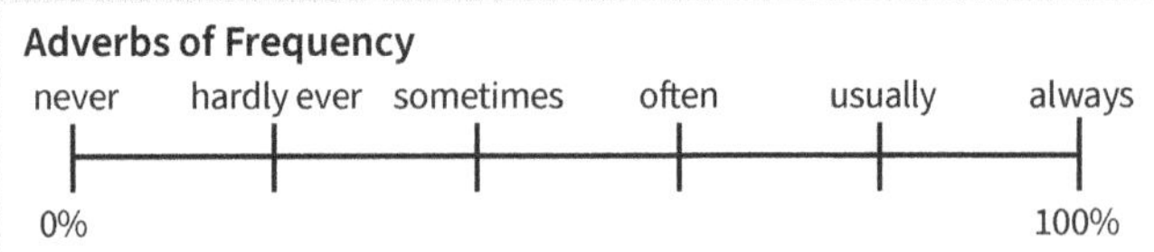

- We use **adverbs of frequency** to say how often something happens.
- We put them before the main verb but after the verb ***to be***.
  I often text my friends.
  There are always music festivals in the summer.
- ***Often, sometimes,*** and ***usually*** can also come at the beginning of the sentence.
  Sometimes, my family, and I listen to music.

Expressions of Frequency

every	day / week / weekend / year
once / twice / three times	a day / a week / a month / a year

- We also use **expressions of frequency** to say how often something happens.
- We usually place them after the verb phrase, but they can also come at the beginning or end of a sentence.
  I see my friends twice a week.
  Every weekend, they give a concert.
- We can use an expression of frequency and an adverb of frequency in the same sentence.
  I usually go on vacation once a year.

Simple Present and Present Continuous

- We use the **simple present** to talk about facts, habits, and routines.
  My sister likes rock music.
  I use my phone every day.
- We use **adverbs of frequency** (***always***, ***often***, etc.) with the **simple present** and ***at the moment*** and ***now*** with the **present continuous**.
  My dad often plays computer games with me.
  My teacher is walking into the classroom now.
- We also use the **simple present** to talk about future planned events if a **future time expression** is used or understood.
  My mom starts work at 10 a.m. on Friday.
  Hannah can't come shopping with me this afternoon.
- We can also use the **present continuous** to talk about temporary future plans or arrangements.
  We are taking a trip to Florida.

Simple Past: Regular and Irregular Verbs

	Affirmative	Negative
I / He / She / It We / You / They	called me.	didn't call me.

Questions		
Did	I / he / she / it / we / you / they	call you?

Short Answers		
Yes,	I / he / she / it / we / you / they	did.
No,	I / he / she / it / we / you / they	didn't.

- We use the **simple past** to talk about completed events and actions in the past.
  I watched the band play last night.
  Three years ago, she had a great party.
- To form the affirmative of the **simple past**, we add *-ed* or *-d* to the infinitive.
  help – helped *organize – organized* *play – played*
- For verbs ending **consonant** + ***-y***, remove the *-y* and add *-ied*.
  study – studied *cry – cried* *try – tried*
- For one-syllable verbs ending **consonant** + **vowel** + **consonant**, we double the final consonant and add *-ed*.
  drop – dropped *chat – chatted*

  For verbs that have two or more syllables, double the final consonant and add *-ed* if the stress is on the last syllable. If the stress is not on the last syllable, do not double the consonant before adding *-ed*.
  tra*vel* – *traveled* *pre****fer*** – *preferred*

  We do not double the consonant in words that end in *w*, *x*, *y*, or *z*.
  tow - towed *relax - relaxed*
- Many common verbs are irregular in the **simple past**.
  get – got *put – put*
  have – had *make – made*
- Question words always go at the beginning of the question.
  When did the concert start?
  Where was your brother last night?

Simple Present and Present Continuous with Adverbs of Frequency

1 Put the words in parentheses in the correct place in the sentence.

1 Do you play in a band on Saturday nights? (always)
Do you always play in a band on Saturday nights?
2 We see our friends at the jazz club in town. (sometimes)
3 My mom gets angry with me when I'm late. (never)
4 I text my teacher when I can't do my homework. (hardly ever)
5 My brother's soccer team wins the cup. (often)
6 Are those music apps free or not? (usually)

2 Complete the sentences with the correct form of the verbs in the box.

do go have ~~post~~ spend study

1 *Does* your sister usually *post* photos on social media?
2 I'm on vacation at the moment and I ______ a great time!
3 How much money ______ you usually ______ each week?
4 What ______ your parents ______ when you get good grades at school?
5 We ______ by bus today because it's too cold to walk.
6 She ______ for exams this weekend, so she doesn't have much free time.

Simple Present and Present Continuous for Future

3 Put the words in the correct order to make sentences about the future.

1 eight / English / at / starts / class / Our / thirty
Our English class starts at eight thirty.
2 begin / time / the / does / tomorrow / What / concert / ?
3 taking / next week / My / Chicago / grandparents / train / to / the / are
4 six / This / closes / tonight / at / store
5 the / trip / We / for / morning / leaving / our / in / are
6 back / teacher / week / We / our / next / essays / the / get / from

Simple Past

4 Use the prompts to make questions and answers in the simple past.

1 When / you see that movie? / last week
When did you see that movie? I/We saw it last week.
2 What time / the girls go to bed? / after 11
3 Where / your parents meet? / in college
4 What / he buy yesterday? / a new bike
5 How / the visitors get here? / by boat
6 When / the last bus leave? / at ten

Simple Past and Past Continuous with *When* and *While*

	Affirmative	Negative
I / He / She / It	was crying.	wasn't crying.
We / You / They	were crying.	weren't crying.
Questions		
Was	I / he / she / it	crying?
Were	we / you / they	
Short Answers		
Yes,	I / he / she / it	was.
	we / you / they	were.
No,	I / he / she / it	wasn't.
	we / you / they	weren't.

- We use the **past continuous** to talk about actions in progress around a time in the past.
  At seven o'clock, I was waiting for the bus.
  Chloe was wearing jeans yesterday.
- We also use ***when*** and ***while*** to mean "during that time" or to connect two events happening at the same time.
  When my parents were studying, they didn't have the Internet.
  While he was eating, the phone rang.
- We usually use ***while*** with the past continuous to emphasize an ongoing action in the past.
- We usually use ***when*** with the simple past to talk about an interrupting action.

Used To

	Affirmative	Negative
I / He / She / It / We / You / They	used to play soccer.	didn't use to play soccer.
Questions and Short Answers		
Did	I / he / she / it / we / you / they	use to be scared?
Yes,	I / he / she / it / we / you / they	did.
No,		didn't.

- ***Used to*** emphasizes that past states, habits, and actions are now finished.
  It used to be a library, but now it's a museum.
  We used to walk to school, but now we ride our bikes.
- We do not use ***used to*** to talk about things that only happened once, how many times something happened, or duration.
  They went to the movies yesterday.
  ~~*They used to go to the movies yesterday.*~~
  My brother lived there for four years.
  ~~*My brother used to live there for four years.*~~
- ***Used to*** does not have a present form. For present habits and states, we use the simple present.
  My cousin drinks coffee in the morning.

GRAMMAR PRACTICE

Simple Past and Past Continuous with *When* and *While*

1 Complete the sentences with the past continuous form of the verbs in the box.

cook look not study ~~snow~~ wear

1 It ___was snowing___ all day yesterday, so we didn't play soccer.
2 We ________ for you after class. Where were you?
3 Marcos ________ – he was reading a magazine!
4 Nina ________ her new shoes for the first time.
5 What ________ you ________ in the kitchen earlier? It didn't smell very good!

2 Write sentences with *when* or *while* and the correct form of the verbs. Some sentences can have more than one answer.

1 Her father / wait / she arrive home
Her father was waiting when she arrived home.
2 The doorbell / ring / I make tea
____
3 The boys / walk home / their teacher drive past
____
4 Our friends / arrive / we prepare lunch
____
5 I / listen to music / I do my homework
____

3 (Circle) the correct option.

1 What *did they do* / *(were they doing)* when *(we called)* / *were calling* them?
2 She *watched* / *was watching* a movie when her computer *broke* / *was breaking*.
3 I *didn't see* / *wasn't seeing* you while I *shopped* / *was shopping* in town.
4 The police *stopped* / *were stopping* her when she *drove* / *was driving* to work.
5 We *walked* / *were walking* to school when the rain *started* / *was starting*.
6 They *shouted* / *were shouting* for ages, but nobody *heard* / *was hearing* them.

4 Complete the conversation with the correct past form of the verbs in parentheses.

JORGE Hi, Lena! [1] ___Did you finish___ (you / finish) your history essay yesterday?
LENA No, I [2] ________ (work) on it after school when my mom [3] ________ (stop) me.
JORGE Why [4] ________ (she / do) that?
LENA Because she [5] ________ (want) me to help her with dinner. Then I [6] ________ (watch) a wildlife show on TV.
JORGE Oh, yeah. I [7] ________ (see) that! So then I guess you [8] ________ (be) too tired!
LENA Correct!

Used To

5 Make sentences with the correct form of *used to* and the verbs in the box.

~~have~~ live not eat play

1 1 Our neighbors ___used to have___ a horse.
2 We ________ in a smaller apartment.
3 Children ________ outside until it got dark.
4 Ollie ________ vegetables, but he does now.

6 Make questions to match the answers.

1 Did you use to go to school by bus ________?
No, not by bus. I went to school by bike.
2 ________?
No, my sister's never eaten meat.
3 ________?
No, my sister played with me, but not my brother.
4 ________?
Olives? No, and I still hate them!

7 (Circle) the correct options.

School teachers in the 1950s [1] *(used to write)* / *used writing* on chalkboards because, of course, they [2] *didn't have* / *weren't having* today's technology. They [3] *used to talk* / *did talk* a lot while the children [4] *were sitting* / *didn't sit* quietly. School books never [5] *didn't use to look* / *looked* very interesting, and there weren't any videos to watch. Many teachers [6] *used to be* / *were being* stricter than they are now, too.

GRAMMAR REFERENCE UNIT 2

Present Perfect: Regular Verbs

Affirmative / Negative			Questions		
I / We / You / They	have walked / haven't walked	to school.	Have	I / we / you / they	walked to school?
He / She / It	has walked / hasn't walked		Has	he / she / it	
Short Answers					
Yes,	I / we / you / they	have.	No,	I / we / you / they	haven't.
	he / she / it	has.		he / she / it	hasn't.

- We use the **present perfect** to talk about actions, experiences, and facts in the past, when the exact time is not mentioned or important.
  The orchestra has played in many countries.
  He has visited the art exhibition.
- We form the affirmative with **subject** + ***have/has*** + **past participle**.
  I've talked to Danielle. *She's asked me for help.*
- We form the negative with **subject** + ***haven't/hasn't*** + **past participle**.
  Max hasn't auditioned for the part.
  They haven't performed in front of an audience.
- We form questions in the **present perfect** with ***have/ has*** + **subject** + **past participle**. We often use ***ever*** in present perfect questions to ask about your whole life.
  Has she ever had drum lessons?
  Have you ever been to the theater?
- We often use ***never*** to say "not at any time" when answering these questions.
  A: *Has he ever met a famous person?* ***B:*** *No, never.*
- Regular past participles end in *-ed, -d,* or *-ied.*
  want – wanted *believe – believed* *worry – worried*

Present Perfect: Irregular Verbs

- Many common verbs have irregular past participles.
  go – gone *put – put* *be – been* *make – made*
  see – seen *hear – heard*
- We use ***go*** (***gone***) for physical actions, to say somebody has not returned from a place or from doing an activity. We use ***be*** (***been***) for completed experiences, to say somebody has returned from a place or from doing an activity.
  They've gone to Rome. (*They are in Rome now.*)
  They've been to Rome. (*They have returned.*)

Present Perfect with *Already, Just, Still,* and *Yet*

- We often use ***already***, ***just***, ***still***, and ***yet*** with the present perfect.
  Jack has already been to the exhibition twice.
  Emily has just started learning Spanish.
  We still haven't chosen a movie to watch.
  I haven't had time to go shopping yet.
- We use ***already*** to explain that something happened before we expected or to emphasize it has happened. We normally put ***already*** between ***have/has*** and the **past participle**.
  She has already bought a ticket.
  I have already seen the show.
- We use ***just*** with the present perfect to talk about very recent events and actions.
  I've just heard the good news. It's fantastic!
  Dad's just gotten home and he's feeling tired.
- We use ***still*** in negative sentences to express that something we expected has not happened, but we imagine it will happen in the future. We put ***still*** directly after the subject.
  My uncle still hasn't seen the new play.
- We use ***yet*** in negative sentences to emphasize that something we expected has not happened. We put ***yet*** after the complete verb phrase.
  John hasn't arrived yet.
  I haven't asked my parents for permission yet.
- We use ***yet*** in questions to ask if something has happened before now. It comes at the end of the question.
  Have you bought the bus tickets yet?
- In short answers in the negative, we say ***Not yet***.
  A: *Have you spoken to the drama teacher?* ***B:*** *Not yet.*

GRAMMAR PRACTICE

UNIT 2

Present Perfect with Regular and Irregular Verbs

1 Complete the sentences with the present perfect form of the verbs in parentheses.

1 A TV celebrity *has opened* (open) a new supermarket in our town.
2 This Chinese circus ________ (not perform) in South America before.
3 I ________ (look) everywhere, but I can't find my phone.
4 ________ the DJ ________ (play) your favorite song?
5 Our teacher ________ (work) as a filmmaker.
6 ________ they ________ (invite) you to their exhibition?

2 Complete the sentences with *been* or *gone*.

1 We've *been* on vacation. We came home yesterday.
2 Felix has ________ to Brazil three times.
3 The children have ________ out, but they won't be late.
4 I've ________ shopping. Please help me with my bags.
5 Where's Jared? Has he ________ to bed?
6 My mom's not here. She's ________ to work.

3 Write questions with the present perfect and the phrases in the box. Then write true answers.

~~be to a science museum~~	make a sculpture	
see a ballet	take music lessons	win a prize

1 *Have you ever been to a science museum?*
Yes, I have. / No, I haven't.
2 ________
3 ________
4 ________
5 ________

Present Perfect with *Already, Just, Still,* and *Yet*

4 Put the words in the correct order to make sentences.

1 written / I've / some / lyrics / just / cool
I've just written some cool lyrics.
2 *Hamlet* / seen / a / just / of / She's / performance
____
3 song / We / just / our / first / recorded / have
____
4 the / started / just / They've / rehearsal
____
5 auditioned / a / for / show / a / just / Mina / has / part / in
____

5 Circle the correct sentences.

1 (a) She still hasn't played in a professional orchestra.
b She yet hasn't played in a professional orchestra.
2 a The concert tickets haven't arrived yet.
b The concert tickets haven't arrived still.
3 a Have you read this review? No, already not.
b Have you read this review? No, not yet.
4 a Janek has already seen that movie twice.
b Janek has still seen that movie twice.

6 Put the words in parentheses in the correct position in the sentences.

1 Esma has heard from the movie director. (just)
Esma has just heard from the movie director.
2 Has she had her audition? (yet)
____
3 Yes, she's had an audition and an interview (already).
____
4 Has she heard what part she's gotten? (yet)
____
5 No, the director hasn't told her. (still)
____

Can, Could, Will Be Able To

- We often use ***can*** to talk about ability to do something in the present.
  She can speak English and Polish.
- We often use ***could*** to talk about ability to do something in the past.
  People could visit the museum for free last week.
- We often use ***will be able to*** to talk about ability to do something in the future.
  I will be able to translate this document tomorrow.

Present Perfect with *How long ... ?* and *For/Since*

How long ... ?

- We use ***How long ... ?*** with the **present perfect** to ask about the duration of a state or activity.
  A: *How long have you known Greg?*
  B: *I've known him since 2012.*

For* and *Since

- We use ***for*** and ***since*** with the **present perfect** to say how long something has been true.
  She hasn't lived in Santiago for three years.
  I've lived here since I was seven.
- We use ***for*** with periods of time.
  Liam's had a new bike for three days.
  My parents have been married for 21 years.
- We use ***since*** with a reference to a specific time.
  We've been best friends since 2009.
  Emma and Anna haven't seen each other since June.

Present Perfect and Simple Past

- We use the **simple past** when the moment in which something happened has ended. When it happened isn't always mentioned, usually because it is clear.
  I went to Monterrey in June. (It's now July.)
  They began the exam two minutes ago. (It's now 10:02, not 10:00.)
  She wanted to ask you a question. (when I spoke to her)
- We use the **present perfect** when something started or happened in the past and continues to be true until now. We can say how long something has been true but not when it started.
  I've been to Monterrey. (When isn't specified, but it continues to be true.)
  They've begun the exam. (and the exam hasn't finished)
  She's wanted to ask you a question for a few days. (She continues to want to.)

GRAMMAR PRACTICE

UNIT 3

Can, Could, Will Be Able To

1 Are the sentences about the *P* (past), *Pr* (present), or *F* (future)?

1 We won't be able to wave goodbye when they leave. F
2 I can translate the instructions for you. ___
3 He will be able to come to the meeting. ___
4 My parents couldn't understand their Brazilian guests. ___
5 She couldn't hear her phone, so she didn't answer. ___
6 We can't wait or we'll miss our bus. ___

2 Complete the text with the correct form of *can*, *could*, or *will be able to*.

> Beatriz comes from São Paulo, so she [1] *can* speak Brazilian Portuguese very well. She speaks English fairly well, but she [2] ________ always understand if people talk too fast. When she was younger, she [3] ________ speak Spanish, but she studied it in school and now she [4] ________. Next year, she's going to stay with an aunt in Luzern. She [5] ________ learn Swiss German there, but she [6] ________ understand people in the French- and Italian-speaking regions of the country.

3 Circle the correct options.

1 We ... hear the speaker because he's talking quietly.
a could b couldn't **c can't**
2 Antonio is so good at languages. He ... speak a lot of them!
a will be able to b could c can
3 My parents ... choose to learn Greek or Latin when they were at school.
a could b can c can't
4 I hope I ... help you later. I'll be free this evening.
a can't b will be able to c could
5 We ... see the video if we miss the next class.
a couldn't b won't be able to c can to
6 ... visit the Art Institute when you're in Chicago next week?
a Able you to b Can you able to c Will you be able to

Present Perfect with *How long ... ?* and *For/Since*

4 Complete the sentences with *for* or *since*.

1 I have known my friend Victoria *for* four years.
2 She hasn't seen her grandparents ________ a long time.
3 We've lived in this apartment ________ 2016.
4 Have you been at home ________ lunchtime?

5 Make questions with *How long* and the correct form of the verb.

1 you / be at this school?
How long have you been at this school?
2 she / know her best friend?
____
3 they / live near you?
____
4 Lucas / have that phone?
____

Present Perfect and Simple Past

6 Circle the correct options.

1 My mother ***has worked*** / *worked* at this museum since 2004.
2 He *has told* / *told* me the same joke yesterday.
3 They *haven't begun* / *didn't begin* the exam yet.
4 *Has she ever told* / *Did she ever tell* lies before?

7 Complete the conversation with the correct form of the verbs in parentheses.

LUIS Sorry I'm late, Alan. How long [1] *have you been* (be) here?
ALAN No problem, I [2] ________ (just get) here.
LUIS [3] ________ the teacher ________ (arrive) yet?
ALAN No, not yet. She [4] ________ (tell) us yesterday that she might be late.
LUIS Oh, did she? I [5] ________ (not hear) that. Your English is very good!
ALAN Thanks! I [6] ________ (study) it since fifth grade.

GRAMMAR REFERENCE

UNIT 4

Quantifiers

Countable	Uncountable
a few	a little
enough	enough
too many	too much

- We use **quantifiers** to talk about the amount of something.
- We use ***a few*** and ***a little*** to express small quantities.
  I have a few messages that I need to reply to.
  I have a little time to watch TV, but not much.
- We use ***too many*** / ***too much*** to say that an amount is excessive.
  There were too many options. I didn't know what to choose!
  There was too much noise, and I couldn't sleep.
- We use ***enough*** to say that a quantity is sufficient and ***not enough*** to say that a quantity is insufficient.
  We have enough players to make two teams.
  I didn't have enough time to answer all the questions.

Should, Shouldn't, and Ought To

	Affirmative	Negative
I / He / She / It / We / You / They	should help.	shouldn't help.
Questions		
Should	I / he / she / it / we / you / they	help?
Short Answers		
Yes,	I / he / she / it / we / you / they	should.
No,		shouldn't.

- We use ***should*** to say what we think is a good idea or important to do – to give advice and recommendations.
  You should stay in bed if you have a fever.
  Laura shouldn't use her phone before bed.
- ***Should*** is the same in all forms. We use the infinitive after ***should***.
  John should get more sleep.
  NOT *John ~~should to get~~ more sleep.*
- We use ***ought to*** when talking about things that are desired or ideal.
  We ought to eat a lot of fruit and vegetables every day.

GRAMMAR PRACTICE

UNIT 4

Quantifiers

1 Match the beginnings of the sentences with the ends.

1 Please be quiet, there's [d]
2 Too many students [ ]
3 Yoga exercises don't take [ ]
4 You'll be tired if you have [ ]
5 Do you think there's [ ]
6 Muscles get weak if you spend [ ]

a too much time, do they?
b too many late nights.
c too many hours sitting at a desk!
d too much noise in here.
e are worried about their exams.
f too much stress in your life?

2 Complete the sentences with *a little* or *a few*.

1 I do ___a few___ yoga exercises every morning at 7 a.m.
2 Jorge can give you ________ help in the gym if you need it.
3 There are ________ adjustable desks in our classroom.
4 You should do ________ exercise during long study sessions.
5 Karla needs ________ more time to finish her homework.
6 Stop working for ________ minutes and take a walk.

3 Put the words in the correct order.

1 the / time / didn't / We / to / test / have / enough / finish
We didn't have enough time to finish the test.
2 bike / enough / buy / Gisela / to / a / money / new / has
____
3 team / make / There / students / a / are / enough / to
____
4 drive / old / you / car / Are / a / enough / to / ?
____
5 me / adjustable / enough / This / high / isn't / desk / for
____

4 (Circle) the correct option.

1 (*A few*) / *A little* new students joined our swimming class.
2 I have *time enough* / *enough time* to help you.
3 These desks cost *too much* / *too many* money.
4 There were *a little* / *a few* problems we couldn't solve.
5 Does everyone have *too much* / *too many* stress in their lives?
6 Emilio does *a little* / *a few* exercise but not much.

Should, Shouldn't, and Ought To

5 Complete the sentences with *should*, *shouldn't*, or *ought*.

1 You ___shouldn't___ worry about the test – it'll be easy!
2 Melody ________ to go to bed early and get more sleep.
3 ________ Emily stay at home if she's feeling sick?
4 I ________ to eat more fish, but I don't really like it.
5 We ________ buy too many sweet things – they're bad for our teeth.

6 Underline and correct the mistake in each sentence.

1 We <u>shouldn't</u> take our coats today because it's really cold.
We should take our coats today because it's really cold.
2 Bella ought be more easygoing; she worries too much.
____
3 You should to stay in bed if you have a fever.
____
4 Who should I to ask when I need advice?
____
5 We shouldn't all drink enough water.
____

7 Complete the text with the phrases in the box.

ought to ask	ought to do	should find
should listen	~~should read~~	shouldn't start

Top tips for improving your English

You [1] ___should read___ English language magazines or websites. You [2] ________ this as often as possible. If you like reading, you [3] ________ English books or stories, but you [4] ________ your teacher for recommendations. You [5] ________ with something that's too difficult. You [6] ________ to as much English as possible too, like podcasts, radio, and TV.

GRAMMAR REFERENCE UNIT 5

The First Conditional

If- Clause	Main Clause
(*if* + simple present)	[*will/won't, may/might* (*not*), *could*]
If I pass all my exams,	my parents will / may / might buy me a present.
If I don't pass all my exams,	I won't / may not / might not go on vacation.
Unless I pass all my exams,	
Main Clause	***If*- Clause**
[*will/won't, may/might* (*not*), *could*]	(*if* + simple present)
My parents will / may / might buy me a present	if I pass my exams.
My parents won't buy me a present	if I don't pass all my exams.
	unless I pass all my exams.
Questions	
Will my parents buy me a present	if I don't pass all my exams?

- We use **first conditional** sentences to talk about possible situations in the present or future and say what we think the result will be.
- We often use ***if*** + **simple present** to describe the possible action or event.
  We'll pass the exam if we work hard.
- We can use ***unless*** + **simple present** instead of *if not.*
  Unless we hurry up, we'll miss the train.
- We use ***will/won't*** + **infinitive** when we are sure of the result and ***may***, ***might*** or ***could*** + **infinitive** when we are less sure.
  If we don't leave now, we won't catch the 8:30 bus.
  If my grandfather doesn't feel better, he may not visit this weekend.
  I might go the beach if it's warm enough.
  If I'm lucky, I could win the race tomorrow.
- When we use ***if*** to start the sentence, we use a comma between the two parts.
  If I have enough money, I'll go on vacation.
- We normally use ***will*** to make first conditional questions. It is unusual to use ***may*** or ***might***.
  Will you chat with me online this evening if you have time?

The Second Conditional

If- Clause	Main Clause
(*if* + simple past)	(*would/could/might* + infinitive)
If I knew him,	I would / could / might ask him.
If I didn't know him,	I wouldn't / couldn't / might not ask him.
Main Clause	***If*- Clause**
(*would/could/might* + infinitive)	(*if* + simple past)
I would / could / might ask him	if I knew him.
I wouldn't / couldn't / might not ask him	if I didn't know him.
Questions	
Would you ask him	if you knew him?

- We use the **second conditional** to talk about imaginary situations in the present and their possible consequences.
- We use ***if*** + **simple past** (affirmative or negative) to describe the imaginary situation and ***would***, ***could***, or ***might*** for the consequence.
  If he didn't like you, he wouldn't talk to you.
- We use ***would*** (***not***) when we are sure of the consequence.
  He would do better in school if he didn't spend all his time playing computer games.
- We use ***could*** (***not***) to express a possibility or ability as a consequence.
  If it was Saturday, we could go out for pizza.
  I could do some volunteer work if I didn't need to study so much.
- We use ***might*** (***not***) to show we are less sure about the consequence.
  If I had more free time, I might take up the guitar.
  Madison might lend you her laptop if you asked her.
- We can use ***was*** or ***were*** in the ***if***- part of the sentence with *I*, *he*, *she*, and *it*.
  If it wasn't/weren't so spicy, I could finish it.
  I wouldn't say anything if I were/was you.

GRAMMAR PRACTICE

UNIT 5

The First Conditional

1 Circle the correct option.

1 If I *have* / *will have* enough time, I'll help you pick up litter.

2 Unless Jenny calls, we *don't know* / *won't know* where she is.

3 Many more fish will die if they *eat* / *will eat* our plastic waste.

4 *If* / *Unless* we use solar power, we will reduce air pollution.

5 We might go swimming later if the sun *comes* / *will come* out.

2 Put the phrases in the correct order.

1 I might / I have enough money, / If / buy a new phone

If I have enough money, I might buy a new phone.

2 come to school later / you feel better / if / Will you / ?

____

3 if / Henry will / he leaves last / turn off the lights

____

4 climate change, / our planet / Unless / we stop / will get hotter

____

5 we'll miss / we don't leave soon, / the beginning of the movie / If

____

6 we collect all the plastic / The ocean / if / might get cleaner

____

The Second Conditional

3 Circle the correct option.

1 Our planet would be in danger if all the insects *would disappear* / *disappeared*.

2 What *would you do* / *did you do* if someone gave you a plastic straw?

3 Where *would you travel* / *would you traveled* if you had enough money?

4 There would be more oxygen if they *wouldn't destroy* / *didn't destroy* rainforests.

5 We could reduce the effects of climate change if we *would use* / *used* solar power.

4 Complete the second conditional sentences with the correct form of the words in parentheses.

1 If I had (have) the answer to the problems of climate change, I would tell (tell) you.

2 She _______________ (not ask) you to come if she _______________ (not like) you.

3 We _______________ (not endanger) animals so much if we _______________ (not destroy) their habitats.

4 If we _______________ (live) near the ocean, I think our home _______________ (be) in danger.

5 I _______________ (not eat) meat if I _______________ (be) you.

5 Underline and correct the mistake in each sentence.

1 What would you do if you had won a million dollars?

What would you do if you won a million dollars?

2 If you didn't work so hard, you would get so stressed.

____

3 Would those animals safer if they lived in a zoo?

____

4 I didn't eat fish unless I lived near the ocean.

____

6 Write second conditional sentences about the problems.

1 I don't have enough money to buy a new phone

have more money / buy a new phone

If I had more money, I would buy a new phone.

2 This coffee isn't sweet enough.

this coffee / be better / if / you add / a little sugar to it

____

3 We're not healthy because the air is polluted.

we all / be healthier / if / the air / not polluted

____

4 There are enough insects to feed everybody.

if / we all / eat insects / nobody / be hungry

____

Simple Present Passive

	Affirmative		Negative			
This bottle	is	made of plastic.	isn't		made of plastic.	
These toys	are		aren't			
Questions			**Short Answers**			
Is	this bottle	made of plastic?	Yes,	it is.	No,	it isn't.
Are	these toys			they are.		they aren't.

- We use the **passive** form to describe actions and processes when we are not interested in, or don't know, who is responsible for the action or process.
  English is spoken in many countries.
  Many plastic bottles aren't recycled.
- To form the **simple present passive**, we use ***is/are*** (***not***) + **past participle**.
  The streets are cleaned on Sundays after the market finishes.
- We form questions with ***Is/Are*** + **subject** + **past participle**.
  Is the main square decorated during the festival?
  When are the results sent to students?

Simple Past Passive

	Affirmative		Negative			
The trash	was	thrown away.	wasn't		thrown away.	
The old chairs	were		weren't			
Questions			**Short Answers**			
Was	the trash	thrown away?	Yes,	it was.	No,	it wasn't.
Were	the old chairs			they were.		they weren't.

- We use the **simple past passive** to describe actions and processes in the past.
  The contest winners were given books and a certificate.
- To form the **simple past passive**, we use ***was/were*** (***not***) + **past participle**.
  The first CD was made in 1982.
  Some of us weren't invited to the party.
- To form questions, we use ***was/were*** + **subject** + **past participle**.
  Were the instructions written in Spanish or Portuguese?

Passive + *By*

- We use ***by*** with the **passive** to show who or what was responsible for the action.
  The Merchant of Venice *was written by Shakespeare.*
  A lot of houses were destroyed by the fire.

GRAMMAR PRACTICE

UNIT 6

Simple Present Passive

1 Complete the conversation with the simple present passive form of the verbs in parentheses.

ANA How much waste [1] *is recycled* (recycle) in your home?

DAN Well, glass and metal [2] ______ (collect) every week. I'm not sure what [3] ______ (do) with the other materials we recycle. Some waste [4] ______ (burn).

ANA Yes, but burning waste isn't great. The air [5] ______ (pollute) because dangerous gases like methane [6] ______ (create).

DAN True, but you can do simple things to help. I never buy fruit that [7] ______ (pack) in plastic, and very little energy [8] ______ (waste) in our apartment.

2 Complete the text with the simple present passive form of the verbs in the box.

~~eat~~ fly not grow pack process produce sell send

A lot of the food that [1] *is eaten* in the UK [2] ______ there. Oranges, for example, [3] ______ in California. They [4] ______ there and then they [5] ______ to airports in Europe. Trucks transport the fruit to towns, where they [6] ______ in supermarkets. Incredibly, some food [7] ______ by ship to China, where it [8] ______ before returning to Europe.

3 Circle the correct option to complete the sentences.

1 Where ... ?
  a did BMW cars produce
  (b) are BMW cars produced
  c produced BMW cars by
2 The equipment ... in a small factory near here.
  a is pack b packed c is packed
3 A very strong tape ... these boxes.
  a is secured b secures c are secured
4 Their work ... every day by the managers.
  a inspects b is inspecting c is inspected
5 The end product ... for many different things.
  a uses b is used c has used

Simple Past Passive

4 Complete the sentences with the simple past passive form of the verbs in parentheses.

1 The Frisbee *was invented* (invent) by American college students.
2 The Shard ______ (build) near the river in London.
3 My favorite picture ______ (paint) by Frida Kahlo.
4 The factory workers ______ (not pay) very much.
5 English ______ (speak) in many of the resorts.

5 Write questions using the simple past passive.

1 what clothes / wear / by teenagers in the 1950s
  What clothes were worn by teenagers in the 1950s?
2 who / that amazing building / design by
  ______
3 where / the American soldiers / send
  ______
4 what / those old wooden boxes / use for
  ______

6 Answer the questions in Exercise 5. Use the information given.

1 blue jeans and T-shirts
  Blue jeans and T-shirts were worn by teenagers in the 1950s.
2 Frank Lloyd Wright
  ______
3 to Europe
  ______
4 packing equipment
  ______

7 Rewrite the questions using the simple past passive with *by* in your notebooks.

1 Who found those beautiful cave paintings?
  Who were those beautiful cave paintings found by?
2 What destroyed the city of Pompeii?
3 Who wrote *Romeo and Juliet*?
4 Who built Machu Picchu?

Past Perfect

Affirmative	
I / You / He / She / It / We / You / They	had forgotten.

Negative	
I / You / He / She / It / We / You / They	hadn't (had + not) forgotten.

Questions		
Had	I / you / he / she / it / we / you / they	forgotten?

Short Answers		
Yes,	I / you / he / she / it / we / you / they	had.
No,		hadn't.

- We use the **past perfect** with other past tenses to talk about actions or states that happened before the main past action or state.
  We hadn't seen the news, so we didn't know about the storms.
  I couldn't call you on Friday because I had left my phone at home.

Reported Statements

	Direct speech	Reported Speech
Simple Present	"I **want** some new jeans."	He said (that) he **wanted** some new jeans.
Present Continuous	"We**'re making** our own clothes."	He said (that) they **were making** their own clothes.
Simple Past	"I **had** a great time."	She said (that) she**'d had** a great time.
Present Perfect	"We**'ve just seen** a live concert."	She said (that) they**'d just seen** a live concert.

- When we report somebody's words, we often have to change the verb forms – see the chart above for how the verb forms change.
- We often need to change pronouns in reported speech.
  "You have to arrive before 7 p.m." – He said (that) we had to arrive before 7 p.m.

Past Perfect

1 Complete the sentences with the past perfect form of the verbs in parentheses.

1 I couldn't go to the performance because I ___had been___ (be) sick.

2 She __________ (not sleep) very well, so she felt tired all day.

3 I was happy because my team __________ (win).

4 We realized that we __________ (meet) once before.

5 He __________ (know) about the event for a long time.

2 Circle the correct option.

1 When we arrived, the party ....
   a already was started.
   b has already started.
   (c) had already started.

2 I didn't want to see the movie until I ... the book.
   a was read   b had read   c hadn't read

3 When we heard the noise, we knew something ....
   a had happened.   b happened.   c happens.

4 They were so late that the performance ....
   a has nearly finished.
   b nearly had finished.
   c had nearly finished.

5 Yolanda ran to the station, but the train ....
   a had just leave.
   b had just left.
   c was just left.

Reported Statements

3 Circle the correct option.

1 They (*say*) / *tell* that it's the biggest fair in the world.

2 Edwin *said* / *told* everyone that he wasn't coming.

3 Did anyone *say* / *tell* you what time the movie started?

4 I have already *said* / *told* you not to do that.

5 The ticket *says* / *tells* that costumes are optional.

4 Write the direct speech in reported speech.

1 "I had an interesting vacation."
   He said (that) ___he'd had an interesting vacation___.

2 "I've already read the movie review."
   Maria said (that) __________.

3 "We're making pizzas for dinner."
   They said (that) __________.

4 "Juan can't leave before eight."
   I told them (that) __________.

5 Write the reported speech in direct speech.

1 She said she'd bought tickets for the exhibition.
   "___I've bought tickets for the exhibition.___"

2 He told me he didn't watch any daytime TV.
   "__________"

3 Jacky said she was waiting for her friend to arrive.
   "__________"

4 We told them we had never heard that band.
   "__________"

6 Read the email. Then complete the reported speech below.

Home   Inbox   Sent   **New**

Hi Diana,

Bernie and I are having an awesome time in Rio! We're staying near the Copacabana beach, so we've swum every day. The festival has been amazing. I've never seen so many fabulous costumes. We've loved every minute! Actually, we don't want to leave!

Love, Susie

I've just gotten an email from Susie, who's in Rio with Bernie. She said they [1] ___were having___ an awesome time. She said they [2] __________ near the Copacabana beach, so they [3] __________ every day. She wrote that the festival [4] __________ amazing. She said that she [5] __________ so many fabulous costumes. She told me that they [6] __________ every minute. Actually, they [7] __________ to leave!

To Be Allowed To

Affirmative / Negative		
I	'm / 'm not	allowed to run.
We / You / They	're / aren't	
He / She / It	's / isn't	

Questions			Short Answers
Am	I	allowed to run?	Yes, I am.
			No, I'm not.
Are	we / you / they		Yes, we / you / they are.
			No, we / you / they aren't.
Is	he / she / it		Yes, he / she / it is.
			No, he / she / it isn't.

- We use ***to be allowed to*** to say that we have permission to do something.
  We're allowed to use my aunt's laptop.
  You're not allowed to take this book out of the library.
- We often contract ***to be*** in negative sentences.
  They aren't allowed to have phones in class.
  He isn't allowed to go to the party.

Must / Must not

	Affirmative	Negative
I / He / She / It / We / You / They	must go.	must not go.

- We use ***must*** to say what we think it is necessary to do, to talk about obligation, and to give strong recommendations.
  I must start studying more.
  You must listen to this song. It's fantastic!
- We use ***must not*** to say what we think it is necessary not to do, to talk about prohibition, and to give strong advice against something.
  We must not forget to buy her a present.
  Tell them that they must not be late tomorrow.
- Questions with ***must*** are not very common as they sound very formal. We tend to use ***have to*** instead.
  Must I go to bed so early?
  Do I have to go to bed so early?
- ***Must*** is the same in all forms.
- We use an infinitive after ***must***.

To Need To

Affirmative / Negative	
I / We / You / They	need to work. / don't need to work.
He / She / It	needs to work. / doesn't need to work.

Questions		
Do	I / we / you / they	need to work?
Does	he / she / it	

Short Answers					
Yes,	I / we / you / they	do.	No,	I / we / you / they	don't.
	he / she / it	does.		he / she / it	doesn't.

- We use ***need to*** to say that there is an obligation to do something.
  I need to go home after class.
- We use ***don't need to*** to say there is no obligation to do something.
  I don't need to take the bus. I can walk.

To Have To

Affirmative / Negative	
I / We / You / They	have to learn / don't have to learn.
He / She / It	has to learn / doesn't have to learn.

Questions		
Do	I / we / you / they	have to learn?
Does	he / she / it	

Short Answers					
Yes,	I / we / you / they	do.	No,	I / we / you / they	don't.
	he / she / it	does.		he / she / it	doesn't.

- We use ***have to*** to say what it is necessary to do.
  You have to answer all the questions on the exam.
  He has to wear a uniform to school.
- We use ***don't have to*** to say that it is not necessary to do something, but that you can do it if you want.
  You don't have to help me with my homework.
  Elsie doesn't have to get up early tomorrow.
- Question words go at the beginning of the question.
  How much homework do you have to do every day?
  When do we have to make a decision?

GRAMMAR PRACTICE

UNIT 8

Can/Can't, To Be Allowed To

1 Write affirmative [+] or negative [–] sentences with *can* or *can't*.

1 Susanna / come with us tomorrow. [–]
Susanna can't come with us tomorrow.

2 we / write in our English books. [+]
______

3 James / use his brother's bike. [+]
______

4 they / play in a professional orchestra. [–]
______

2 Write sentences with *to be allowed to* and the verb in parentheses.

1 We *'re allowed to wear* (wear) boots in the winter.

2 Andrea ______ (have) her laptop in class.

3 Franklin ______ (not / drive) his father's car.

4 Children ______ (not / be) rude to their parents.

3 Make questions and short answers with *to be allowed to*.

1 your teachers / give detention / yes
Are your teachers allowed to give detention?
Yes, they are.

2 your little sister / wear makeup / no
______
______

3 they / use online dictionaries / yes
______
______

4 we / eat all these cupcakes / no
______
______

5 Carlos / play soccer with us / yes
______
______

To Have To, Must, and To Need To

4 Underline and correct the mistake in each sentence.

1 She don't have to sit at the front of the class.
She doesn't have to sit at the front of the class.

2 You have be well-behaved on the school bus.
______

3 Luis and his friend needs to finish their homework.
______

4 Must we to come into school on the weekend?
______

5 Circle the correct option.

1 It isn't necessary to write a thank-you letter.
(a) You don't have to write a letter.
b You must not write a letter.

2 I can go to the gym by bike.
a I need to take the bus.
b I don't need to take the bus.

3 It's important for me to study for exams.
a I don't need to study. b I must study.

4 We're not allowed to run in the hallways.
a We don't have to run, but we can.
b We must not run.

5 You must watch this video!
a I strongly recommend it.
b I don't think you'll like it.

6 Complete the swimming pool rules with the phrases in the box.

don't have to use	don't need to bring	have to have	have to wear	must remember	~~must not come~~	must not run	need to pay

You [1] *must not come* into the pool area in outdoor shoes. You [2] ______ rubber shoes around the pool. You [3] ______ attention on wet surfaces, and you [4] ______ at any time. There are lockers in the changing rooms, but you [5] ______ them. You [6] ______ your own towel because towels are provided. However, if you do use ours, you [7] ______ to leave them in the basket provided. Finally, swimmers under the age of ten [8] ______ an accompanying adult.

GRAMMAR REFERENCE

UNIT 9

To Be Going To

Affirmative / Negative			Questions	
I	’m / ’m not	going to tell him.	Am I	going to tell him?
He / She / It	’s / isn’t		Is he / she / it	
We / You / They	’re / aren’t		Are we / you / they	

Short Answers			
Yes,	I am.	No,	I’m not.
	he / she / it is.		he / she / it isn’t.
	we / you / they are.		we / you / they aren’t.

- We use ***to be going to*** to talk about future actions we have decided to do.
  After we finish school, I’m going to travel to Australia.
  My grandparents are going to stay with us this summer.
- We use the appropriate present form of ***to be*** (***not***) + ***going*** + ***to*** + **verb**.
  I’m going to wear my new jeans and my red T-shirt.
  We’re not going to take the bus.
- We form questions with ***to be*** + **subject** + ***going*** + ***to*** + **verb**.
  When are you going to start studying for the exams?
  Is she going to get here before nine o’clock?

Present Continuous for Future

- We use the **present continuous** to talk about future arrangements when they have a fixed date.
  They’re getting married this summer.
  What are you doing this weekend? I’m going shopping with my parents.

Future Continuous

Affirmative / Negative		
I / You / He / She / It / We / You / They	will / won’t	be lying on the beach this time next week.
	may / may not	
	might / might not	

Questions			Short Answers
Will	I / you / he / she / it / we / you / they	be lying on the beach this time next week?	Yes, I / you / he / she / it / we / you / they will.
			No, I / you / he / she / it / we / you / they won’t.

- We can use the **future continuous** to talk about actions in progress at a point in time in the future.
  My sister will be living in Mexico next year.
  Next Saturday, we’ll be sitting on the beach.
- We use ***will***/***won’t*** when we feel sure about the action in progress, and ***may*** (***not***) / ***might*** (***not***) when we’re less sure.
  They’ll be answering questions online at 7 p.m.
  We might be having dinner at 9 p.m.

Relative Pronouns and Relative Clauses

- We use **relative clauses** to make the person, place, or thing we are talking about clear.
  My aunt has a friend who makes beautiful bags.
  This is the song that I told you about.
- We use **relative pronouns** at the beginning of relative clauses. We do not repeat the subject pronoun when the subject of the pronoun and following clause are the same.
  We know a lot of people who live in the village.
  NOT ~~*We know a lot of people who they live in the village.*~~
- We use ***who*** or ***that*** to talk about people.
  The man who/that lives next door works at night.
  She’s the scientist who’s/that’s moving to Antarctica next year.
- We use ***that*** to talk about things.
  I don’t like books that have sad endings.
  I want boots that I can wear all year.
- We use ***where*** to talk about places.
  That’s the office where my uncle works.
  Try the restaurant where we had my party.
- We use ***when*** to talk about time.
  That was the day when we were late for school.
  It’s the holiday when everyone is happiest.
- We use ***why*** to talk about reasons.
  You studied a lot. That’s the reason why you passed!
  I lost my passport. That’s the reason why I’m so sad.
- We use ***whose*** to talk about possessions.
  Do you remember the name of the guy whose phone charger I borrowed last week?

GRAMMAR PRACTICE

UNIT 9

To Be Going To

1 Complete the sentences with the correct form of *to be going to* and the verb in parentheses.

1 We are going to visit (visit) our old neighbors on the weekend.

2 She ______ (not come) with us to Peru.

3 He ______ (leave) for the station at nine.

4 They ______ (deliver) the products by drone next year.

5 Flights ______ (not be) cheaper in future, are they?

6 ______ you ______ (buy) the train tickets online?

Present Continuous for Future

2 Put the words in the correct order.

1 train / traveling / on / to / the / night / Madrid / We're

We're traveling to Madrid on the night train.

2 meeting / the / friends / their / They're / on / bus

______

3 on / summer / going / I'm / trip / this / school / a

______

4 for / you / Are / birthday / having / a / your / party / ?

______

5 tonight / isn't / our / Stella / to / concert / coming

______

Future Continuous

3 Complete the text with the phrases in the box.

will be building	will be cycling	~~will be driving~~
will be making	will be using	won't be doing

More people [1] will be driving electric cars in the future. Transportation companies [2] ______ driverless trucks, too. But I wonder how teenagers [3] ______ their daily trips in 20 years? Many believe that they [4] ______ more, but they [5] ______ that unless road conditions are improved. Today's cyclists hope that town planners [6] ______ more bike lanes by the time their children are teenagers.

Relative Pronouns and Relative Clauses

4 Circle the correct option.

1 I didn't know the person (*who*) / *whose* sat next to me.

2 She's the girl *who* / *whose* mother is from Chile.

3 Is August the time *which* / *when* it rains a lot in Scotland?

4 This is the book *that* / *whose* was banned in the 1940s.

5 That's the place *why* / *where* they used to meet.

6 It's the summer and that's *where* / *why* I'm happy!

5 Underline and correct the mistake in each sentence.

1 Do you know <u>who</u> bags these are?

Do you know whose bags these are?

2 She can't remember when she wanted to buy.

______

3 That is the language school she will be studying.

______

4 I'll never forget the time why I met Adele.

______

5 Is there a reason where you don't want to fly?

______

6 Complete the conversation with the phrases in the box and the correct relative pronoun: *where*, *why*, *that*, *whose*, or *who*.

father was the artist	she recommended	told us
was the artist	we could wait	~~you took~~

ALEXIA Are those the photos [1] that you took on vacation?

KARL Yes, I took this one in Paris, remember?

ALEXIA Oh, I remember! We found a museum [2] ______ for the rain to stop.

KARL That's right! This was the girl [3] ______ about the exhibition.

ALEXIA I don't remember her. Was she the person [4] ______?

KARL No, it wasn't her father, but she knew the man [5] ______. That's the reason [6] ______ the exhibition.

LANGUAGE BANK

STARTER

Vocabulary

Technology

app device emoji screen
social media video chat

Feelings

angry bored embarrassed
excited nervous upset

Music

bass guitar country DJ drums fans
heavy metal jazz keyboard rap reggae

Grammar in Action

Simple Present and Present Continuous with Adverbs of Frequency
Simple Present and Present Continuous for Future
Simple Past

Writing

Useful Language

Writing a Review of an App

… is a(n) … app
It's great because …
In my opinion, there are a couple of problems with it.
Overall, I think it's …
I really recommend it.

UNIT 1

Vocabulary

Describing People

active ambitious calm cheerful
confident helpful inspiring patient
sensible sensitive sociable talented

Phrasal Verbs

cheer (somebody) up
deal with
depend on
get along with
give up
hang out
look up to
take care of

Grammar in Action

Simple Past and Past Continuous with *When* and *While*
Used To

Speaking

Everyday English

Go ahead.
Good for (her)!
I'm with you there.
The thing is …

Useful Language

Can I ask you a few questions … ?
Can you tell us … ?
First of all, …
One more thing …
That's all …

Writing

Useful Language

Writing a Letter to a Magazine

For me, …
In my opinion, …
In my view, …
Personally, I think …

LANGUAGE BANK

UNIT 2

Vocabulary

Visual and Performing Arts

architecture contemporary dance exhibition fashion design filmmaking gallery illustration musical theater performance photography sculpture street art

Music and Theater

audience audition lines lyrics orchestra part rehearsal scene show studio

Grammar in Action

Present perfect with regular and irregular verbs
Present perfect with *already*, *just*, *still*, and *yet*

Speaking

Everyday English

dunno
ginormous
kid
nope
tons

Useful Language

It isn't supposed to …
It looks like …
It makes me feel …
It probably shows …
It seems a little …

Writing

Useful Language

Writing a Review

I recommend it because …
It's playing at …
It's the best show I've ever seen.
I've never seen anything like it before.
What I liked / didn't like about it was …

UNIT 3

Vocabulary

Communicating

describe gesture greet interpret post shake hands shout smile translate wave whisper

Collocations with *To Say* and *To Tell*

Say: hello / something in Italian / sorry / yes/no
Tell: a joke / a lie / a story / someone a secret / the truth

Grammar in Action

Can, Could, Will Be Able To
Present Perfect with *How long* … ? and *For*/*Since*
Present Perfect and Simple Past

Speaking

Everyday English

Oh, no!
Phew!
Sure thing.
Yep.

Useful Language

I need them to …
It's a kind of …
They're similar to …
You use it to …

Writing

Useful Language

Writing a Listicle

all (his) life
before
later on
over the last few years
since
soon
these days

LANGUAGE BANK

UNIT 4

Vocabulary

Health and Fitness

cough get better get enough sleep get sick get stressed go jogging have a fever relax sneeze sweat train warm up work out

Healthy Eating

a balanced diet calories carbohydrates dairy products fat fiber nutrition protein vitamins

Grammar in Action

Quantifiers
Should, *Shouldn't*, and *Ought To*

Speaking

Everyday English

I'll give it a try.
… isn't really my thing.
Seriously?
Tell me about it!

Useful Language

How about … (+ *-ing*)?
Make sure you …
Something else I find useful …
… works for me.
You could just …

Writing

Useful Language

Writing a Post on a Forum

Have you tried … (+ *-ing*)?
I recommend … (+ *-ing*)
That way, you can just …
Why don't you … ?
You could always …

UNIT 5

Vocabulary

Planet Earth

carbon dioxide climate change endangered species energy marine life oxygen pollution solar power the environment the planet waste wildlife

Natural Environments

bay cave cliff coast iceberg rainforest stream valley volcano waterfall

Grammar in Action

The First Conditional
The Second Conditional

Speaking

Everyday English

I'll have to pass.
I'm off to …
It's not cool.
Wanna join us?

Useful Language

Don't forget that …
I see your point, but …
Let's agree to disagree.
Maybe you're right, but …
Remember that …

Writing

Useful Language

Writing an Opinion Essay

Furthermore, …
However, …
In addition, …
In my opinion, …
In my view, …
In summary, …
Some people believe that …

LANGUAGE BANK

UNIT 6

Vocabulary

Making Things

add boil cover dip freeze increase place pour press pull reduce remove stir

Materials

cardboard glass leather rubber silk tin

Containers

bag box can case jar tube

Grammar in Action

Simple Present Passive
Simple Past Passive

Speaking

Everyday English

any old …
Go for it!
Hang on a sec!
I get it.
kind of tricky

Useful Language

Giving Instructions

And there you have it!
First of all, …
Once (something is done), …
The next part's …

Following Instructions

Let me get this straight.
Oh, I see.
Then what?
What's next?

Writing

Useful Language

Writing a Review

The glasses look like …
The lenses are made from …
What I like about them is …
However, I should point out that …
Overall, I think it is / they are …

UNIT 7

Vocabulary

Festivals

atmosphere ceremony costume crowd decoration fair fireworks float lantern parade program stall

Music Festivals and Live Music

band member campsite encore gig headliner stage supporting act tent track venue

Grammar in Action

Past Perfect
Reported Statements

Speaking

Everyday English

at my place
Count me in.
It kicks off at …
I won't say a word.
The more the merrier.

Useful Language

I'd love to.
I'll be there (at/around) …
Should I bring anything?
What are you up to … ?
What time should I be there?

Writing

Useful Language

Writing an Email to a Friend

Anyway, that's all from me.
Bye for now,
It was great to hear from you!
Thanks for your email.
Write back soon!

LANGUAGE BANK

UNIT 8

Vocabulary

School

cheat on a test   fail an exam   get detention
get good grades   give (somebody) a talk
hand in homework   pass an exam
pay attention to the teacher   study for a test
take an exam   write an essay

Attitude and Behavior

careful   careless   disobedient   disorganized
immature   mature   organized
polite   rude   well-behaved

Grammar in Action

Can/Can't
To Be Allowed To
To Have To, *Must*, and *To Need To*

Speaking

Everyday English

How come?
Kind of.
That's no big deal.
Yeah, right!

Useful Language

Anything else I need to know?
What are the rules about … ?
What happens if you do?
Why's that?

Writing

Useful Language

Writing an Essay

In this essay, I outline …
On the one hand, …
On the other hand, …
Others argue that …
Some say that …

UNIT 9

Vocabulary

Travel

abroad   accommodation   backpacking
book   cruise ship   destination
journey   resort   sightseeing
tour   tourist attraction   trip

Travel Phrasal Verbs

check in   check out   get away   get back
get in   go away   look around   set off   take off

Grammar in Action

To Be Going To and Present Continuous for Future
Future Continuous
Relative Pronouns and Relative Clauses

Speaking

Everyday English

… and so on.
bucket list
… right in the middle of …
the usual stuff
What were you saying?

Useful Language

How long are you going for?
I'm really looking forward to … (+ *-ing*)
… in two weeks
We're going to try …
What are you planning on doing?
Where will you be staying?

Writing

Useful Language

Writing an Email to a Host Family

Best wishes,
Dear Mr. and Mrs. …
Do you know … ?
I'm writing to …
Thank you very much for (+ *-ing*)